Long Beach Island
Chronicles

Trish Craig

Edited by
Margaret Thomas Buchholz

DOWN THE SHORE
PUBLISHING
WEST CREEK N.J.

The words "Down The Shore" and the Down The Shore Publishing logo are registered U.S. Trademarks.

This book is co-published with The SandPaper, Inc. of Long Beach Island, NJ.

For information, address:
Down The Shore Publishing Corp., Box 100, West Creek, NJ 08092

www.down-the-shore.com

Printed in the United States of America on recycled paper,
FSC certified mixed sources, 30% post-consumer content.
10 9 8 7 6 5 4 3 2 1

Book design by Leslee Ganss

Library of Congress Cataloging-in-Publication Data

Names: Buchholz, Margaret Thomas, 1933- editor.
Title: Long Beach Island chronicles / edited by Margaret Thomas Buchholz.
Other titles: Beachcomber. | SandPaper.
Description: West Creek, New Jersey : Down The Shore Publishing, [2018] |
    Includes bibliographical references and index.
Identifiers: LCCN 2018024518 | ISBN 9781593221140 (pbk. : alk. paper)
Subjects: LCSH: Long Beach Island (N.J.)--History. | Long Beach Island
    (N.J.)--Social life and customs. | Seaside resorts--New Jersey--Long Beach
    Island.
Classification: LCC F142.L65 L65 2018 | DDC 974.9/48--dc23

LC record available at https://lccn.loc.gov/2018024518

ISBN 978-1-59322-114-0

Contents

The Environment 194-241

Way Back When 242-273

Contributors' Notes 274
Acknowledgments 279

Barnegat Light Historical Museum

*October 22, 1920: View from the Oceanic Hotel, looking north toward Barnegat Light-
house and its keeper's house (with tall chimneys, undergoing demolition). The Oceanic
— from which vantage this photograph was taken — was also being demolished, as
beach erosion undercut the hotel.*

Introduction

O ver the past half-century, I've published and edited a Long Beach Island newspaper and written and edited books about Jersey Shore storms, shipwrecks, and travelers' tales about historic visits to our coast.

I grew up in Harvey Cedars and now am back in that house on Barnegat Bay. Although I have traveled frequently and lived away many winters, I've never missed a summer. My roots are deep in the sand and water. I always return to this Island, both in person and in the stories I value.

In the 2006 pictorial book *Island Album* I presented a large collection of photographs combined with oral history from old-timers who remembered when this island was largely undeveloped. *The Long Beach Island Reader*, published in 2015, offered some of the best writing from *The Beachcomber*, first published in 1950. I owned that paper from 1955 to 1987, and continued as editor until 2014. Both of these books were fun to research, and for you, fun to dip into — on a stormy night, or on the beach, or far away from these shores when thoughts of Long Beach Island were calling. And now I've had the great pleasure of gathering another batch of stories for this new collection. I've included historically intriguing articles from *The Beachcomber* and *The SandPaper* — a publication that was a rival upstart when it launched in 1976.

At that time, *The Beachcomber* was the dominant summer weekly, with fat issues delivered to every doorstep on the Island and nearby mainland each week. *The SandPaper* was the skinny new kid in town, with a scrappy young staff just out of college, with new ideas about journalism and print, and it was threatening my domain. It's a small island, especially in the off-season when we are a tight community, so it's funny (but perhaps not surprising) how rivals become friends and colleagues. In 1987 *The Beachcomber* merged into *The SandPaper* family, and I continued to happily edit my old paper and had opportunities to work on book projects as well.

With this new collection, *Long Beach Island Chronicles*, I had a chance to page through many bound editions of *SandPapers* and become engrossed in stories I

had never read. I've included subjects as varied as the troubling environmental problems of the 1980s; Tiny Tim's visit to the Island; birding before so many trees lost out to development; Leroy Lewis' years at the organ; Mick Taylor at Rick's; essays on sailing, fishing, summer jobs; and my favorite story — a drunk trying to get away from the cops by swimming due east in the ocean.

And storms and history: I couldn't edit a book without including these topics. There are a handful of hurricane and northeaster stories from the 1930s up to Sandy in 2012. The most fascinating is taken from a long letter written by an unknown man detailing his family's close escape during the 1944 Hurricane. The earliest historical report is from a Pennsylvania paper in 1833. I have a rum-running story from the late 1920s which include the shenanigans of local Coast Guards, and a German U-boat off the coast during World War II.

In addition to stories in *The SandPaper* and *Beachcomber*, I've also included selections from *Echoes*, public domain historical accounts, museum archives, and other publications. I tried to contact all the authors, but there were several who have left no trace. I thank all who were so pleased to be included and who helped me update information where needed.

M.T.B.

The building in the foreground is the Ashley House, a boarding house built in 1822 by Bart Sleight, one of the first on the Island, along with the Mansion of Health in Surf City. John Maxon Brown bought it in the 1850s and sold it in the 1860s, when John Warner Kinsey became the owner/manager. It was abandoned by the late 1870s, when this photograph was taken, and torn down in 1887.

Up and Down
The Island

Polly's Dock, Beach Haven, circa 1980.

Ray Fisk

1978 The Joy of Crowds

Roy S. Wolper

Whenever it is known that we have a house in Beach Haven someone always says, "Lucky dogs — you have those weekends in September." June and September — those are the months that everyone longs for. Then the beach is something shared with spindly legged gulls and the nights are so quiet that you can hear the ocean's surf as you fall asleep. In September the water is warmer than ever, and no lifeguard whistles you to swim between the narrow flags; and the sunlight, which is softer than its summer's glare, makes everything lovelier — the house fronts, the twilight haze, the tranquil bay.

But, it is in July and August, when the crowds are thickest, that I love the shore the most.

I don't walk to Jack's Bakery when I get up at 7:30 on Sunday mornings, even though the doughnuts have just been made and are so hot that you need a napkin to hold them. I go about nine or ten when you have to take a plastic number and wait for one of the four counter girls. I usually ask someone — anyone — "Would you like to split a dozen sticky buns? With nuts." They come in dozens, too many for us. The person I ask usually says no, but another customer in the crowded shop overhears us and is happy to share: her husband doesn't like sticky buns either, but she and her daughters do.

On weekends, our beach overflows with day-trippers — those who motor down for the day — and expands into the adjoining ones at Centre and Norwood.

The Brannigans, who own a house and are from New York, say that we're becoming another Coney Island. They say, disapprovingly, "We remember when you could count the people in the water on both hands." I remember those days, too.

But without the trippers on the weekend, we couldn't have our late-af-

from *The Beachcomber* • July 23, 1978

11

Beach Haven.

ternoon volleyball games on the beach. Because of an ordinance, any activity with a ball is prohibited during the time that the beach is patrolled. After the guards leave, you can sail a Frisbee or fly a kite or play volleyball (but with the latter, you need ten to twelve people). There are about a half-dozen of us who want to play volleyball, and from the stragglers who have not left the beach we can always recruit a handful, usually college students, for a game. And volleyball with bare feet on sand and with the ocean as a chaser — could one want more?

But it is not just for selfish reasons that I like the crowds. As a fair or a market is bedraggled if it lacks people, so too the beach. I like lying on a towel, looking at the different shapes of the bodies, listening to the talk of the Phillies, the high price of celery, or the new front of the Hand Store. Each blanket or umbrella or row of towels marks an apartment, even more transparent than in a theater with its invisible fourth wall; at the beach, four open walls.

Because we go to the same beach each day, there are communities. Even though many of the people rent, they come back to the same apartments every summer and are as reliable as the homeowner.

The Weinrybs, who have rented the cottage across the street for more than ten years, sit to the right of the pavilion. The McKaigs, our neighbors, to the left and in the afternoons only. Dr. Meyers' wife is a beachie; she's there all day. The Karlens are to the right and close to the wet sand so that they can keep their children in view. As I lie there, Charles McKaig walks past; "One more time?" he says, his shadow stopping. Though my bathing suit is not dry from the last time, I go in again. Swimming, unlike volleyball or baseball, is private. The joy is catching a wave as it breaks, the water's chill on a hot forehead, and a sky very large and blue and not marked by tall buildings.

Before I go home, I pass Dr. Zitser, who takes a room at the oceanfront motel each year, and say, "C'mon in, Stanley. It's not too late."

I don't ever mind the crowding in the center of town. I love going to the Island Book Store on Sunday morning even though the line for newspapers is beyond the sidewalk and into the street. After you little-step your way past the stacks of Jersey and Philadelphia papers to the thick Times, there is another line to pay for them. The owner, jowly and white T-shirted, is not too busy for the same teasing he does on weekdays. As I pay, I say, "I remember when I could buy this for a quarter."

"These days," he says, "ink's expensive."

When I go to the laundromat, I do not mind the wait for one of the dryers. Because I know that they will all be taken, I never go without a book: It is on the green bench in front of the laundromat that Rennie Morgan died as the result of an abortion, that Alison rejoined her husband Jimmy to play squirrels and bears, that Dr. Eduardo Parr bought sunglasses and the beginning of Maria's love. I could read at home, but there, cracks cry for spackle and paint scruffs look like gashes. At the green bench there is nothing one can do but read.

Even the noise from the nearby houses, each bursting with people, can be pleasant. In the evenings windows are open, radios and stereos are louder than the listeners in the room realize and parties start late and go on and on. Our bedroom window is close to the McKaigs's porch, and often, when we are ready for sleep, we hear the laughter as the McKaigs and their friends bring back the fun of the day. Barely awake and too tired to do more than move slowly, we enjoy their spirit. It catches the happiness that thousands have found at the beach and is a pleasant soporific.

1967 It Was the Summer of Love

Kathryn M. King

"It was twenty years ago today ...
Sergeant Pepper taught the band to play ..."

When the Beatles album *Sergeant Pepper's Lonely Hearts Club Band* hit the charts in June 1967, it opened the eyes of young people all over the country to the beginning of what is now called the Summer of Love.

It might not seem that "Lucy in the Sky With Diamonds" and "Lovely Rita" have been around that long, but it's been two decades since Indian gurus, rock stars and media hipsters led the youth of America on a dance to a different drummer.

1967 was the year of the Central Park and San Francisco gatherings called "Be-Ins," the flaming guitar of Jimi Hendrix at the July Monterey Pop Festival, Janis Joplin wailing and ex-Harvard professor Timothy Leary advocating "Turn on, tune in and drop out."

On the saccharine side, Donovan (that was his only name) sang about "Eee-lectrical Bananas," and others tried to smoke them. Haight Ashbury became the capital city of youth, and that summer the national social climate took seed and bloomed right here as Long Beach flower power.

Hippie was the label someone affixed to the proponents of peace and love that spawned the anti-Vietnam War movement and the long-running Broadway musical "Hair." The '40s generation was "hep," this one was "hip." To some, the young were "long-haired freaks," but to those devouring Herman Hesse, Ken Kesey and Richard Brautigan, they were just expressing themselves. Dig it. Didja put up your black light? I've got my day-glow, Robert Crumb "Mr. Natural" poster and my patchouli incense and we can all trip on the vibes, man.

It was the summer of love for youth, and the summer of fear for parents. All of a sudden their kids turned into foreign beings, boys stopped

from *The Beachcomber* • September 3, 1987

"Harmonic Convergence," Surf City, August 1987.

getting haircuts and girls dressed like maidens from the Middle Ages —
without the chastity belts.

Lee Yarnell and Beach Haven art gallery owner Richard Jeffries opened
a coffeehouse on Engleside Ave. in Beach Haven. They were only in business thirteen days when they were forced to close by borough officials.
Non-conforming zoning was the official reason, but Yarnell said it was
really a reaction to residents' irrational fears about drugs.

"We served coffee, lemonade and sandwiches. We opened at about six
or seven o'clock and closed at two in the morning. We were packed. We
wanted to give kids a place to go. We weren't up to anything. We passed
the basket to pay the guitarists," Yarnell said. "The walls were all painted
black, and we had posters and candles and we scrounged all the furniture.
Nothing matched except the tablecloths. Dick's wife made them. But the
thought of kids coming together in a coffeehouse made them crazy. We
were young and it was our first business venture. We believed them, and
later found out we weren't in violation at all."

There were other, isolated businesses touched with the ambiance of
flower power, places like Stop the World that sold the beads necessary to
make the hippie jewelry. Or Blow Up, a Harvey Cedars boutique that sold
the Mod clothing style made famous in England by designers like Mary
Quant.

The Trip Shop occupied a tiny storefront in Beach Haven and sold paraphernalia and the requisite leather goods necessary to evoke the natural

look. Bit of Soul in Beach Haven featured sewed-to-order long dresses in colorful African fabric.

But the hot spot on the Island was Le Garage Discotheque Au Go Go, opened the year before on 23rd Street and the Boulevard in Spray Beach by cousins George and Joe Laputka with Bob Kusek and Bob Fleming.

George recalls the six years they operated the business with fondness: "We did have the Jefferson Airplane about that time, and it was later that Bruce Springsteen played at the Garage. We had a lot of what were called psychedelic bands. Some became famous, some didn't.

"We got the bands through Bill Graham, who was running the Fillmore in San Francisco. He later got the Fillmore East in the Village, and we met him there. He brought the bands out from the West Coast. They weren't expensive, because they weren't well known."

Le Garage got the groups during the week, usually for one performance. The audience were all young people, and no alcohol was served. George explained, "We had all the best sound and lighting equipment available. We had strobe lights, and big round colored ones that shot light all across the room. I have nice memories of those days, but we got other responsibilities and we grew up."

The popularity of surfing as a sport bloomed that year. Although individuals like Stretch Pohl, Earl Comfort and Ron DiMenna had been surfing for years, by 1967 it had evolved to a point where both surf shops — Ron Jon's and Koseffs — had surfing teams that traveled to meets up and down the Jersey coast.

But Renny Koseff and *Beachcomber* writers recall there was friction between municipal officials and surfers over the uses of the beaches. The last week of June 1967, about twenty surfers held a "surf-in" on a Long Beach Township beach to protest against limiting the hours they could surf. Police were called and surfers resumed the protest at the police station.

"It is the same thing as today. The surfers wanted to be able to surf all day. Surfing was allowed on Township beaches only from 7 to 10 a.m. and after the lifeguards left the beach in the afternoon. I think they had one beach they could surf all day, in Holgate," said Renny Koseff, who today is owner of Pier 18.

In the *Beachcomber* account, Chief Pete Bohan told the surfers that the

Township was more than lenient with surfers. He went on to explain that "many towns along the Jersey coast had banned surfing and that is might happen on Long Beach Island if they (the surfers) did not start conducting themselves like gentlemen and obey orders from lifeguards the same as bathers do."

By the end of that summer something wonderful had happened, a harmonious spirit united young people. But it was never that naive again. Riots killed forty people in Detroit in July and activists like Abbie Hoffman urged youth to openly defy authority. Young men were called up to serve in Vietnam, and the innocence was gone.

Two decades later, many who attended the celebration of a so-called "Harmonic Convergence" this summer on 5th Street beach in Beach Haven described it as reminiscent of those halcyon days of the late '60s. The hippies might be thickening in the middle and trying to juggle raising teenagers and working, but somewhere inside is still the long-haired, flower-powered person of twenty years ago, holding up a hand with two fingers raised in the peace sign.

Ray Fisk

Holgate.

1980 Night Beat with Men in Blue

Sue Paynter

"Long Beach to thirteen; Long Beach to thirteen. An officer is requested at a breaking and entering at the following address…"

Patrolman Jim Falkowski pulls out of Barnegat Light onto the Boulevard, heading south to Loveladies. Turning into a dark bayside road, he switches on the spotlight and slowly drives toward the bay. Houses are hidden behind the dense shrubbery and curving driveways.

"This doesn't make it easy when they don't put numbers on the houses," he mutters.

"Thirteen to Long Beach. Can you give me that address again? Do you know which side that's on?" he asks, exasperation growing. "Well, do you have a name?"

Finally the house is located. Falkowski steps out of the car, shining a flashlight on the ground as he walks to the door. After speaking with the occupants, he begins searching the grounds. "This is a lot easier in the day. Sometimes when they get scared off, they'll drop the stuff outside," he says.

The initial search turns up a cartridge dropped from the stolen videotape machine, and several fresh footprints made by a sneaker with a ridged sole. Falkowski re-enters the house and checks the occupants' shoes to make sure the prints are not theirs. They're not.

Cautioning the residents to stay inside, he walks over to question the neighbors. "They say they heard more noise than usual tonight, but they didn't report it. Well, I'll call in the ID man to take the prints, but if we don't locate the stolen property tonight, it will be well off the Island by tomorrow," he says. "Witnesses! They either don't want to get involved, or they say 'He went this way' or 'No, he went that way.' They see everything and they see nothing."

So begins another night of routine patrol. No high Kojak-type drama here, just a night that can be very frustrating, gratifying, tragic, or humorous.

from *The SandPaper* • August 20, 1980

"You can see an altogether different light of the Island at night. At four or five in the morning, it is very still, very quiet, and very mysterious. Even normal sounds are strange," recalls former Patrolman Harry Slick. "Your whole equilibrium and body cycle is different. Everything is going in the opposite direction. You may stop in a diner at 6 a.m. to get a hamburger, and people will look strangely at you. It can be very lonely, especially in the winter."

Lonely perhaps, but all agree that the job is never boring, although eight hours cruising the dark streets alone is not exactly the most exciting profession.

"The job runs hot and cold. Sometimes you'll think that you will be busy and you'll be all psyched up, and nothing happens. Sometimes you can feel that you'll go a little crazy on a Wednesday night in December when it's really quiet," jokes Patrolman Allan Walton. "Even during the winter, it's not really boring, but you have to make your own work by rattling windows and doors, checking that houses are locked up, and sometimes it will pay off. Quiet nights can be disheartening, but that one night when you catch a guy coming out of a house carrying a television, it makes it all worthwhile."

Break-ins of empty houses take up much of the time and attention of patrolmen during the winter. "You get used to exactly what cars should be on which streets, and you observe that a closed-up house remains visibly the same with drawn curtains and blinds," says Walton. "At night on patrol, we are looking for any visible differences in the house or the area."

Falkowski, who worked for four years in Elizabeth and has been a member of the township department for four years, adds that he really prefers and requests the night duty, because he doesn't have the traffic to contend with and he feels that he can accomplish more police work during that time in checking residences and businesses. Prowler calls are fairly routine and Walton and Falkowski recently responded to one. "We split up, and I was walking around one side of the house when the woman tapped on the window," Walton recalls. "Don't you hear him out there in back? Listen, she said. I was listening, but I didn't hear a thing. When we got there, we found six frogs in the swimming pool."

Falkowski picks up the story.

"We have to make preliminary reports on all of the calls, so what the heck, I made it out — officer responded to reported prowler call, observed six unidentified green frogs entering the swimming pool from the south end, etc."

During the summer, some of the most frequent calls concern noise complaints and loud parties. "Sometimes we get calls at 9:30 p.m. complaining about loud parties. I think that's a little drastic, but a large part of our work is to go up to a house where there's a lot of hootin' and hollerin' going on, and request that they keep it down," says Walton.

As Walton heads out for the night, he cruises around the back and side streets of the township. "I want to get a feel of the area, see where the kids are tonight, and I'll have an idea what to expect later on," he says. "We have our regular trouble spots on the beach where they have the most parties. They can be a real pain in the neck."

Walton, a township cop for four years, is a study in concentration as he patrols. The patrol car radio and a scanner connected with other local departments are constantly broadcasting. Even during a simultaneous broadcast of a mixture of seemingly unintelligible words and indecipherable codes, he grabs up the radio, answers his call, and responds to the destination.

A station wagon is parked behind St. Francis Center. As Walton shines a light on the car, a man's head and shoulders appear and disappear. The patrolman gets out of the car, and cautiously approaches the vehicle. He appears to be more wary than at other times. "Sometimes, things just don't look or feel right to you, and this was one of those times. But the guy was just eating doughnuts and getting into his sleeping bag for the night," he laughs afterwards. "Told him to find another place to sleep. He'll probably be back."

Most cops attribute an instinct to spot trouble to experience. "It isn't a natural thing that you're born with, but it comes from experience. You might see a guy that looks okay, and you find that he is a real bum, and vice versa," says Stick. "But if you're a good cop and sharp, you feel it when something is wrong and most of the times you are right."

"It's the small things that catch your eye," adds Falkowski. "I can watch a kid on a moped, and just by the way he is acting and reacting to me, I

Long Beach Township police officers drop in on a beach party.

know whether or not he has a moped license or whether he is fifteen or fourteen."

The types of calls that the patrolmen get run the gamut of every human experience. "We really meet all kinds of people. Most don't even know what our job is all about. Maybe they think we just sleep in the car or something, but we're there first whether their baby swallowed something or their oil burner went out. You meet the ones who want to help you and the ones who want to stab you in the back. It's the ones who appreciate you that make it all worthwhile."

Walton estimates that only twenty-five percent of the calls have to do with crime, the rest are public service calls. Even as he patrols the streets, he is flagged down for directions and even by one man who wants to know where he could play pool. "See, we have to know everything," laughs Walton. "We even have to know where the pool tables are."

The police think they have foiled one little game played by vacationers who have used the department as a messenger service. "People come down here and don't have phones, so they devise codes," Walton explains. "Some-

Ray Fisk

Long Beach Township police officers on the night beat, August 1980.

one in north Jersey will call the department and say that their grandfather died and would we send a car over to inform the vacationers in a certain house. In one week the same grandfather died three times. If the grandfather died, that means the kids aren't coming down for the weekend, or if the grandmother died, that means that they'll be here." This year, by order of Chief of Police James Hartmann, all death calls must come through the hometown police department.

Asking any cop if he sees a difference in people during a full moon will bring a torrent of descriptions and anecdotes. "There's no question about it. When the moon is full, the jails are full. People really get flipped out and goofy," jokes Slick. "We would get these incredible calls, and someone in the station would say, 'Hey it must be a full moon tonight,' and it always was."

Sometimes the moon brings out spaceship sightings. Falkowski says that within the past few weeks, a man called in to inquire if there had been any reports of a black and orange spaceship in the area. He thought he had seen one on the beach and was just curious if anyone else had seen it, too. "Probably the best one was several years ago when a guy called and reported that a spaceship had just landed, and he was afraid of getting zapped by the rays," Falkowski recalls. "Someone in the station grabbed the phone from the dispatcher, said that we would send over a car, and that the guy should wrap himself in aluminum foil for protection. When the cop got there, the guy was really wrapped in foil."

Even the trained, professional police officer isn't immune from things that go bump in the night. "One morning around 5 a.m., I was driving from Brant Beach to Surf City to meet another patrolman for a cup of coffee," recalls Walton. "I saw a very bright light in the sky shooting down over the bay at a fantastic speed. When it got to Surf City, the point of light broke into three lights — one blue, one green, one white. I sat down to have my coffee. The other cop and I looked at each other for a while. Finally, I said, 'You see that?' He nodded. I said, "I'm sure glad that you saw it, too." Neither of us wanted to mention it first.

Slick recalls seeing a bright light off the north jetty in Barnegat Light several years ago. "As you approached the beach, the light went down. And as you drove away, the light went up into the sky. Every time I moved, it moved. And it wasn't there every night," he says. "It really looked strange and caught all of my attention for a while. I think it was Venus, but of course I still wonder."

However, most nights do not produce so much diversion. It is regular, routine business. As Walton drives around, stopping an occasional speeder, three kids come up to the car. They greet him, ask him if he knows where Joe is that night, peer into the car, and beg him to turn on the lights and siren. After a few minutes of banter, he drives off.

Good friends of his? "I never saw them before in my life," he says.

He answers a noise complaint, stops and asks a kid who is occupied in setting fire to a milk carton to please put it out, and suddenly stops the car.

Backing up, he looks closely. "I know that license plate," he muses. "I arrested him last year, and thought that he had gone out west. Wonder what he's doing back." He calls in the information to have the license plate checked — it turns out to be the car that he remembered. "It's something that you don't consciously think about, but you can have maybe two-hundred plate numbers filed in your head," he says. I'll keep an eye on that now."

The night goes on. He helps a woman who has locked her keys in the car, checks parking lots. "This is a prime place to siphon gas. Last year there was a shortage, and this year it is the price." And then the three kids come running back to the car. More begging for the lights, and finally Walton flips the flasher and siren on for a total of seven-tenths of a second. "Okay, are you happy? Now get out of here and give me a break," he commands with mock sternness.

A call comes in to respond to a possible drunk driver. Three patrol cars arrive on the boulevard. "Whenever we see another car pulled over we check to see if everything is all right," says Walton. "This time the original officer didn't say how many people were in the car, so that is why two extra back-ups arrive."

Whenever Walton has a car pulled over, within a minute, another patrolman drives slowly by with the standard greeting, "You okay?" A strong rapport is also held with members of other borough departments. They help each other help others.

For example, Falkowski and a Harvey Cedars officer spend half an hour helping a young woman who has gotten the tire of her car stuck across a concrete parking block. After much trial and error, the car was freed and Falkowski was awarded a kiss for his efforts. "Sure, we could have called a wrecker, but what the heck," he said. "A little time and a little muscle, and it saved the girl fifty bucks. I think that this is part of what our job is all about. We all work together. During the winter in the north end when we can't even get a cup of coffee at night, we'll stop in Harvey Cedars. We talk over some coffee, exchange information, and the rapport is very good."

Each cop has a certain amount of leeway in his performance while on duty. With speeders, for example, sometimes the officer feels that a warning will be sufficient, and the attitude of the driver also figures into the picture. And, yes, even a cop will accept extenuating circumstances, that is, if the story holds water. "I picked up one guy going forty-five in a twenty-five-mile zone," recalls Walton. "The guy said he was speeding because his wife was very ill and he had to get her home. When I asked where they lived, he said Cherry Hill! 'What are you going to do? Drive twenty-five over the limit all the way there?' Incredible!"

Walton thinks that the best excuse he has heard to date is the woman who justified speeding because she had to get home to the bathroom.

Besides the high-speed chases, frightening times, and lighter moments, perhaps the most poignant calls are for rescue or first aid. Every time a rescue squad is called, the nearest patrol car is also dispatched. Often, the officer will be the first on the scene. "Of course it is gratifying every time you do CPR and save a life," says Walton. "But it's the other times that stay with you. I get more excited about trying to save a 16-month-old baby who is choking to death than I do about breaking up a bar fight. Driving along here, I could probably point out every house where I failed to pull someone through."

The memories of some of these episodes can haunt a cop years later. "Any cop who can leave the job after eight hours and not think about it is like a robot. Things still bother me today," says Slick, who was a township patrolman for ten years. "You're so involved at the time. Accidents with children and dogs — especially children — would really tear me up. Sometimes you would have to go into the courts later to testify and relive everything months later. It's really tough to come home and be happy, cheerful, and normal."

But it's all part of the job, and something that every cop must deal with and have perspective on. "It's incredible how close you can get to an accident victim in fifteen minutes when you are trying to save a life. You just care so much. Sometimes I know I drive the hospital crazy calling over to check on the condition of someone I have just worked on," says Walton. "It's rough and you can't put it out of your mind. But these are the things that I hope I never get used to or lose the compassion that I feel."

1981 Hashish on the Beach

Sue Paynter

Beachcombers mobbing the sand recently may have been looking to get high on life and the great outdoors, or they may have been looking to get high on something else — the bales and packages of hashish which have been washing ashore during the past week.

"I have never seen so many people on the beaches at this time of year," said one Island resident with mock innocence. "We have the usual Derby fishermen, but so many people are now jogging, taking beach walks, and trying their hand at beachcombing. I think it's wonderful that everyone is returning to nature and becoming so health conscious."

Investigating officials, including the U.S. Customs Department, the U.S. Coast Guard, the Ocean County Prosecutor's office and local township police departments, surmise that the bales may have been dumped overboard north of the Island from a boat carrying the illegal drugs which the current washed south. Bales and broken packages have been found on beaches from Point Pleasant to Lavallette to Island Beach State Park and Long Beach Island. "In excess of three bales," each containing 30 kilos (60 pounds) of hashish, have either been found by or turned in to the Coast Guard and local police departments, according to Long Beach Township Lt. Robert Berkheiser. Most of the drugs have been found on the northern half of the Island.

Area residents, as well as sightseers from miles away, flocked to the beach in hopes of cashing in on the new-found wealth scattered over the sand. After dark, flashlight beams streaked across the high water line, often followed by the glare of headlights from police beach patrols who were searching for the searchers.

Local gathering places were more popular than usual as the hopefuls plotted and shared their ingenious plans to make a killing. These comments were overheard in an Island bar:

from *The SandPaper* • October 21, 1981

"I think I'll get some fresh air. You know, sorta stretch my legs on the beach."

"You mean you're going to take a dope walk."

"That's a waste of time. The junk would be all broken up any way. What about taking out the boat?"

"I wonder if a plane could spot it?"

"Is there any way someone could rent one of those police sniffer dogs?"

Allegedly, several dog owners are trying out their talents as K-9 police dog trainers, with some "home-grown" hidden in various places. Ideally, doggy will learn to find it behind the couch or under the dresser, then during the next beach walk, prove he really is man's best friend. Long Beach Township has been running extra patrols on the beach due to the new popularity of the area. "There are a lot more people down there and most appear to be fishermen," said Berkheiser, "but some of them act like they don't even know one end of the pole from the other."

Investigating officials have not yet found the boat or boats in question. It is suspected that the drugs may have been thrown overboard to lighten a boat during unusually high seas, or out of panic if a Coast Guard or marine police boat was sighted. The bales are wrapped in plastic and burlap, bearing the flag of either Iran or Turkey, and marked with Arabic writing.

Although the Coast Guard in Barnegat Light had stopped all pleasure craft in the inlet late last week, that cautionary action has been suspended, according to Petty Officer Doug Sharp. "We believe everything has been found that's going to be," he said.

One Ship Bottom resident found a two-pound package last Thursday morning. "I first saw it 300 yards away, and by the time I got there, it was almost completely buried in the sand," he said. "It must have come from one of the bales that broke up a jetty. If those two pounds washed in, there has to be more that wasn't turned into the police. It's a good question whether the rest of it is buried or if people have walked away with it."

Being suspicious, plus a good citizen, the beachcomber opened the package and found "a fine brown powder," which he took to the police station. "If you take it home, and it's dope, you can be in a lot of trouble. I didn't want it in my possession. I didn't want to get caught." He also said it was quite probable that "hundreds of packages" could be buried in the sand one or two feet deep until the next storm cuts the beach away.

After being waterlogged, the hashish loses its potency, according to Berkheiser. "The active ingredient is THC. When we get these packages, they weigh more because they're water logged and the water that runs out is brown, meaning it's losing its content."

The lieutenant had a final word of warning to any finder-keepers: "If a citizen finds any of the hashish, we expect him to turn it in and there will be no indication of prosecution. However, if anyone withholds it, we will prosecute to the fullest extent."

And they will be losers-weepers.

1981 Old Hotel Hosts Memories

Cathie Cush

"There aren't many of these around," bartender Ron Betrix says, tossing a leather room-key tag onto the bar of the Acme Hotel. The key tag is a souvenir from the good old days, when Lou Gehrig liked nothing better than to sit on the Acme porch and sip a little whiskey on a summer's evening. That was back in the 1930s, when the Tueckmantle family owned the dining and drinking establishment on Dock Road in Beach Haven, and rented rooms to the likes of Gehrig and Babe Ruth. "They were good 'skates'," says Ernie Tueckmantle, remembering the baseball heroes fondly.

The Acme was old even then. The weathered building has seen more than a few famous faces and a lot of changes in its day; the exact date of construction is not known for sure. Although a borough tax map marks the date as 1919, it is generally agreed that the building is much older.

John Cramner was the original owner, says Joseph Sprague, who has lived in Beach Haven all his life. "I'm going back to 1908, 1911. I was in the cradle in those days. It's always been there as far as I'm concerned." Beach

28

Havenite Margaret Lovett's memories of the Acme go back to the 1940s. "It was said to be one hundred years old at that time, but this is only hearsay," she notes. A photograph of Dock Road in the Beach Haven Library Museum shows the neighboring Hotel De Crab standing alone. Although the picture is not dated, it is known that the Hotel De Crab, a lifesaving station built in Harvey Cedars in 1848, was moved to Dock Road in 1872. How long it stood alone before the Acme was built is not certain.

A historic search was conducted last fall by Michael May, an architectural historian with Heritage Studies in Princeton. The resulting document, which nominates Dock Road, as well as other sections of Beach Haven, to the state and national registers of historic sites, places construction of the Acme Hotel in the late 19th century.

"The Acme Hotel," it reads, "built in sections, has a shingled and clapboard exterior containing Queen Anne elements. The building is crowned by a mansard roof and dormers, and like many houses along the shore, porches are found on both the first and second floors ... the Dock Road area came into being as such shortly after the founding of Beach Haven in 1874."

Local memories don't stretch back that far anymore. Existing information about the emporium is sketchy until Prohibition days. In 1925, John and Ruby Cramner sold the hotel to Gustave Tueckmantle. Ernie Tueckmantle doesn't remember what his father paid for the Acme, but does remember Wida's Restaurant and Hotel in Brant Beach being offered for sale at about the same time for $6,500.

Back in those days, Dock Road was surrounded by water and swampland. A canal ran along the dock to the back of what is now the Colonial Theater. "Dock Road was houseboat alley then," says Bill Gee, who was raised in Beach Haven. "In the late 1920s or early '30s the houseboats were all moved out and the land filled in."

A trolley used to run from the Baldwin Hotel on Engleside Ave., down to Dock Road — that was one way to get there. "I used to come up on a boat." Joe Sprague remembers. "There was only one road to the dock — nothing on either side of it but marsh, meadows and water. I lived on 2nd Street. I

Ray Fisk

Ernie Tueckmantle outside the Acme in 1981, its last year.

could just take a little sneakbox."

"You used to be able to go right up to the back of the hotel in a rowboat. When the tide comes up you can still go up in a boat," Leon Lovett says wryly.

Before Dock Road was filled in, the Acme was on pilings — a fact that came in very handy while the 18th Amendment was in effect. "Bootleg booze came in Beach Haven Inlet from Atlantic City and Tuckerton," says William Morris Hart, better known around town as "Hardy." Born in Burlington, Hardy first came to the Island in 1908, and moved here permanently in 1919.

It seems no one on the Island was dry, thanks to the rumrunners who brought bootleg liquor in on their garveys. For a disgruntled clammer, the money was good, and night trips into the bay to meet suppliers were exciting if, as Hardy reminds, one didn't get caught. "The Hudson House is a little over one hundred years old. It's always been a bar. Even during Prohibition you could always get a drink there," Hardy says of another Beach Haven watering hole. "The old Antlers used to be a gunning club way back. In Prohibition days it was a bootleg place."

The Antlers, adjacent to the Acme, was built slightly later than its next door neighbor. In the '60s it was renamed The Rip Tide, and in the '70s it provided the Tide Lounge in Bay Village with a liquor license.

But until 1933 nobody had a liquor license and the Acme had its share of Prohibition business. "The sheriff would call us up if we were going to be raided," Tueckmantle recalls. That gave them plenty of time to put liquor in sacks and drop it through a trap door in the floor of the bar. The contraband hung suspended in the water below the hotel until the inspection was over. "We got the license back after Prohibition ended," he says. "A busload of National *Turn Verein* [a German club] came down to celebrate. Dinner was on my father."

Hardy doesn't remember the day the 18th Amendment was repealed, but he guesses "everybody on the Island was drunk. After whiskey came back you got a beer for ten cents and a shot of booze for fifteen. You could get a load on for a dollar.

Modern-day patrons, sent back in time, wouldn't recognize the place. "There was a big, high bar that ran east to west," Margaret Lovette relates. "I remember it used to be heavily varnished, very well-kept." Until the mid-'70s, the interior of the bar was done in dark woods. The location of the mahogany bar was moved to run parallel with Bay Ave. sometime before 1959, when Bird and Betty Clutter bought the Acme. "That was a nice barroom," Hardy relates. "Wealthy people came there — all men. There were no women in barrooms in those days."

"The Acme was the last vestige of this hunting-fishing thing. In the main it was catering to men who spent the day on the water, and enjoyed themselves," Bill Gee says of the days when the Acme and places like Bond's Hotel catered to visitors who came to the Island to get away from the urban scene. "There were quite a number of judges," Gee says, who came to relax in the anonymity the Acme offered. "Almost all their customers during their heyday came from party boats."

"Party boats were different than they are today," Lovett recalls. "In those days they were private boats." The boats could be hired for $50 or $75 a day, and were chartered by one group, rather than by many individuals the way they are today. When the boats returned to the docks at the end of the day, weary fishermen would stop at the Acme for a drink.

Many were also guests of the hotel. Until the mid-'60s, the eighteen upstairs rooms were rented. In the 1930s the rooms went for a buck-fifty a night. Tueckmantles, and later Clutters, lived in an apartment over the bar. A wrought-iron grate in the floor allowed Gustave to keep an eye on goings-on in the bar below. A stove provided heat during the winter.

A number of celebrities have crossed the Acme's threshold. John Barrymore stayed there in the 1920s. "We used to have Babe Ruth, Lou Gehrig, Steve Allen, Skinny D'Amato of the 500 Club in Atlantic City," Tueckmantle reminisces. "Clare Luce, the actress, came with her husband. Don Vorhees, the orchestra leader, used to come down here too." Babe Ruth — he'd come down and stay drunk for weeks," Hardy snorts.

There were rockers and flower boxes out on the porches. The baseball heroes used to sit on the porch with a bottle and have a few drinks. Tueckmantle remembers. "I shoulda took pictures of them," he sighs. "They used to be on the porch at five in the morning waiting for the restaurant to open."

The Acme was well-known for its kitchen in those days. "We used to sell about a hundred breakfasts. And we had to get up at four to do the box lunches. "Three sandwiches, fruit and a pickle cost a fisherman 65 cents. We had all German chefs. One of 'em gave me the recipe for marinated herring." His herring has since become a local legend. Mount Olympus has nectar and ambrosia — Long Beach Island has Ernie Tueckmantle's marinated herring.

"The Acme had the best food on the Island in those days," Hardy says. "You could get great big steaks for a dollar and a half." A clam bar, adjacent to the kitchen, sold six clams on the half shell for ten cents.

Bill Gee remembers the Acme was "much more a restaurant than a bar," and also that the dress code for the two was quite different. "In the bar, people would come in off the boats. In the restaurant you wore white shoes, white pants and a blue jacket. You didn't go slopping around in the dining room."

Rules of the house were stricter than they are today. "My father wouldn't serve anybody that came in with a big beard," Tueckmantle confides. "When we had it, it was a real high class place. They were all dressed up when they came in the bar. The fishermen were dressed better than they are today."

"The old man wouldn't allow music. He wouldn't even allow television," Hardy remembers. Tueckmantle tells a story about the time Al Meyers, the orchestra leader at the Engleside, brought a piano into the Acme bar. "My dad said 'Get it out of here!'"

"People didn't want that noise," Tueckmantle adds, explaining his father's reasoning. "It was all older people back then."

"Old Mister Tueckmantle didn't care about having a young crowd in there," Eleanor Cramner corroborates. "It was down by the dock and catered more to people who were interested in going fishing."

"The kids didn't drink in them days like they do today," Tueckmantle notes. Tastes have changed, too, over the years. "There's a lot of different things they drink now — they drink these whiskey sours," he shudders. Back in the old days, martinis, Manhattans and old fashioneds were the big sellers. Budweiser and Ballantine were the big names in beer.

The Acme had a reputation as a quiet sort of place, and the bar appealed to a more local crowd than the Engleside or the Baldwin did. It was a place to relax and unwind after a day on the boats, and it was also a place to pick up any news that might be floating around.

Lovett recalls the Acme of the 1940s, after Gustave passed away and Ernie took over. The Boat House Restaurant used to be McArthur's boat house. The diner was built in the early '30s, as Dock Road was filled in. The Acme porch was a sort of gathering spot.

"Sitting on the willow rockers, watching people go up and down Dock Road — this was how you kept up with goings on." She qualifies her remark. "Now we are boat people, not beach people — there's a distinction. We gravitate toward the dock." There may still be a distinction between boat people and beach people, and folks may still frequent the Acme to find out what's happening around town, but more has changed than has stayed the same.

In 1959 Tueckmantle sold the Acme Hotel to Bird and Betty Clutter. They continued to rent rooms until the mid-'60s. By then the price had risen to about $10 a night. The Acme was one of the last of the grand hotels in Beach Haven — Bond's Long Beach House and the Baldwin were lost to fire, and the old Engleside was torn down. Only the Street Rita still operates as a hotel. Young drinkers began to gravitate toward the Acme, which was sold to its present owners, East-West Inc., in 1975. A boisterous, college-age crowd now frequents the bar. Nightly drink specials keep the place crowded, and a line of patrons waiting to get in often stretches out to the street.

Today the Acme doesn't attract many celebrities, but it has become a celebrity in its own right. Kevin McGorty, director of the Ocean County Cultural and Heritage Commission, says Beach Haven recently passed a resolution supporting Beach Haven's nomination to the national and state registers of historic sites as a multiple resource district. The Acme is a pivotal building, which means it is central to the nomination. McGorty says it is very likely that the nomination will be accepted on both state and federal levels by this summer and this fall, respectively.

If the Acme is placed on the National Register, it offers its owner several advantages. Historic sites are available for federal and state restoration funds (although the prestige does not protect historic buildings from demolition). A prospective purchaser would also receive a substantial tax break, and McGorty says inquiries to this effect have been made concerning the Acme.

The future of the Acme is as hazy as its beginning. Whatever its fate, a lot of water has gone under its pilings, and it's not quite the same place Gustave Tueckmantle bought in 1925. Now Space Force and pinball machines occupy the area that was once the kitchen. The old mahogany bar is gone, replaced by a large L-shaped structure which dominates most of what was the original barroom. A big rectangular bar takes up much of the space in the old dining room, and the interior has been painted white.

The upstairs rooms have accumulated fifteen years' worth of dust and junk. In one there are old dishes and other kitchen paraphernalia; in another, a staircase lies on its side. Detex boxes, where watchmen clocked in on their rounds, are still nailed to doorjambs at the end of the hall. An old bar sign leans up against a wall.

"Who knows how old this sign is? Everything should be dated," Betrix sighs. "This had to be a classy place."

He picks up the key ring and shakes his head.

The Acme mystique has seduced another generation. Who knows how many more will follow?

The summer of 1981 was the Acme's last. When the establishment opened its doors for the 1982 season, it had been transformed. Michael Battista and a group of other local businessmen had purchased the place, renovated it and reopened it as The Ketch — a bar and live music venue. They gutted the first floor, opening it up to one large room with a second-floor balcony on the east side of the building.

Later that summer, they opened a restaurant on the west side of the building with a deck overlooking the bay. It continues today. For many, drinks on the upstairs deck at sunset has become the quintessential Ketch memory — and few remember the rich history of the building.

1981 Rooms for Rent, Not Parties

Gary Reed Price

Next April and May the high school and college students now packing footlockers for the fall semester will be back looking for the job that will enable them to stay on Long Beach Island all summer. They'll also be looking for a place where they can afford to live on minimum or slightly above minimum wage. With motel rooms running from $30 to $75 a night, and cottage rentals averaging 4300 to $550 weekly, lodging for those on a strict budget is scarce — and getting scarcer.

For years, big old houses with names like "The Magnolia," "The Spruces," "The Pillars," "The Green Gables" and "The Holly House" took in youngsters who didn't mind doubling up with a friend if the rent was cheap enough.

With the advent of the so-called sexual revolution during the early '70s, and the widespread use of drugs that became socially acceptable in young circles in the years that followed, many houses began closing their doors to singles, in favor of families.

Marie Coates, owner of the Street Rita Hotel in Beach Haven, had a six-bedroom structure on the back of the hotel which she rented each summer to six young women. One year, she recalls, a sad, inhibited young woman slashed her wrists with a razor blade in a suicide attempt. After a pep talk and a few words to her family, who evidently had no idea of the depth of their daughter's feelings, all was happily resolved. "It made me feel good that I could help," she says, "but that's the problem when you rent to kids for the summer. You end up playing housemother. It's impossible not to become emotionally involved.

"Sometimes it's not the girls, but the creeps they pick up on the beach," she says. "I used to hate it when these unwashed-looking types would come in the hotel and ask for 'Susie or Mary,' and if I asked what the young lady's last name was, they never seemed to know. And they're nearly always

from *The SandPaper* • September 2, 1981

The Green Gables.

drunk! ... One time, a 17-year-old's drunken boyfriend turned out to be a Long Beach Township cop. He could hardly walk when he came into the lobby. When I told him not to come into my hotel in that condition, he gave me a lot of verbal abuse. I asked to see his badge number, but he refused. He said he wanted to start a party for a couple of the girls, but he didn't know anybody's last name.

"Another time," she laughs, "we had a really rough looking bunch come in looking for girls who were staying in the back. These guys wore headbands, with feathers like Indians, and were swinging bottles like weapons. I chased them out, but they congregated in my alleyway on the side of hotel. When my husband, who had just come out of the shower, ran outside in his white terrycloth bathrobe, one of them said, 'Well, if it ain't St. Rita in the flesh!' My husband was mad, but we had to laugh.

"Last year, along with other problems, we had two girls of different sexual persuasion. One afternoon I heard a lot of screaming coming from the driveway and I ran to see what was happening. By the time I got there, the two had ended their quarrel and were making up with a great deal of ardor. I told them to confine that sort of behavior to their rooms and not to disturb my guests. I was answered by a string of foul words, and my husband had to tell one of them to leave. Within the next few weeks the fountain in the hotel lobby was discovered overturned; all the hanging plants on the porch were stolen, and some wicker furniture disappeared.

"After last year my husband and I decided we'd had it with renting to kids, and the day after Labor Day, he went into the building and started converting it into an apartment. We only rent it to families now."

Coates was the first to originate a blacklist of the worst-behaved renters, both young and adult alike. The list is now kept up by several other rental establishments, and those who behave badly one summer have a difficult time finding a place to rent the next.

For Lucille Reddington, owner of Green Gables Guest House, 1972 seemed to be the summer of wild kids. "I had a bunch of girls from Pottstown, Pa., who looked sweet and clean and attractive and turned out to be just the opposite.

The highlight of that summer was a two-week barbecue on behalf of Southern Ocean County Hospital. "Mrs. R," as she is known by her tenants, purchased hundreds of hot dogs, blueberries and ears of corn, made buckets of Manhattan and New England style clam chowder and sold it to all comers. "We had two girls staying at the house who were folk singers. They were really good, and stayed on the porch much of the day to entertain the people who were buying food. The thing was, some people came

The Magnolia.

and never left. We had Philadelphia cowboys complete with hats, boots and brown bags full of ol' red eye, and a potpourri of other select weirdos."

That year was also remembered for a fabulous feast. Two young fishermen stopped by one day with an enormous fresh tuna they had caught. Reddington filleted the fish, cooked all the leftovers in the house and invited anybody who wanted to, to sit on the front porch and have dinner. "Everybody who went by came over for a piece of fish, an ear of corn and a cold drink," she recalls. "It was a lot of fun. I sometimes wonder if some of these kids ever got a proper meal when they were down here on their own. They spent their whole pay on their rent and partying."

Over the past nine years, Reddington says, she has acquired some repeat tenants and made some nice friends. "Once in a while you get a bad apple, the girl who sneaks friends upstairs to spend the night without paying, or makes a lot of noise and keeps the others awake, but now I've got a lease with everything spelled out. They agree to the rules before they come in, and if they don't behave themselves, out they go. As a result, my house is one of the quietest on the street."

When Dee Poletti took over The Magnolia on Centre Street, the house had a reputation for being a "party house." When asked if any of the old tenants came looking for rooms the following summer, Poletti replies "all of 'em!" adding, "and some of them were really scary!"

Poletti, a registered nurse, has a background in psychiatry, having worked at Northwestern Psychiatric Institute in Philadelphia. "It doesn't take me long to size up a person or what's going on," she says. "Nowadays, you can pretty much pick and choose your tenants carefully. I know just what questions to ask when I interview them, and I'm usually sure of what I'm getting, although sometimes you can never tell. The thing is, now that the houses that rent to kids are becoming fewer and fewer you can afford to be selective.

Although she didn't have any troubles with her tenants last summer, there was a lot of drug traffic on the street, and late in the season a state narcotics officer asked to stay upstairs to survey the action. One major drug bust was made in a nearby apartment, but a large one planned for Labor Day weekend did not pan out.

Coates said she, too, had police staying in her place one year. There was a rapist who traveled up and down the Garden State Parkway getting off shore exits at random and picking up hitchhiking girls; he chose one of her young tenants as his victim. The girl got away, but had made the mistake of telling her would-be assailant where she was staying. The trooper had the area staked out, but the rapist never came to reclaim his victim.

"I don't know if they ever caught that guy," she says.

Poletti says that aside from the "narc" upstairs last August, and the noisy street on Friday and Saturday nights, her first summer as a landlord was pretty quiet, but that this year's tenants have an entirely new set of problems. "This is a preppy crowd. They all come from upper-income families and are extremely competitive. They compete about everything, and there is no loyalty to each other."

But so far she's had a minimum of trouble, although she says she is considering bumping one youngster who repeatedly climbs out "onto the more than 100-year-old roof."

1985 Not Just Any Old Shack

Curtis Rist

In the middle of the bay, at the eastern end of the Causeway, is a smooth stretch of wetlands that is undeveloped except for a long billboard, a decaying shack and a sun-bleached truck.

The shack is empty, save for some overturned furniture, and has no windows or doors to speak of. Outside, there is only an outline on the one wall where the electric meter used to be. A dock runs from one side of the house out into the bay, and a large rain barrel flaked with red paint is connected by gutters to the roof.

The house is no longer habitable, a large chunk of it having fallen off over the winter. It stands empty, and bears the marks of countless vandals. But the clam shack, as it is known locally, had a glorious past that dated back before a bridge was built, and before the Island was populated by people other than tenders of lifesaving stations.

"The building has quite a bit of historical value," said August Landi of Edgewater, "but now it has fallen into a sad state of disrepair." Landi, along with several others, owns the clam shack and the tract of land where it is located on Cedar Bonnet Island to the south of the Causeway. Because the land is valued more for real estate development than for preservation of the structure, it seems inevitable that the building will someday be razed.

"The plans are up in the air right now," said Johanna Colasante, another of the property's owners. "The stretch of land there is about 133 acres, and better than 50 or 60 acres of that is uplands! There is a man interested in buying and developing it, but right now the whole thing is tabled."

According to Stafford Township Zoning Officer Martha Kremer, the land on Cedar Bonnet Island is currently zoned for coastal wetlands, meaning no additional development can occur. "However, last year there was a petition to the Planning Board, and the Planning Board recommended to the council that the area be zoned for Planned Residential Develop-

from *The SandPaper* • May 22, 1985

ment," Kremer said.

A rezoning, which has not been adopted by the council, would affect only the land to the south of Route 72. Under the proposed rezoning, six units could be built on each acre, which would make the density of development similar to Beach Haven West. "Right now we're still talking about zoning and rezoning," said Colasante. "I have no idea and my partners have no ideas to restore the building."

The future of the shack may be uncertain, but so is its past. Ed Hazelton, a lifelong Manahawkin resident whose father once owned all of the neighboring Cedar Bonnet Island, said the building has been there for as long as he can remember. "It was built by some boys from upper bay, near Point Pleasant or Bay Head. One older fellow I know tells me the house was built over on the other side of the Island, what would now be the north side of the Causeway, then moved to the spot it's at now." The building was used as a gunning and fishing club when it was built, and was known as the Happy Days Lodge. "I would guess it was built in the early 1920s, or maybe earlier," Hazelton said.

In recent years, the house was rented for the summer, according to Colasante. "Then we had some people who tried to restore it a few years

The Shack, late 1970s, with summer resident on the deck.

Ashley Vosseller

The Shack, in its last years, before Superstorm Sandy washed it away.

ago, but they gave it up because it was getting too expensive for repairs." She said the shack has been empty since about 1980.

According to Barb Michallis, who lived there for two summers in the late '70s, the house has a special place in the Island's history. "It holds a spot in a lot of people's hearts, because as long as people have been coming to the Island, the shack is the first thing they see after they cross the bridge," Michallis said. "It holds on a lot to the past, as opposed to modern houses and condos that you see everywhere on the Island. This is something different."

The Shack remained a causeway landmark until Superstorm Sandy washed it away in 2012. As recounted in the book Surviving Sandy, *resident Ed Hoffman was leaving the Island with a group of evacuees in the back of a National Guard truck. He caught a glimpse of the shack; only two walls were standing, Then, as he watched, it collapsed into the rising tide.*

1986 Life with a Little Dampness

Roy S. Wolper

Wherever you look — at newspaper advertisements, billboards or racks of postcards — it's the same image: Behind the sweep of sail off Beach Haven, the bikini-clad blonde in Surf City or the rolling sand dunes of Barnegat Light, there is sunshine. Always, the Jersey Shore is wedded to the sun.

But even in the clear, hot season, visitors become aware of the moisture. A friend who once stayed with us at our Jersey Shore house was unable to see the time on his watch one morning because of the water that had formed under its crystal.

"Time may march on," he told us at breakfast, "but no one can prove it here. I can't see the hands."

For the vacationer, dampness is a matter for a transient joke. However, to those of us who live at the shore, dampness is as palpable and omnipresent as the tropical air.

Knives and forks washed after dinner and then left in the drainer overnight to dry need to be toweled dry in the morning. In the bathroom, the bar of soap sinks into the ribs of its plastic holder. When my outside door is shut at bedtime the swollen lower ledge rasps as it crosses the lintel.

Like the cigarette ash on the plate of a friend, these are not more than irritating afterthoughts. But no house owner can afford to overlook moisture. My next-door neighbor built a shed but did not use galvanized nails: one day later like tears on mascara, streaks lined his new wood. Even two coats of paint were not able to contain the shedding metal.

The dinette set purchased secondhand may have been a good buy, but not for the shore. Within a few seasons, its chrome legs developed ineradicable pitting, even though we waxed them regularly. Soon the whole set — unmarked plastic top and all — went to the curb. If you own the house, you know that you live under siege. (It was the same in Saskatchewan.

from *The Beachcomber* • August 13, 1986

Ray Fisk

Little Egg Harbor Bay in fog.

Except that the enemy was cold. You never touched metal in the winter unless you were wearing gloves and you kept apples or candy bars in the car's glove compartment because you were afraid of a breakdown on empty country roads.)

Because of the dampness you learn how brake cables work and where they have to be oiled. You learn about screening and screws and nails (copper, for instance will not rust but its softness makes the nails less durable). You also become aware that leather has a life. Every day, I check (overcompulsively) to see if the leather-covered banjo above our bed is growing a beard. At the hardware store you become alert to the word "coated" on the packaging.

You come to enjoy the battle, although sometimes the victories are expensive. For example, our replacement for the dinette was a butcher-block table and chairs held together by pegs, but they cost twenty-five times the price of our chrome set. And sometimes those victories are just chancy — our wooden bathroom cabinet is a discard from a boat.

And some of these victories are psychological.

When I have to put on a limp T-shirt or drooping slacks I think of my hitch in the army, when the sheets were as stiff as cardboard and my shirt collars as hard as a ruler. Limp is better, I tell myself. The paper on which I prepare notes for my lectures curls at both ends, the top taking its configuration from the book it had rested against. I smooth the paper, but it remains misshapen, curved and rumply.

But my great rewards are due to the battle.

My three-speed bicycle, which I purchased more than twenty years ago, spends most of its life outside. Before leaving the shore each year, I flip it on its back and oil it carefully. In the spring, wheels on the pavement, I check it for life.

The left handbrake always works, and I try it first. More coy, the right one often refuses to budge, and so I oil its cable again. After waiting a little while, I pump the right hand-brake. It releases.

At that moment, as my fingers hit my palm, I am so excited that I almost stroke the bike and say, as I do to my Malamute friend Ilsa, "You're fine, old girl."

When the Millers, who came to the shore for the Memorial Day weekend, wanted beach chairs we walked to the shed. I inserted the key and it went in as easily as my feet into loafers. I turned it. The lock sprung open with the suddenness of light.

For the Millers, the experience was nothing more than a long pause. But for me, the day was a triumph. Squat, heavy and discolored, the lock has been under attack by moisture twenty-four hours a day from the first year I bought the house twenty-five years ago. Its innards, oiled every month, kept their verve. I was overjoyed.

Such pleasures, I suspect, the day-tripper or renter rarely feels. For them dampness is a nuisance, the mainspring of a wry joke. But for those of us who battle it every day, when we win (rarely), we feel, to paraphrase Shakespeare, "the perfectest heralds of joy."

1987 Best of Beach Haven

Carole Garibaldi Rogers

We are about to begin a summer vacation on Long Beach Island. That certainly does not make us unusual; thousands of other New Jersey families can say the same. Nor is it particularly newsworthy in our own family history, as we have spent many vacations in Beach Haven.

We have taken vacations elsewhere, but as the boys grow old enough to remember the various places they've been and to make their own comparisons, they invariably choose to return to Beach Haven. They're quick to list their reasons:

"The surf is the best there," says one,

"And they have great cheese steaks," another will add.

"We can ride our bikes everywhere."

"We can get sticky buns."

"Besides, we get to hear such good stories down there."

So we return. And we do all the things we promised we'd do. The boys spend hours in the ocean and confirm that the riders are best in Beach Haven. We eat cheese steaks and sticky buns. We ride our bikes to breakfast, lunch or dinner — and also to Holgate. The boys go fishing and crabbing with my husband. We eat steamers and corn and blueberries. Nothing unusual, really. We could be in Bay Head or Stone Harbor or many other Jersey Shore towns. But Beach Haven is different — and for us, better — because that's where our memories are.

When we get on our bikes and travel up and down the quiet streets, we are taking our own tour, noting our own historical markers. We see the present, but we're thinking of the past. My husband, who spent many bachelor summers in Beach Haven before we met, points to a newly refurbished, gray-shingled guest house similar to all the other Victorian houses on the block. "Many a weekend I stayed on the top floor up there," he tells the boys. "The man who used to own the place knew Hemingway when he was

from *The Beachcomber* • July 30, 1987

Beach Haven, 1984.

in Paris. Bill always told wonderful stories."

On another street he points to a nondescript brown house. "That used to be an old convent," he says. "We rented that house the first year after the nuns moved out. There were still pews in the chapel." And he goes on to tell of the group of eight single people and one married couple who came together to share a summer's lodging and have stayed friends for close to twenty years.

Our boys know these stories; so do I. We know the people, too, so we listen and laugh at the escapades of that summer and the many that followed. The magic envelops all of us, for these are my husband's memories.

Mine begin at the corner where Coral meets Beach — in a green, Victorian-style house. The year before we were married, when I was first introduced to Long Beach Island, I stayed there on weekends. It was a charming guest house in those days; each bedroom had pastel walls, matching chenille bedspreads and ruffled curtains. We called it "Cozy Corners," an offhand tribute to the extra homey touches. The following year, after a June wedding, we chose to rent a cottage in Beach Haven for the summer rather than take a more exotic, distant, two-week vacation.

The cottage has a new coat of paint now and is almost obscured by the pines we loved even then. The boys pay it no mind; they're much more

48

interested in the next few places on our tour. The memories continue to intertwine — his, then ours, now theirs.

We stop our bikes on Atlantic Ave., pointing like tourists in Malibu at the rear of an oceanfront house. And we tell them again of the summer Matthew had an ear infection. He does not remember crying most of every night, but we remember taking turns, one night on, one night off, pacing the length of a very small living room. We saw many a sunrise that summer.

"Do you remember when we walked out into the dunes to look at the sunrise?" we ask.

"No," he answers. But when we mention the pink medicine that we gave him every four hours around the clock ... "That pink stuff? I remember that," he says.

Gradually, as the boys grew older, we introduced them to our favorite things. They were still toddlers when we took them to the Bayview Manor to watch the sunset. The Bayview was a restaurant with a spectacular western view and an outdoor waterfront bar that was seldom crowded. There our group gathered. Fortified with carrot sticks and saltines that we'd brought in baggies, the boys would sit on picnic benches watching the boats come and go while the sun slid down behind the marshes and we talked and sipped.

The Bayview has given way to condominiums. We gathered last time on the deck at the home of an old friend. The sunset was wonderfully familiar; so were the stories. Seven of the ten members of the original group were there; they had come from Florida, New York and Pennsylvania, as well as New Jersey. I don't think old friends set out to reminisce. It just happens,

"Have you seen ..."

"Not since Christmas ..."

"How did we meet him anyhow?"

"Don't you remember that night at Joe Pop's?"

And they're off. Our son Doug has an unerring instinct for when the stories will begin. He may be down on the street or on the upper lookout deck, but let my husband launch into a story, and Doug will appear. Both boys love that kind of evening. It is one of the reasons, they say, they like to return to Beach Haven. And they're right. Evenings like that are fun —

and all too rare.

Our sons are already beginning to stockpile their own memories. As we prepare to return to the Island, they interrupt each other to tell of the spectacular fireworks we watched from our deck or the day our canoe capsized on the Wading River.

My husband and I are still lured by faraway places. We will travel elsewhere and so, I hope, will the boys. The Island will continue to change, growing more crowded, and thus less appealing to those of us who liked the old days. But the intertwining of all our memories — his, ours, theirs — will pull us back again to Beach Haven.

1987 Overexposed: I Was Warned

Sidney Jones

When I was a little girl, we spent our summers here at the shore. After a long winter in the city, we motored to our cozy cottage by the ocean. It was a typical shore home, just behind a big sand dune. White with green trim, it was on 4th Street in Surf City. Dad's hand-painted sign over the door read, "Saltie Sprae."

I remember playing on the beach with my brothers and chasing the fiddler crabs as they scurried to find their holes in the sand. And sometimes we scooped up a couple of dusty miller plants that grew so profusely on the beach to plant in Mom's little garden. The diamondback terrapins came out of the bay in June and crawled across the Island to lay their eggs. It was a large procession and lasted several weeks every year. Sometimes a few got squashed by cars as they crossed the road, but there weren't many cars then, so most made it safely back to the bay.

My dad was a big man, or so it seemed to me, and we used to go for a walk most every day down to the Surf City Hotel. Walt Searle tended the bar while his wife Mable ran the combination grocery and candy store. We always went into the bar and I'll never forget how I always smelled the odor of stale beer about half a block away before we got there.

Several other local men stood at the bar drinking and talking and laughing. Everyone sure did enjoy themselves at Walt Searle's bar. My dad always had a beer and a shot and he usually gave me a couple of nickels to play the pinball machine. Oh, it was fun.

One day as Dad and I left the bar, he said there was a fortune teller in town on vacation. It was a typical shore day, bright and sunny with a refreshing breeze off the ocean. When we got to her cottage just a few blocks up the boulevard, I saw a colorful sign with a hand holding face cards. Under the hand, it said, "Fortunes Told." Dad knocked and a small woman with straight black hair, wearing a beautiful gypsy dress, answered the door and invited us in. The three of us sat at a table with a red and white checkerboard cloth and she told our fortunes.

We were going to have exciting lives, according to the fortune teller. The only disturbing thing she told me was that when I grew up, the whole world would be able to see me naked. Well, I positively knew that would never happen. Dad and I had a lot of fun together. Guess I was special because I was his only daughter.

As the years rolled by, the shore changed and many, many more people discovered its fascination. Hundreds of new homes were built, most on pilings high in the air. They went up all around us, and our little cottage looked so small. I went into several of them over the years and I always looked out the windows to see the view, but all I ever saw were the roofs of all the small houses.

Dad and Mom are in Florida now, and I live here in our little cottage with my own family: Jeffrey, Lloyd and Lori. First thing when I get up in the morning, I like to shower. The big window in the bathroom is always open to let the ocean breeze in, which adds to my enjoyment. The other morning I was enjoying my daily ritual, soaping my body as the water bounced off my breasts and arms, and I looked up out of the window and there were half a dozen teenaged boys standing on the deck of a high-piling house next door watching me shower. They were laughing and having fun — at my expense.

I guess fortune tellers know what they're talking about.

1987 Summer in Freeze Frames

Robert A Freedman

Summer always seems to end before it ever really gets going. Too soon, the back-to-school specials are appearing in newspaper advertising, and the days become noticeably shorter. It's all a whirl, a lovely whirl, rich in memories to be mined in later years. My brain stores these summer times in freeze frames, black-and-white photographs in an album that exists nowhere in reality.

Snap: There's my father on the beach, wearing a white captain's hat with a plastic brim. He is smiling. Dad never wears that hat anywhere but on the beach, and doesn't smile much the rest of the year.

Snap: My cousin Michael, my brother Paul and I are rolling down a sand dune, one mass of wrestling, youthful humanity. We are grinding sand between our bodies and laughing so hard that we're no longer sure where one of us begins and the other ends. Michael is diagnosed as having leukemia two years later.

Snap: I am casting a surf pole on the beach at Ship Bottom. The pole is three times as long as I am. I catch a blowfish. We are both hooked.

Snap: My friend Lenny and I sit at the end of an old wooden pier. We are fishing. By the end of the day, we have caught only a few ugly spider crabs and our bare feet have become lanced with scores of jagged splinters. My father patiently removes the sharp slivers with a tweezer that night, and paints my feet with Mercurochrome.

Snap: I am on my first bicycle, a three-speed British job with brilliant crimson paint. I can hardly believe my parents have been this generous. I am twelve years old but have never owned a bike before, as there is no place to ride one safely in our West Philadelphia neighborhood. Now we have a place of our own at the shore and I have a bike. Later, I crash my beautiful bicycle on Beach Ave., riding with my friend Billy the Juvenile Delinquent, whom my parents hate.

Snap: Carolyn, my first girlfriend. Blonde curly hair and freckles and a smile that knocks me into mute submission. We go to the movies in Brant Beach, and after an hour of agonizing over whether I dare, I take hold of Carolyn's hand. I think I've died or wish I would, 'cause life will never again be so perfect. Then the movie ends. My mom waits outside to pick us up. Neither of us speaks on the way home.

Snap: I am at third base for the infamous Shapiro Pirates, our short-lived Little League team. A ball comes rocketing on the ground to my corner. I pick it up smoothly and hurl it to first base. I watch as the ball soars twelve feet over the first baseman's head. We lose the game, and when the coach takes us out to the A&W for ice cream cones, I refuse mine. I don't deserve it.

Snap: The whole clan is crabbing at a bayside bulkhead. My Uncle Jack has led us here and is keeping everyone laughing with a constant stream of jokes and banter; I think I will cry, I am laughing so hard. And we are catching crabs so quickly we have to wait to use the landing net. Sometimes there are even small bass or eels in the crab traps when we haul them up.

Snap: Toads in a shoebox. Paul and I have collected them. They are tiny, no bigger than nuggets of salt-water taffy, babies. Us city boys watch in amazement as the toads jump in the carton. Mom makes us let them go. They leap out to freedom on our front lawn.

Snap: The mosquito man is coming down the street in his jeep; a thick cloud of smoke billows out behind him. He is spraying the thickets where the mosquitoes live and breed. Paul and I run after the jeep, losing our-

Ray Fisk

After a day of crabbing and fishing, Causway Boat Rentals, mid-1980s.

selves in the cloud of gas. All the kids love the smell of DDT.

Snap: There is a sky full of clouds, black and threatening. The air is thick around us as the adults whisper among themselves. But we know what is happening. A hurricane is on the way and they are discussing whether we should get in the car and leave the Island. "I want to stay," I announce. "It'll be fun." I am told to be quiet. We stay and the hurricane passes us by.

Snap: Three kids with smiling faces and burnt noses are standing with their backs to the surf. Mom is taking their picture. Smile, she says. I try hard, but can't. I am frozen like my snapshots, and this is someone else's picture, someone else's summer. I am all grown up, and gone away.

1987 Residents Like It Like This

Margaret Daley

Crossing Barnegat Bay eastbound via the Route 72 causeway bridge, just beyond the grassy stretch that follows the main causeway, there is a sign hidden among the trees on the right that boldly announces "Entering Cedar Bonnet Island." A cluster of cottages appears on both sides of the highway for the few seconds it takes motorists to zoom by. Most people speeding by probably don't notice the Island, let alone the sign. And anyone curious enough to explore Cedar Bonnet would be hardpressed to do more than circle it once.

No useable beaches are found on Cedar Bonnet, and no marina is located there, although the adventuresome can rent a rowboat from Duke's Boat Rental on 1st Street There's no place to buy bait, pick up a newspaper or a quart of milk, or even make a pit stop for cigarettes or gas. Its only draw and, not surprisingly, its unofficial landmark, is The Dutchman's, a German restaurant and bar.

Yet there is something unique about Cedar Bonnet, an aura that replaces the monotonous drone of the highway almost at once, and suggests that time, like the highway, has passed it by. The narrow streets, their squatty painted cottages with pitched roofs and names like "Cozy Corner" and "Bay View," the mailboxes disguised as sitting ducks and the weary bulkheads and piers all resemble the kind of family resort that was popular in the 1950s. Longtime summer residents of the Island still refer to the older cottages that were built in the late 1920s by the names of their original owners, like the McCann house or the Pages' place. Except for an occasional raised house or the wooden decks or fresh additions that stand out in some places, Cedar Bonnet shows no signs of the modern development apparent everywhere on Long Beach Island.

One obvious reason is that there's no place left to build. The only undeveloped land remaining there consists of wetlands on its north end that are

from *The SandPaper* • July 29, 1987

livelihoods. Hired by the state to operate the drawbridge between Cedar Bonnet and Long Beach Island, Adams arrived in 1922 and moved his young family into a four-room house that sat right on the bridge. That same year, Charlie Fackler appeared. Fackler, originally from Pennsylvania, had been a baker in Bordentown and was lured to the shore by his love of fishing. He recognized the importance of Cedar Bonnet's location and bought a piece of land alongside the western end of the auto road where the Dutchman's parking lot now stands. The family lived in the Bayside Club, a modest hunting lodge and one of the few shelters on the Island. Fackler did odd jobs for the railroad until the house was built and in 1924 went into business selling bait and tackle.

In those days, the population on that tiny island, between the Facklers and the Adams family, hovered around ten. The Island's future lay firmly in the hands of C. H. Cranmer of the well-known Cranmer/Hazelton clan. Cranmer owned a country store in Manahawkin but preferred to play out his hunches about the land. He had bought up most of Cedar Bonnet and was selling it off in small lots, about 25 feet by 30 feet, like the one Charlie Fackler bought. In the late 1920s the lots went for about $800 on the installment plan. For $500 more Cranmer would put up a house. As Cranmer attracted buyers, mostly from the Trenton and Philadelphia area, the population swelled to about thirty in the summertime.

The Island offered all the fishing, crabbing, duck hunting and clamming one could ask for, but the real challenge was coping with everyday life. Neither Charlie Fackler nor Burrel Adams is alive today, but their sons are. Jack and Bill Fackler, both in their 60s, recall a bittersweet childhood trying to stay one step ahead of Mother Nature while reaping the bounty of her land.

Winters were desolate and brought northeasters and in the summers greenheads and mosquitoes struck like a plague. There was no running water and what came up from the artesian well was potent with chemicals, "You couldn't leave the clothes in it too long, let alone make tea," Bill Fackler recalled. The brothers, along with Bill's twin sister Betty, made countless trips in a rowboat to get water from the Bonnet Club, which in those days served as the private playground of a group of wealthy industrialists.

In the winter, since kerosene was expensive, the Fackler kids, along

Charlie Fackler's bar, at the foot of the old Causeway on Cedar Bonnet Island.

with young Burrel Adams, would collect the loose pieces of coal and hot coke that were left on the railroad tracks after a train passed. Even in those days Cedar Bonnet was no more than a whistle stop. The train would drop off newspapers and kerosene and supplies for the Bayside Club, but the only people who got on or off were family members on their way to or from the mainland to shop. Still, the railroad, along with the original causeway, looms large in the memories of these men — all retired now and still living in the area. Those memories include fishing off the railroad bridge and scrambling down the trestle when a train came, often getting doused with steam, and watching a train approach after a storm when "the whitecaps would cover the tracks and it looked like the train was running on the water," Adams remembered. Some old-timers recall hearing the rumbling of the wooden planks of the Causeway all the way from Mud City (a similar housing tract along East Bay Ave. near the bay front in Manahawkin) where the cars started across.

The railroad and causeway linked the Island to the outside world and exposed the Fackler and Adams children to life beyond Cedar Bonnet more intimately than any newspaper or radio could. The city folks who traveled to the Island in the summer represented more than bread and butter to the Facklers' bait and tackle business or young Adams' paper route. They were also the source of vivid recollections like the one Adams still cherishes of Billy Richmond's silver grey Auburn Cord auto and the times Burrel got to ride in it when Billy picked him up hitchhiking to Manahawkin for the family's mail.

When the Great Depression caught up with the often extravagant life-styles of those from the city, the families on Cedar Bonnet were ironically spared its devastation. "We didn't really feel the Depression because we lived off the land. There were no industries around, and the game wardens looked the other way. We took care of each other. We didn't know how poor we were until the Depression was over and people told us how bad it was," said Adams.

The end of the Depression, and more importantly the repeal of Prohibition in 1933, marked the start of what could be considered Cedar Bonnet Island's only heyday. Charlie Fackler's business had survived, even grown a bit. With his kids now old enough to mind the store, Charlie decided to expand. During Prohibition he had brewed nearbeer, the only thing legal, to sell to the local fishermen. Afterwards, he obtained the first liquor license issued by Stafford Township, which put up little opposition thanks to Cedar Bonnet's remote location. Charlie had already established a reputation as a colorful character (his son, Bill, describes him as "the world's first hippie"), and it wasn't long before everybody knew about "Charlie's place."

Among other things, Charlie was an inveterate collector, and the tavern became his own private museum with whale bones serving as bar stools and scores of old rifles and guns, some dating back to the Civil War, hanging from the ceiling, along with an aerial bomb from the first World War. "People would come in to show my father something they'd found on the beach," explained Bill Fackler, "and he'd take it off their hands for a couple of drinks. Then they'd come back later with a friend to show off where Charlie had hung it on the wall." As Charlie's collection grew, so did the business.

Charlie's was the kind of place where you didn't worry about decorum, not with a dozen pet rattlesnakes in the window and the local fishermen who stepped up to the bar with the day's catch in tow. It was the place to gather on Friday and Saturday nights. "The bar would fill up, and there wouldn't be three people who didn't know each other," recalled Jack Fackler, who spent more hours than he cares to remember behind the bar. Fishermen would belly up with industrialists, $100 bills commonly crossed the bar, and Billy Richmond drank from his own private bottle of scotch. Often, tempers flared, mostly between the Mainland "stump jumpers" and the Long Beach Island "clamdiggers," but slug fests often came to a sudden halt when somebody knocked over the pot-bellied stove and everyone scrambled to gather up the still burning coals.

While the Fackler brothers insist the bar brought them little besides headaches, they did have their fun. Jack recalls a certain Canadian tourist who came down every year and ordered a crab sandwich. Jack would grab a live crab from out back and stroke its belly until it fell asleep and then lay it on a piece of bread and cover it with lettuce. When the waitress delivered the sandwich she would purposely set the plate down with a bang, startling the crab, not to mention the customers, and send it scurrying, lettuce and all, down the bar.

By the late 1930s, other businesses had sprung up along the auto road including another tavern, a couple of restaurants and even a small hotel. But World War II meant another turning point for Cedar Bonnet. After the war, more and more people came to the shore. The Fackler brothers and Burrel Adams had all married, and only Jack still lived on the Island. He and Bill continued to help Charlie with the business, even expanding it further to include a restaurant. Eventually, it proved too much to handle, and in the early 1950s, Charlie sold the business to Otto and Thekla Schmid, who changed the name to the Bay Shore Bar. The 1962 storm forced the Schmids to rebuild, and they reopened with The Dutchman's. Meanwhile, Charlie Fackler and his wife remained on Cedar Bonnet, living in a house their sons had built for them until they died.

The building of the current bridge, in 1956-'57, and extension of Rt. 72 wiped out the other businesses along the old road and brought Cedar Bonnet full circle to its original status as a stepping stone. Not much remains from the past except the old road that runs along the highway. Even the last of Cranmer's lots were finally sold a couple of years ago, and when Adams

Esther Rinear's sons Douglas and David at home on Cedar Bonnet Island, about 1949.

stopped by one day looking for the old railroad bed, he couldn't find it.

Cedar Bonnet's legacy now rests in the handful of summer and year-round residents like Rinear, who first came as a kid and remembers the Facklers and the Adams family, Charlie's place and the rumbling of the wooden planks on the old causeway.

According to them, except for the highway, Cedar Bonnet hasn't changed all that much. Considering the fact that Rinear's son owns the house next door to hers, and her grandson represents the fourth generation of the family there, one wonders if Cedar Bonnet ever will.

1987 AT&T Lays It on the Line

Marion Figley

While beachgoers along the Island sunned themselves — or tried to under the haze brought by humid weather early this week — people along Beach Haven's surf watched more than the waves and an occasional gull. Working off the surf on the first leg of a transoceanic job, AT&T technicians and engineers were carefully and laboriously laying out the initial twenty miles of a new cable that will carry the equivalent of 40,000 simultaneous telephone calls between North America and Europe.

Officially christened the "Eighth Atlantic Undersea Cable System," or TAT-8 for short, the $335 million project is a far cry from the first transoceanic telegraph cable laid back in the 19th century or even the older copper lines currently in service.

"A fiber-optic cable is a whole lot thinner than a standard cable," said John Satterfield, AT&T's public relations manager. "It is an extruded glass that can carry a far higher volume of telecommunications. Fiber optics enables us to convert communications to beams of light and transmit at the speed of light. The best copper cables can carry between 400 and 500 telephone circuits on a piece of cable about an inch in diameter. On six, hair-thin filaments, we can carry 40,000 separate circuits: 10,000 on each of four filaments with two filaments in there for spares." By contrast, TAT-7 — which was built in 1973 and runs from Manahawkin to England — carries about nine thousand simultaneous calls.

TAT-8 originated at AT&T's cable terminal in Tuckerton last October when 4,000 feet of line was laid to the east side of Rt. 9. From here, another length of one-and-one-quarter miles took it over the salt marsh to the western edge of Little Egg Harbor Bay where a reel of the cable was loaded on a barge and laid out over the stern of the vessel. Another 4,300 feet of cable ran from the bayfront of Beach Haven to a temporary resting place on the oceanside at Taylor Ave.

from *Beachcomber* • July 16, 1987

"The cable used in this portion of the project is the light-wire armored version of TAT-8," said Satterfield. "The cable is covered with a layer of steel wires to protect it from such underground hazards as excavating equipment and burrowing animals, and from anchors, fishing equipment and other hazards in Little Egg Harbor." That underwater portion in the bay was buried to a depth of four feet with special electronic equipment called sea plows that leave the bottom virtually undisturbed.

And while the three weeks of this installation project were going on, similar work was underway at the two TAT-8 shore terminals in Europe. Those stations are in Widemouth, England and Penmarch, France, a distance of about thirty-six-hundred nautical miles. "Both England and France have laid cables to a branching repeater about 280 miles off the coast of Europe," said Satterfield. "When the Cable Ship *Long Lines* arrives there, it will splice into the repeater."

When the freighter *Marion C* arrived off Beach Haven on Monday, the cable was channeled through 1,500 feet of existing conduit previously buried under the surf and beach and spliced into the terminal at Taylor Ave. "The ship lowered a jet-sled sea plow to dig a trench four-feet deep, and it's playing out the cable as it goes," said Satterfield. That going is slow — a tenth of a knot per hour to allow the plow to bury the cable. To steady the ship's course at the slow speed, two anchors are used off the bow and the ship is winched toward them. Yesterday, the freighter was about a mile off the beach, carrying the 130,000 feet of cable needed to lay the first twenty miles of TAT-8. The process should take about two weeks, said Satterfield.

From the twenty-mile mark to the edge of the continental shelf, a distance of about 80 miles, the Canadian Coast Guard ship *John Cabot* will lay the cable with a sea plow but only to a depth of two feet. "The additional depth of the water out there probably means that there will be less chance for a ship dragging an anchor and snagging it or for a trawler accidentally bringing it up," said Satterfield.

AT&T distributes free charts so fishermen can give a one-mile-wide berth to an active cable, and official navigational charts also mark undersea cable corridors. A five- to ten-ton hydraulic clam dredge and other boats used to spread nets on trawlers can break cables. For international callers, that's no problem: AT&T immediately shunts the calls over satellite channels or other cables. For the company, however, the repair bill is usually six figures. When not installing cable, the *C.S. Long Lines* is on maintenance duty on the Atlantic Ocean.

"The only alternative to cables right now are satellite transmissions, and cables — particularly the fiber-optic cables — offer a very good alternative to satellite transmission," said Satterfield. Besides the economic advantage of the cables he added, "It's also a bit more certain. You don't have to worry about atmospheric interference. Anytime you're transmitting through the air instead of a wire, you can run into interference problems that can disrupt your signal. The cable is very reliable and relatively economical."

That's not to say that cables aren't without their own problems. The ocean bottom of this relatively young planet is constantly shifting and heaving with seaquakes and seaslides. And when AT&T ran test lines of the new fiber-optic cable between the Canary Islands off the coast of Africa, engineers checking the lines discovered sharks' teeth embedded in the cable sheathing. Apparently, the sharks preferred the high-tech cables over the older copper lines which have gone untouched on the ocean floor. Company engineers blamed the sharks' snack attack on the higher current that runs through the fiber-optic cable.

Because the cable here will be buried for its first one-hundred miles, there should be no problem with sharks, Satterfield said. And when *C.S. Long Lines* finally retrieves the end of the cable at the continental shelf, splices it into cable stored on the ship and lays the remainder of TAT-8 across the Atlantic, there will be no shark worries either, even though the cable will not be buried. "The water isn't shallow there like it is on the shelf," said Satterfield. "We don't expect them to feed in this area." No trouble is expected from the weather, either. "*Long Lines* doesn't turn back; when it hits a storm, it just rides it out," said Satterfield.

And unlike the days when it carried the thicker copper cable, the ship does not have to return to port to pick up more cable: all 3,160 nautical miles are stored on huge spools in special bins located in the hull. At a speed of five knots an hour, *Long Lines*' trip should take less than three weeks. The new cable has a life of about twenty-five years, said Satterfield, and will replace retired or retiring cables.

TAT-8 will be owned by twenty-nine companies and telecommunications administrations in North America and Europe. AT&T will own about thirty-seven percent of the system and is constructing eighty percent of the project. By next July, area residents should be able to reach out and touch someone in Europe via TAT-8.

TAT-8 was the first transatlantic telephone cable to use fiber optics.

1992 **What We Do All Winter**

Larry Savadove

Summer people, even spring people, always wonder: "What do you do here all winter," the implication being that the only thing to do here all winter is wait for summer in a sort of hunkered-down, bunkered-in hibernation.

Usually we just point a chin at the checkerboard or mumble something about knitting afghans. One or two might gush over walking alone on the wind-swept beach and a few admit to indulging in a penchant for alchoholism, but the last thing we want to do is let you know that in the winter this place is such a churn of activity we barely have time to get it back the way you remember it before summer.

But since idly curious minds want to know, we decided to pull back the curtain, throw off the covers and cough up the truth. Heck, you probably won't believe it anyhow.

One of the big events is the All-Island Cat Catch. Since people are forever leaving or losing their cats here, we end up with an enormous feral feline population. Around the middle of January, two teams start out from

from *The Beachcomber* • May 16, 1992

opposite ends of the Island, appropriately padded against tooth and claw and bayberry brambles and provided with old frying pans. They advance toward each other banging on the pans and howling like dogs, flushing out cats that they try to lasso. Those that elude them come together in the middle of the Island where, stirred to a frenzy, they fall upon each other in a fury of furballs until only one bleeding but triumphant survivor is left standing. They let him go to wait for next year's crop of pretty kitties. Then they cook the losers. This year Martha Digadak created a puss mousse that had us all raving.

Another popular pastime is to build sand igloos which we cut out of the frozen surf line and then sit in for long hours waiting for the seals. This winter, to everyone's astonishment, a seal did show up, so we're thinking of waiting for polar bears next year.

Every weekend we pick a different "closed for the winter" house and have a hell of a party. We always clean up the next day, except for one little clue we like to leave to make people think. Rat skulls are always good.

On clear Saturdays we have races down the Boulevard. The direction depends on which way the wind is blowing. Fastest time so far is five minutes, twenty-seven seconds, set by Burt Farfellow, but it didn't count because he mounted his pickup on rollerblades.

Sometimes we all go down to Fantasy Island and ... fantasize.

A new thing we're just playing around with is bungee-jumping off Barnegat Lighthouse. We discovered the wind has to be just right to do this and there have been suggestions we switch to the water towers. Jimmy Gibber is studying it.

At least once a year we play all the miniature golf courses on the Island in one day. It's more fun without the obstacles. Since the golf clubs are locked up, we use baseball bats and croquet mallets. Balls were a problem for a while. We found that sand crabs didn't hold up too well. We finally decided we didn't really need balls and since then it's been, well, a ball.

Fish-tossing is always good. It's something like Frisbee tossing but you can't let the dog go after them. The trick is to toss them by the tail, catch them by the gills. An accomplished fish-tosser can put a spiral on one, like a football, so the gills make a whistling sound, but it takes practice. And velcro hands.

Broom hockey on a frozen Barnegat Bay, Harvey Cedars, New Year's Day 1984.

There is sand skiing on the dunes and, lately, there's a wonderful ski jump off that great sloping roof in Loveladies, but ice dancing is far more challenging. It's called ice dancing but it's really more like ice hopping or, as some people call it, bay-plopping. The object is to get from here to the mainland by hopping from ice floe to ice floe.

It does take some ingenuity to entertain ourselves when our only link to civilization is cable TV but we're a hardy lot and used to deprivation and we think being thrown on our own resources builds character. It can take a toll, though. There was the time the Tolliver twins, Solly and Polly, built a pyramid of lifeguard stands. They'd gotten it up higher than the lighthouse when the tide turned and toppled it, throwing Solly way out somewhere into the Gulf Stream, still clutching a stand. It finally washed up on Cape

Race in Newfoundland, but without Solly. Polly went off to the west coast of Scotland to wait.

It may sound like all we care about is just having fun, but come summer we're as sober and proper and boring as everybody else. If you want to sample some of the good times, though, come down here for the winter. Oh, and bring some frying pans. With more people taking shorter vacations, it looks as if we're going to have a lot more cats this year.

1993 The Cat Who Walked Alone

Larry Savadove

Her name was Sam. She was green-eyed, tawny, sleek and spoiled — spoiled the way favorite pets get, spoiled with treats for doing little more than looking good and yawning indifferently every now and then.

She came and went as she pleased, pleased with herself and, generally, with life.

Then — she was abandoned.

Maybe the family thought she was in the back of the van, curled up on a beach towel as she often did. Maybe everybody thought somebody else had seen to her. Or maybe, unthinkable as it may be, in the end-of-season rush to pack up, board up and be off, she was just, well, overlooked.

For when Sam returned from her dune-side stalk of late butterflies and plume grass that September afternoon and bounded up to her own private entrance in the bottom of the back door she found it shut. Tight.

She pawed at it a few times, her claws raking the metal with a screech

from *The Beachcomber* • July 3, 1993

of impatience. She sat and looked at it for a while in haughty non-compre-hension. She mewed again, louder, several times. By now the situation was not merely annoying, it was an outrage.

She raised her tail high and straight, her flag, her colors to the world, and marched around to the front porch. But instead of the screened-in bubble of creaking rockers and laughing children and radio music she found a bare and silent deck on which the only sounds were the echoes of the surf from across the empty beach and the faint whistle of the rising wind.

And Sam felt a chill.

When life is a set of routines, any change in any one is disorienting. A breakdown of all is immobilizing. Sam sat on the edge of the deck, confu-sion already replacing outrage, hunger beginning to clutch at her gut, and utterly no idea of what to do. She sat there as night rose out of the ocean to creep up the beach and wrap her and the house and the Island in dark-ness that had, heretofore, been Sam's to embrace or ignore as she chose.

Her eyes quickly adapted; some things are inborn. But her body remained frozen in place, its muscles tense — another instinctive reac-tion — ready. But all the night through nothing attacked her, save for the hunger and the realization that sometime that afternoon her life had drastically changed. She was suddenly in a world that didn't care whether she was there or not.

On the first day of her new life she began to register things she had known before but only as part of the atmosphere. The wind from the beach brought a familiar scent. There has been no whine of the can opener that once was her dinner bell, but the odor was umistakable.

She stood, arching slowly in the sun. There was an unfamiliar ache in her bones but she soon stretched it out again. Then she padded down the steps and back out over the dunes to the beach, toward the smell.

The first few nights she came back to the porch, pulled by the inertia of habit. But it was an exposed perch, and as the days grew shorter the winds grew longer. She took to sleeping under the porch for a while, but then discovered the small caves made by the tilted jumble of jetty where she could hunker into the sand and out of the increasingly chilly wind. The waves washed bits of food into nearby crannies and the sun warmed the rocks for midday naps.

And she grew accustomed, drawing on an instinct that had been hibernating somewhere in her genes. She roamed the surf line, scavenging what the gulls left or chasing them away from a newly cracked clam. On days when the wind was still and did not turn the long, dry grasses into whips, she prowled the dunes for mice and insects.

She discovered she shared the jetty with rats. Less shy of the water, they were sometimes caught in a crevice when a sudden wave would take them by surprise, and Sam would dine, as if at a buffet, picking her next morsel at will from the skewered carcass. The gulls were too fast for her, but now and then one would crash against the rocks on a bad take-off into a cross wind, smashing a wing, and Sam could vary her diet.

Thus passed the winter. One snowstorm kept her in her burrow for two days, but she had learned how to pry open mussels by then. The pad of fat that had accumulated under her fine fur during her domestic years was replaced by muscle. She kept her sleek coat groomed but it was now thick and, despite her best efforts, gnarled with burrs.

Her ears could pickup the sound of a clammer over on the bay, the Dumpster behind the supermarket, the trash truck. Once she heard some radio music and sat bone still, listening, until it stopped. Once she came upon an old wicker chair, half buried in the sand, its seat half torn out, and she sat in it for the morning. Once when she was crossing the boulevard a car stopped and a figure got out. Its silhouette fit a pattern somewhere in Sam's buried consciousness, something associated with warmth and comfort and ease and predictable dinners, but she shied from it nonetheless and fled into the bush.

Now and then she would come across another cat pacing the beach or rooting in the same Dumpster. Backs went up, hisses went forth, lips curled back from teeth, until the proper distance was re-established and the two went separate ways, true descendants of The Cat Who Walked by Himself. Or Herself.

Long before the unfamiliar cries of geese sounded across the Island, the scent of opening buds and shedding pollen told Sam the season was turning. The light lasted longer, which made hunting easier. The days were warmer and she was pulling great swaths of fur off her coat with each grooming. And there were more sounds, more activity.

The day the family returned, she had gone back to the house on her afternoon hunting circuit. It had been a long time since there had been any scraps to be found, but habit still took her on a reconnaissance tour under the porch.

The slam of the car door stirred something at the bottom of a memory that had been long enshrouded by winter winds, lashing grasses, screeching gulls, scratching rats, and layers of instinct that had built up like armor to protect her. She gathered herself into a tight wad of alert intensity. She peered out of the slats by the steps.

"Do you think she's still here?" The voice rang an echo inside memory cell. "Sam ... Saaaaamm."

"Don't be silly. If we did leave her she's dead by now."

"Sammmm. Oh, Saaamm ..."

Sam crouched in place, as immobile as the landscape. She placed the voices, more or less, something to do with her past, back beyond the wild beaches and the quiet nights. They were joined by others, all part of the memory which grew stronger with each chorus. Still she did not move.

All that day she remained at her post under the porch. Now and then the first voice would call out "Sammm," but each time with less conviction.

When darkness overtook the scene again and the house was quiet, Sam crept out and made her way back over the dunes. Another instinct inside her dropped the house from her hunting circuit. The memory that had circulated briefly in her consciousness receded and spun into the discard pile.

It was, after all, of no practical use to her.

1993 Rescuers Finally Get Their Man

Take the end of a long week, a day of beer drinking, add a gallon of vodka and shine an almost full moon over it all and what do you get? A middle-of-the-night craziness with the aspect of a three-ring circus.

In one ring — the one on the beach — frustrated police and firemen pulled from their homes and interested spectators. In the second — circling about two-hundred-fifty yards offshore in a rescue vessel — the U.S. Coast Guard from Barnegat Light and lifeguards attempting a rescue. And in the third, smaller and center ring — an angry man swimming in the ocean, yelling to be left alone and that he wanted to die.

According to Harvey Cedars policeman Tom Preiser, several anonymous calls came in to the borough dispatcher at 12:20 a.m., alerting the station to a man in the water who might be in trouble. One witness said the fracas began at the ocean end of 80th Street when a man started yelling obscenities at a woman walking to the beach with her brother to watch the moon on the ocean. When the brother chased the man onto the beach and apparently into the water, his sister called for the police.

When the police arrived, three borough lifeguards who were on the beach went out to search for the man, towing a rescue buoy from the police car. The swimmer yelled that if the police would turn off the searchlights being used to keep him in sight, he would come in. Preiser said they doused the lights, waited about five to eight minutes and he didn't move closer, so they put the lights back on but couldn't locate him as he'd swum further out.

When the incident started, the man was about 100 yards out and kept swimming east. Next, the High Point Volunteer Fire Company was called in with its stronger searchlight, and the Coast Guard was alerted. The sea was calm and the rescue vessel arrived in fifteen minutes, shot up a flare and, according to Preiser, it was as light as day. The recalcitrant swimmer

from *The Beachcomber* • August 7, 1993

was now being circled by the Coast Guard and the Harvey Cedars guards about 250 yards off the beach.

The man refused all pleas and rationalizations to come aboard, verbally threatening anyone within earshot. He started to swim under the boat and the Coast Guard cut the engine so he wouldn't be chopped up by the propeller. Meanwhile, the guardsmen also tried to convince him to swim ashore if he wouldn't come on board.

Now enter the Long Beach Township Beach Patrol with an inflatable rescue boat, with the Barnegat Light First Aid Squad standing by. Again at the swimmer's request, all lights went off except the moon, and the man edged closer to shore. He lay quietly in the surf, like he was hurt or playing possum, said Preiser. When the lights were switched back on, he saw the police and dived back into the surf and swam out just to the outer edge of the breakers.

It took two hours before he finally came in, and when he did four police officers grabbed him. Preiser said the first aid squad checked the swimmer immediately as the water temperature had dropped ten degrees in the past twenty-four hours and squad members feared hypothermia. (The Harvey Cedars guards had gone aboard the Coast Guard vessel, and the township guards were protected by wet suits.) Observing the scene, 80th Street resident Gary Hermann said, "It's lucky the firemen didn't get their hands on him."

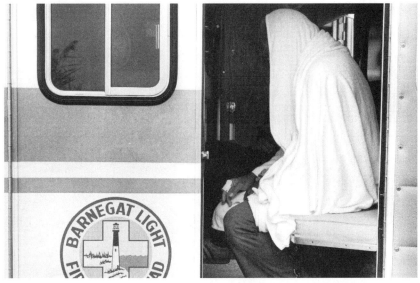

Ray Fisk

1994 **Screaming About Ice Cream**

Marjorie Amon

L enore Weiss of 25th Street in Spray Beach is hot under the collar when it comes to ice cream trucks parading past her home.

At Friday's commissioners' meeting Weiss said she started complaining about the influx of trucks when the total number cruising by reached six per hour. "This is my fourth — or is it my sixth? — appearance. I complained again when there were eight," she said. "This summer I counted between twelve and fourteen trucks an hour on summer weekends going by my house. That's a lot of bells and clangs and jingles every hour. Just to give you an idea of what it is like on my street," said Weiss, "the ice cream trucks start going by my house about 11 a.m. and come by about every four minutes. We cannot stay out on our decks, and neither can our neighbors."

Weiss said it is unpleasant when one vendor in particular leaves his truck running in front of her home while he runs up to the beach to ring a large cowbell to attract customers. "This gives me about four minutes of gas fumes in my living room," said Weiss.

"I've tried speaking to some of these fellows about being more considerate and some of them are nice. They say they can't shut the trucks off because the ice cream will melt. But the Good Humor man said to me, 'This is my route, and I can do anything I damn well please.'"

Weiss said if she can't get any peace from the ice cream invasion next year, her only recourse will be to move. "I'd hate to give up living here because of ice cream trucks," she implored the mayor. "Something has to be done."

Mayor Mancini said that he would continue to look into this ongoing problem.

from *The SandPaper* • October 26, 1994

1995 Frozen Assets in Good Humor

Marjorie Amon

The thermometer rises and the heat is on — to eat ice cream. You can, of course, come in contact with quarts of the cold, craved confection at your favorite ice cream parlor or supermarket. But for those not inclined to venture any farther than the end of their driveways for frozen refreshment there is another alternative which just keeps rolling along — the ice cream truck.

Keeping those wheels of fortune rolling along are the modern-day mobile emperors of ice cream, the vendors whose business credo is similar to Mohammed's: You scream, I scream, but if we won't get to the ice cream, then ice cream will come to us.

For some, the idea of driving around all day in an ice cream truck has a melting appeal, but that part of the vendor's job is just the tip of the iceberg. In order to make cold cash while the hot sun shines, an ice cream vendor needs not only a clean driving record, but the skills of a foreign diplomat.

Frank Sirianni, president for the past forty years of Bay Berry Ice Cream Co. of Toms River, one of several ice cream truck services that cruise Island streets, attests to the fact that his people — mostly schoolteachers and college students — are more than just ice cream vendors. "You need to be an entrepreneur, yes," said Sirianni, who has a summer home in Brant Beach. "But mostly as an ice cream vendor you are a student of human nature. And you'd be surprised how many of our former drivers have come back to us and said the interpersonal skills they have learned are useable in other areas of their life."

His 20-year-old son, Erik, who's been driving a Bayberry ice cream truck for the past three years, agrees to the entrepreneur part. "It's a job that requires a lot of self-motivation, how long you want to work and all that," the Ship Bottom resident said. "If I wanted to, I could park my truck in the shade all day, but I wouldn't make any money."

from *The SandPaper* • June 28, 1995

Bill Fackler, son of Charlie Fackler, on Cedar Bonnet Island, where he grew up.

Jerry Ellson/The SandPaper

off limits to developers. But there seems to be another more subtle force at work on Cedar Bonnet, as if the Island preferred, like the mostly hidden sign, to go unnoticed.

"We're in a world of our own here," admitted Esther Rinear, a retired schoolteacher who has spent close to sixty summers on the Island. Rinear and others claim that despite the proximity of Rt. 72, the Island is still the haven of serenity it has always been. Indeed, it doesn't take long for the cries of the local wildlife or the sight of a perfect sunset to make a visitor forget about the traffic whizzing by.

The serenity, plus a rare bit of obscurity, seems just rewards for Cedar Bonnet. Less than a half mile long and about a city block wide, this tiny island that represents the easternmost edge of Stafford Township has from the very beginning served as a handy stepping stone between the mainland and Long Beach Island. Bisected first by the 1880s railroad tracks, then the 1914 causeway and finally by Rt. 72, Cedar Bonnet Island has endured an endless flow of people passing through.

In the beginning the few who came to stay, like Burrel Adams and Charlie Fackler, depended on the Island's transportation links for their

He said he's been "around the trucks" since he was ten, likes ice cream but doesn't eat much of it. He likes being an ice cream man, though, despite the tedious nature of the job. "You always have to drive very slowly and you can't really listen to the radio," he said. "That way you can see people or hear them yell 'stop.' But it beats sitting behind a counter somewhere with a boss hanging over your back."

Erik considers his job a happy one simply because he is selling what just about everybody wants. "You deal with people, lots of kids and families, who are happy because they're buying ice cream." His biggest group of customers — kids ten and under — also provide him with the greatest satisfaction. "Every little kid, convinced ice cream tastes better when it comes from a truck, looks at you with a big smile trying to decide what they want."

But young or simply young at heart, customers who buy their ice cream from a truck tend to be a particularly loyal bunch, bonding with their vendor like hot fudge to a scoop of vanilla. "The regulars will wait for you," said Erik. There's one elderly man who always waits for him on a bike in order to buy 14 ice pops and then speed home to stick them in his freezer. "Or sometimes people will wait for you just because you have something another truck doesn't have. It helps to have an advantage over the competition."

Erik said he has long-time repeat customers. "I see people I remember first meeting years ago," he said. "Each summer I see some of the same kids and each summer they grow up and change."

What doesn't change is the time it takes kids to make up their minds which variety they want. It seems that half the fun is trying to make up your mind. "Usually you just have to wait and watch the little kids stare at the menu," said Erik. "For some, even if they always choose an ice cream sandwich, it takes a very long time to decide."

Although adults tend to stick to the traditional stuff such as vanilla bars covered in chocolate, the treats kids ultimately go for are confections with cartoon faces, "characters like Bugs Bunny," said Erik.

Sno-Cones, the second most popular ice cream menu item, unfortunately are also the most frequently dropped. "It's happened three times already today," Erik said. "The way the kids open them, the Sno-Cones just fly out of the package. I always give them another one, not because I have to, but it's better business."

Frustrations do abound for a nice ice cream man who takes his work seriously. Take kids whose ice cream appetites are bigger than their pocketbook.

"You get the kids who come and say, 'I don't have any money, give me something for free,'" said Erik. "My father's logic, and it's true I guess, is once you give away a free ice cream you never live it down because those kids never leave you alone. But I let it go if they're a few cents short."

Another frustration is motorists who don't stop for his truck — ignoring the red stop sign that swings out from the side of the truck. "That sign is required by law," said Erik. "People ignore it all the time and that's bad. Kids see an ice cream truck and they run towards the truck and it's really frustrating that people ignore it. Cops will give them a ticket."

Don't discount the heat the ice cream man has to take. Despite the fact that its cargo is frozen, the vehicle is no ice box on wheels for the driver. "This truck hasn't been turned off all day," Erik said, "and the engine makes it hot."

As with most things, there are class differences in the ice cream business. "You never see anyone from the bigger, fancy houses come out to buy ice cream," said Erik. "If they see you, they just stare at you. It's the families in the little houses who always buy from you." He has also noticed it's tourists rather than locals who buy ice cream from a truck. "You go on vacation, you see an ice cream truck, you gotta buy your kid an ice cream," he said.

Erik said he has vacation plans of his own once the season ends a few weekends after Labor Day. What does an ice cream man plan to do when he stops being an ice cream man? "I'm going to take off and drive out west."

Did he say drive?

"Yeah," said Erik laughing, "I'll be driving around the United States for a couple of months."

Listen for the bells.

2009 My First Winter on the Island

Christine Rooney

On Labor Day 2008, I watched as neighbors, friends, and guests packed up and departed in a caravan of SUVs and minivans, heading west across the Causeway. I was filled with an unfamiliar mix of anticipation and trepidation. My friends from the Northern Virginia neighborhood that we had just recently left behind for good asked, "You sure you want to stay there all winter?" My summer neighbors warned ominously, "It'll drive you crazy here all alone." Many made the emphatic statement, "I know I couldn't do it!" Amid the dire warnings and forecasts, the year-rounders just smiled and winked.

We had always planned to someday retire and live here year-round. But my own bout with cancer, my husband's sudden illness, and a strong desire to get out of the rat-race speeded up the process and prompted us to take immediate action. After thirty years in the Washington, D.C. area and a long teaching career, I resigned, sold our house, canceled my library card and moved north to our second home in Ship Bottom — the site of many a childhood summer vacation. The mysterious rhythm of life was telling us the time for bold action had come, so we went.

As the assault-of-the-guests season closed, I realized for the first time in decades I had time. I now had choices on how to spend, manage and wile away my time, choices of those with whom I wanted to spend my time. After a lifetime of being over-scheduled, overworked and living by the calendar, I had time. Time could now be appreciated and molded, not dreaded. I vowed not to over-schedule myself, not to fill my time with 'must dos' and 'should dos.' In this new chapter of life, time was going to be savored. So, I made myself four Island Promises:

- I will walk the beach every day.
- I will watch winter sunrises and sunsets as often as I can.
- I will take the time to observe, record, and reflect.

from *Echoes of LBI* • Summer, 2009

• I will live in the present.

This was my time to re-invent, rejuvenate, and restore. I was putting my life in slow, but deliberate, motion.

Did I have concerns about wintering on a desolate barrier island? Absolutely! I wondered if I'd be providing 24/7 entertainment for a bored husband. I worried I'd find myself addicted to daytime dramas and cooking shows. Now that I had left my chosen profession, I fretted about how I would respond to the question, "What do you do?" The dire warnings of friends, neighbors, and family wandered and snaked their way through my thoughts, at times taking a chokehold. What did I need in order to live a happy, connected life? Starting over at fifty-five was a daunting task. I reflected on these worries and concerns, begrudgingly validated their existence, and moved on. In my experience, worrying is a waste of time and energy. I did not want to squander my time; I wanted to use my time wisely.

I did all the things newly arrived transplants do. I joined a gym, connected with my year-round neighbors, volunteered and booked a cruise. I signed up for tap dance lessons, lectures and computer classes. Not to be out done by my Generation X kids, I joined Facebook! I was settling in for the winter. My husband, thankfully, decided to pursue a Master's degree in history. I reminded myself of my Island Promises, and I was determined not to over-schedule my days.

On Long Beach Island winter creeps up slowly, in stages. Summer residents pack up. The traffic lights are set to blink. The Causeway is drivable anytime. Businesses shorten hours or close. Chowder Fest gives the Island a brief, illusory return of summer. Snowbirds head south. Only the stouthearted remain. By December, winter has descended quietly.

I thought I'd dread winter storms, but it turns out I love them. The greatest surprise was an eight-inch snowstorm in March. The thought that I did not have to get dressed, get out, and go to work made me appreciate being retired at the shore like nothing else. I grabbed my camera, snapped a few pictures, and settled down in front of the fireplace with a good book and my computer.

The best things about a winter day on Long Beach Island are the unexpected, small pleasures. Having a coffee and conversation in the middle of

Harvey Cedars beach in a snowstorm.

Ray Fisk

the day with neighbors — something I could never find the time to do in the past — became something to which I looked forward. Never having to wait in line, now that is priceless! Watching an injured seal on the beach being rescued thrilled me in an unfamiliar way. I learned the value of good neighbors you can call on, and I learned that some neighbors are better not called on. I learned the beach is a solitary, peaceful place and that it is all yours for the taking.

I also learned I am good company for myself. I can slow down. I am a better wife, mother, daughter, friend, and sister. My conversations with friends and family are no longer just brief news bulletins of my life events and current stresses. They are untimed conversations. I'm in a time and place that allows me to listen carefully and to speak unhurriedly. I have the time to decide: Should I? Will I? Or, should I just do what I feel?

As the days grow longer and seasonal residents begin to return, I look forward to the hustle and bustle of the summer. It was in the summer days at the shore that my romance with Long Beach Island began. But in the back of my mind, I feel a slight sadness and I utter a sigh. This is the end of private walks on the beach, quiet, dark nights of star-gazing, and zipping up and down an island with no stoplights. I'll miss winter at the shore, until it returns. Next year, I'll make more Island Promises. I'll work out more. I'll volunteer more. I'll read more and relax more.

Well, maybe. Who knows what the Island promises for next winter?

Polly's Dock, Herman's Dock

Maggie O'Neill

Walk down West Street in Beach Haven and just before you get to the Boat House or the Ketch you will see a driveway running between chain link fences.Behind the fence are a few clapboard buildings, a turn-of-the-last-century house, and a dock with rows of boats and Jet Skis for rent. At the edge of the dock there's a table for cutting bait and cleaning fish. Perched on its edge is a very large egret. His name is Big Bird. Out from one of the gray-blue ramshackle buildings walks Herman Joorman. His full head of wild gray hair, spiraling out of an old visor, is matched only by the length of his beard. Glasses sit amid the cloud of grey. He has an uneven gate, courtesy of polio as a child; quick, gnarled hands that wave hello and an ease that lets you know he is no stranger to this spot. Indeed, Herman grew up here, among the clapboard buildings and the bay. This is his home. This is Polly's Dock.

Herman takes a seat on one of the many chairs haphazardly strewn around a deck situated between the buildings. Four or five long-time locals sit on the porch railings or casually lounge on the chairs. There are two old refrigerators; one is marked 'bait' and the other holds cold German beer. Someone hands Herman a Becks. The conversation is easy; the weather, how rough the water is today, who came by last night, remember when Big Al took the boat, has anyone seen Flynn, where is Pat, etc. Time passes and the beers flow, full then empty, like the bay tide.

The small, front hut holds guitars both old and new, tambourines, a washbasin drum and a microphone. Herman shuffles into the shack, picks up his fourteen-year-old guitar and starts to strum. The others join him and music fills the salt air in and around the dock. The songs run from country, to beer hall, to classic rock and finally, to gospel. Voices come together over the common ground of music. The voices are good. The washbasin drum keeps a beat along with newer instruments as the music

Polly's Dock and the West Street bayfront in the 1960s.

melds with the bay. Smoking is definitely permitted here and the camaraderie is undeniable.

Herman grew up in the narrow, old house that sits next to the bait and tackle building. His family has owned and worked this piece of land for more than sixty-six years. He is as much a part of Polly's Dock as the water and salt air. He has lived a bayman's life that few of us today could ever imagine, and it has served him well.

Herman's father and mother bought Polly's in 1943 when he was eight years old. Back then it was known as Kelly's. "My mother's name was Mary, but everyone called her Polly. So we renamed the business Polly's Dock," explains Herman. As a child, he contracted polio and spent many months in a hospital, relearning how to eat, move and walk. "I just got sick one day and had this pain in my neck. They didn't know what was wrong. I collapsed and they brought me to the hospital in Atlantic City, where I was quarantined," he says matter-of-factly. "After a few days I felt I could move a little. It took me six months to learn to feed myself again." Through sheer will he regained the use of his legs and spent his childhood years working the dock with his father, renting boats and catching minnows to sell as bait.

When the time came for college, Herman chose the prestigious College of William and Mary. After his first year there, he decided to return to Long

Beach Island. Although college may not have been his cup of tea, within a short time in his company you don't doubt his mental ability. From his extraordinary vocabulary to the breadth of ideas that he so effortlessly formulates, there is obviously a keen mind under that old visor.

His early 20s were important years in his life; he met his future wife, Gerri, and he bought Polly's from his parents. As Herman tells it, "My father said to me, 'Do you want it? Here are the terms.' I just said yes! Back then you could make a good living on the bay, catching mussels, clams, and minnows. I can remember when they used to ship out boxes of fish to Philadelphia. One box could hold up to fifty pounds. In those days, two fluke would fill it up to the max, weighing in at twenty-five pounds each."

Herman goes on to say that when he first took over the business, the boats were all rowboats. "They didn't have motors back then. We would rent boats to people and they would row out to fish. When they went out at night, they used kerosene lanterns. During the day when they were done and wanted to come back, they would hold up an oar as a signal and someone would go out and tow them in." Herman laughs a salty laugh at the memory. "Outboards were one of the biggest changes to the business."

Beach Haven history reveals that Herman is known for catching more minnows than anyone else. It is this claim to fame that provided him with the lifestyle he loves. "We built up the business on the minnows in the summer and it gave us the freedom to travel all winter." I asked him where he traveled and his itinerary was one to be envied. "We went to Mexico many times," he said, showing me a dozen or so pictures of himself and Gerri in aqua-blue waters, enjoying a world far away from New Jersey winters. "We would just up and go. We didn't have a plan or a schedule; we didn't need one," and from the joy evident in the photos, this certainly seemed to be true. "I'm partial to Australia," Herman says when I asked him to name his favorite place. "We would travel for three months every year and come back broke," he laughs. "Then we'd start working and saving for next year's trip."

I asked Herman where he would like to go now if he had his choice. "Anyplace I've never been," he quickly answers.

Touché, I think. "And your philosophy of life?"

"You're only here for the moment."

Herman is known for loyalty to his friends, always winning at chess and a love of freedom. Being a bayman and working hard at what he does gave him the ability to live life on his own terms — nothing fancy and nothing pretentious. His years were filled with love for his wife, Polly's Dock, friends, travel and a world outside the boundaries of Beach Haven.

When the time came for Herman to decide just how he wanted to set up life for his remaining time in this world, he found the perfect answer. Polly's Dock is a prime piece of bayfront real estate and he had floated many offers over the years. All were turned down until just the right offer came along. Pat Damiani, owner of The Hydrangea House B&B in Beach Haven, made Herman an offer he didn't refuse. Pat bought Polly's Dock to run as it as it has always been run; boat rentals, bait and maybe a Jet S   ki or two. The buildings are the same with the addition of some very welcome bathrooms. The major stipulation in the deal was that Herman would continue to live in his house on the dock for as long as he so chooses.

On this particular night, like most, Herman and his friends gravitate to the music shack. Someone plays the washbasin, the guitars are fired up and someone else starts to shake a tambourine. Herman leads a song, fingers flying over the strings, beer-laden voice clear and strong. Here at Polly's Dock, not all that much has changed. It's a step back in time. The buildings echo its history — a way of life built on the bay. As the night wears on and the music filters out over the water, this spot in old Beach Haven is new again.

So, for the most part, life at Polly's Dock ebbs and flows pretty much the same as it always has for the past sixty-six years. Sadly, Herman recently lost his beloved wife. But the dock is the focal point of his life. He works the boats, strums his guitar, drinks his Becks and, on a rare and wonderful night, shares his story with a few lucky souls.

"Herman," I ask, just before leaving. "Any regrets?" "NO WAY!" he cheerfully roars. "'NO WAY!"

I smile. You have to admire that; life lived on his own terms. And what a life it is!

_____

Herman Joorman died in 2014. Big Bird is still hanging around Polly's Dock.

On the
Water

Ray Fisk

1945 WWII: Snagging the Enemy

William J. Kunze Sr.

Fishing Long Beach Island beaches at night during World War II was very scary, risky and sometimes lonely. The Island was practically deserted. Most people were engaged in some kind of defense work, and few lights were to be seen because of the black-outs.

There were many rumors about German submarines surfacing and trying to land saboteurs onto our shores from rubber boats which did not make a lonely fisherman feel too safe. The beach was off-limits to anyone but the Shore Patrol at night. If you did manage to get fishing on the beach, anyone approaching you sent shivers up and down your spine, because you did not know whether it was friend or foe. People living on the beachfront watched what was going on in the daytime and reported any strangers or unusual activity to the authorities. At night it was a different story — the beaches had to be patrolled.

It is hard for people living in cities to visualize what went on at the shore in wartime. It was our front line of defense, so to speak. Maybe a few stories would give you a better perspective of what it was like.

One night while sitting on the beach with my rod in a sand spike, hoping to catch a few blues, I fell sound asleep. I woke when two terrific explosions rattled my eardrums and shook the beach. My hair stood on end. I did not have the slightest idea of what had happened. Looking out to sea I saw a glow about a mile or so off shore. A ship was on fire and lit up the whole beach. Explosion after explosion followed, and then the ship disappeared. A German sub had planted two torpedoes into the ship's hull, sank it, and was now sitting on the surface under the full moon, in clear view of anyone watching from shore.

Hearing voices, I decided to make myself scarce. Patrolmen, civil defense workers and private citizens were pouring onto the beach to assist any survivors who might make it ashore, and to check them out, too.

from *The SandPaper* • May 27, 1981

U.S. Marines arrest crewmen of the German submarine U-858, *captured 50 miles offshore Cape May on May 10, 1945.*

Sometimes the subs sent some of their men ashore as survivors, figuring no one would know the difference.

I returned to my lodgings and decided to try Holgate the next evening. The dunes were fairly high, and once you got away from the watchtower there was little chance of anyone knowing you were on the beach. Gas rationing was in full effect, and anyone caught using a vehicle for anything other than work or in an emergency could have his stamps confiscated. I owned an old Army ambulance which was still painted olive drab, so I had little trouble making it to Holgate that evening.

I parked my vehicle in the driveway of an empty house, swung my knapsack over my shoulder, picked up my rod and started walking down the beach. A half-hour later I reached the place where I wanted to fish. I baited my hook with cut bunker, cast out and then put my rod in the sand spike. The tide was about a half-hour in and my chances of catching some blues would be very good as it got higher. Settling down on the beach with my back up against a sand bank, I waited for a hit. The moon was full and I could see my rod very clearly.

An hour passed without a hit. The tide was coming in very fast, so I moved higher on the beach, to the top of a sand bank. When the clouds did not cover the moon I could see far out over the ocean. There was hardly a ripple on the water — just an occasional ground swell crashing on the beach. Another hour passed. I caught two sandsharks but no blues. My legs were getting stiff and the sand was very damp so I decided to move around a little. While walking back and forth I heard voices that seemed to be coming from out over the water. A bank of clouds hid the moon which made it very dark close to shore, but further out to sea where there were no clouds I could see a submarine silhouetted against the sky for a few moments before it disappeared. The voices I had heard were probably coming from a landing party in a rubber raft, but I could not see them.

I figured if I could not see them, they could not see me or what was on shore. As loud as I could, I cried out, "Halt! Who goes there?" Then changing my voice slightly I shouted, "Sergeant, you take a squad south along the beach, and corporal, you take one north. A loud response of "Yes Sir! Yes Sir!" must have been heard by someone in that raft, because the voices stopped and a sharp command of "*Mach Schnell!*" followed the frantic splashing of oars, and then all was quiet.

Rushing back to where my rod was setting in the sand spike I found it bent way over. Good! The Germans were gone and the bluefish were in, so I picked up the rod and heaved back to set the hook, but no soap! That line just kept pulling off the reel. This was no ordinary bluefish! I heard many voices and a sharp order just as my line went limp. Reeling in slowly, I came to the end of my line, and there on my hook was a piece of cloth. Mulling over what had happened in the last fifteen minutes I came to the conclusion that what I had hooked into was not a fish. Those guys in the raft must have snagged my line.

I picked up my gear and started back to my vehicle where I saw two uniformed men. I identified myself and found out I knew them both. I told them what had happened. They believed I had seen a German sub offshore, because they often surface to recharge their batteries; but as far as the story about the raft, the men just laughed. In fact, one of them asked me if I had any more of that stuff left. It was getting a little chilly and they said they could stand a nip or two.

Well that did it! I never brought the subject up to anyone after that, but to this day I still believe I hooked into a rubber raft full of Germans, which would have been one of the biggest catches ever made with a fishing pole if I could have beached it. Of course I would also be very dead, because what could one lone fisherman do against a half dozen desperate invaders?

I did manage to fish the beach a few times after that, but then I stopped fishing at night until after the war was over.

I can still visualize a rubber raft mounted on my living room wall with the name tags and serial numbers of six Germans hanging below it, and a plaque that says, "Hooked and Landed at Holgate During the Last Great World War." But then again, maybe it's for the best that I didn't land the raft. Our living room walls are small and I would have to remove everything from them to accommodate my trophy.

1964 That First Fish

Dick Clements

A little kid came in with his father the other day and they wanted to catch some fish. They wanted to fish from along the bay, and about all we could suggest was that they try for snappers, so they got the hooks and the shot and the bobbers and the spearing and set off for the bulkhead behind the Acme. The youngster was very eager to catch a fish, and in a way that only the anticipation of youth can make it the biggest event of the year. He had never been fishing before, and so they set off with stars in one pair of eyes at least.

A few hours later they were back, and if there was ever a happy boy, this was him. They hadn't caught a single snapper. They had fished hard, really gave it the old college try, but there just weren't any snappers around that

On Cedar Bonnet Island, early 1950s.

day. Finally though, just about as they were ready to quit, he caught a fish, and I have no doubt it hit as hard and fought as strongly as any fish ever did. It was a sea robin.

One stinking, lousy sea robin, or so you or I would describe it, but to that boy it was the most beautiful thing that existed at that moment. We

from *The Beachcomber* • August 13, 1964

would be completely disgusted with this result from a fishing trip, but to him it was a sparkling success, one that he'll talk about all winter. A fisherman was probably born that minute, and I hope he has a long, long life.

As clearly as I'm sure that boy will in years to come, I can remember my first saltwater fish. It was nearly thirty years ago, but to me the experience is as vivid as though it happened last week. My family had come to the Island for the day, and my father took one of my brothers and me out in the bay to fish. No motors in those days. We rented a boat from Ed Kane down in Beach Haven and my father rowed us out to the fishing grounds. It was cloudy and threatening, but Pop had promised.

Once we started fishing I immediately caught a nice sea bass, and so did my brother. What with rigging us up and all I don't think Pop even got a line in the water before it began raining like the hammers of hell. So, up anchor and in he rowed with us kids huddled under a raincoat on the rear seat. All the way in we couldn't take our eyes off those two beautiful fish on the stringer, swinging in the water behind the boat.

Two lousy, stinking sea bass.

Look at the faces of a couple of youngsters with a few snappers on a string, or the complete absorption of a bunch of kids with their heads bent over a bait seine full of wiggling minnows. Here is complete, uninhibited enjoyment, uncomplicated by any adult sophistication. It makes me wish, not that I was that age again, but that I could enjoy again the wonders of discovery that is the prequisite of every child at the seashore. Truly, as the Victor Herbert song says about childhood, "Once you pass its borders you can never return again."

Now I'm not happy unless I'm catching the biggest, or the most, or the most extraordinary. What I wouldn't give to be thrilled all over again by one lousy, stinking sea robin.

The author prefaced this "Fishing Around" column by saying: "This isn't at all what I intended to write this week. It just sort of happened to me, and I hope you'll excuse me if I should have written all about how great fishing is or something. I'd rather write about this."

1969 Stretch Pohl, Master Surfer

T he Beachcomber *interviewed the granddaddy of Long Beach Island surfers, Stretch Pohl, when he was fifty-eight years old.*

Beachcomber: *When did you start surfing?*

Pohl: In May, 1932, I got my first whitewater ride at 20th Street in Ship Bottom. I rode a 12-foot hollow, pointed-tail board which was made by Tom Blake. From the 12-footer we went to the 14 and they weighed around a hundred pounds. No cutting, just straight in.

BC: *Where are your favorite places to surf on the Island?*

Pohl: Years ago, we'd run up and down the Island looking for what we thought were good waves. Surf City, Ship Bottom and South Beach Haven have given me some of the best rides I ever had.

BC: *Who were some of the guys you surfed with in the 1930s?*

Pohl: Mike Howes, Charley Lang, Morrie Clark, Jack Lounsberry, Tony Steele and Gary Lincoln.

BC: *What type of board do you ride now?*

Pohl: I just converted to a mini-board and find it out of this world. It is a 7-foot, 8-inch, 23-inch wide board which I made myself. For a 6-foot 2, 195 pounder it is quite a thrill to master the "toothpick."

BC: *What do you think of surfing contests?*

Pohl: Surfing contests are excellent for the manufacturers. They get their professional riders to compete and travel the circuit extolling their boards. If the contests were for the kids, judged by the kids, then they would be purposeful. Otherwise, in my opinion, they are just promotional and business events. Remember, that there are more excellent surfers who don't compete in contests because they'll never displace the name boys. Contests prove nothing.

BC: *What type of surf do you prefer?*

Pohl: Six-feet high with a glass front. Of course, on this Island you don't always get that type of surf, so you take anything that comes along. I detest the shore-break, which I also consider dangerous.

Members of the Malalo-Akula Surfboard Club in Ship Bottom during the summer of 1941. They founded the club on the Island in the 1930s. Left to right: Mike Howes, Cary Lincoln, Erle Jackson and Stretch Pohl. Behind them is Wright's Pier, commonly called the Ship Bottom fishing pier, at 20th Street, which was destroyed in the 1944 hurricane.

from *The Beachcomber* • July 17, 1969

BC: *Why do you surf? What compels you to devote so much of your life to surfing?*

Pohl: I have surfed since I was 21. To me, it is a way of life. I can get more relaxation out of six rides on a surfboard than some people can get out of a gallon of gin. I like the challenge, the unexpectedness of events, the sound of the wave and the exhilaration of beating the wave which tries to destroy you. I'll surf as long as I am able to walk. Of course, I'm slower and can't get up as fast as I once did, but that is all in the game. I know of no sport that gives me as much satisfaction as surfing does.

BC: *What was your hairiest experience?*

Pohl: The first time I got caught by an 8-footer during a northeast storm. I was sucked under and held down by the boiling water for a longer time than I like to admit. I thought that this was it and then I suddenly popped to the surface, half drowned. I barely made it to the shore. I know better now.

BC: *Do you think the surfer makes the board, or the board makes the surfer?*

Pohl: A good surfer can ride a plank made out of two-by-fours. I have discussed this with many top-notchers and they like boards that can do their thing. Some like to bottom turn, drop in on a wave, climb it and so on. The best surfers are always experimenting. For conventional riding, you select that board that is for that purpose. If you want to do acrobatics, then you must have a board for that purpose. Basically, it comes down to what you want to do with a board.

BC: *Manufacturers are building boards from six feet to ten feet; when is this going to stop?*

Pohl: The mini-board is good for waves up to 12 feet. Beyond that you need a longer board. I look for a happy medium. The mini-board has a tendency to spin out, that is the seven-footer or less. A board around 9 feet long will probably become the standard board for all-around surfing.

BC: *What tip can you give for a beginner who wants to learn to surf?*

Pohl: A beginner should get good instruction before he buys a board. The average person goes to a surf shop, buys the latest model and finds he can't handle the board. If one goes to a reliable surf shop and explains his problem, the shop pro will guide him correctly. All beginners should start out with a floater, as it is called in the trade. Once he masters this board, he is ready for the faster models. Also, you can't learn to surf reading books or sitting on the beach. Get involved, get out in all kinds of water and learn to handle your board under all conditions.

1973 A Mystical Experience

Dick Clements

I'm mildly surprised when I reflect on the fact that I've been fishing for about 60 years of my life, which is more than somewhat, as Nathan Detroit might say. Anything that has held one's attention for that length of time can't be all bad, but then Willy Sutton robbed banks for something approaching the same timespan, so where does that leave you?

One could suppose that some atavistic emotion still lurks in the human skull from some dim and distant millennium when it was catch fish or go hungry. That being the case, most present-day fishermen, or fisherwomen, would get a recurring case of the miss-meal cramps for their efforts. It ain't all that productive, as you may have noticed.

No, in this day and age the pursuit of food has to be ruled out. It just won't do the job, especially when the economics of fishing are taken into consideration. Then it becomes downright ludicrous. Employing a 50-grand-and-up sportsfisherman, not to mention the expenses of operating same plus an array of tackle that would buy the spouse a ring with a stone the size of a modest ice cube seems excessive. Especially when one views the catch which may or may not be a grand total of about three pounds of edible flesh. At about four hundred bucks a pound. Of course

from *The Beachcomber* • July 5, 1973

Early off-road adventures: fishing at Barnegat Inlet, from the Island Beach side.

all fishing isn't done on such a grand scale. The kid with the cane pole is the other end of the spectrum and there's a large gradation in between. But either way there are an awful lot of people who spend a little or a lot of time each year with a line in the water. When you stop to think about it, the amount of nonproductive hours spent attempting to convince a fish that the chrome plated thing with the little tuft of feathers on the back end is something good to eat boggles the mind.

I've thought a lot about the fishing phenomenon, without any conclusion. Something that's so absolutely watertight and utterly unproductive has to have some rational explanation, or at the very least an extenuating circumstance or two. I think I may have hit upon the underlying rationalization — it is the Puritan Ethic. Bear with me, it's stunning in its simplicity.

Ever since its founding, this country has been driven by the Puritan Ethic: "Life is real, life is earnest. Early to bed, early to rise, makes a man healthy, wealthy and wise. A penny saved is a penny earned. Up with the cows, to bed with the chickens," and numerous other nauseating exhortations. One must work hard and, more to the point, be seen to work hard.

Fishing is the perfect answer. A man should be back at the cottage painting the front porch, but instead he's standing on the beach, rod in a sand spike, line stretching into the breakers. He's gazing resolutely to sea. He feels not the slightest guilt about the porch. He's otherwise engaged. He's doing something, and more to the point, he's seen to be doing something and thus is immune to criticism. The presence of fishing gear is an explanation in itself. Ownership of a fishing rod gives one carte blanche to shuck all the world's troubles for a few hours, and this is no bad thing. If a few fish are brought home for the frying pan now and then, well, that's all to the good.

Or perhaps fishing is an aesthetic phenomenon. Some of the most beautiful moments of my life have been while fishing. One evening in Great Bay with my older daughter was one of them. We were fishing a small creek that wandered back into the salt marsh, and the creek was full of weakfish. We would motor up the creek, shut off the engine and drift slowly back to the bay casting small bucktails. It was warm and dead calm, and the salty, wet smell of the marshes was like perfume. The sun was on the horizon, its golden light turning the water to ink and the muted greens of the marsh grasses to velvet. We were catching weaks like crazy.

The sun set and slowly it got dark, and then out of the ocean rose a giant pale orange moon, its image shimmering on the water. Off in the darkness we could hear the occasional squawk of a heron and soft undefined plops of feeding fish. It was completely calm and utterly silent. I stopped fishing and just stood there, completely captivated by such beauty, and a moment later Linda did, too. Soon I said, softly, "Well, this is something." And she replied, "Yes." Anything further would have been superfluous.

And there were numerous other times. Fishing the beach in the fall, the sun painting the clouds a garish pink as the sun set behind me, the water clear as green glass in the curling breakers. Casting for weaks, again with Linda, a hundred yards off the beach in a fog bank that turned the world into a Japanese print. The wild excitement of a huge school of striped bass that stretched as far as sight would allow. Casting for big bluefish by the

North Jetty one brilliant June morning with large swimming plugs, the fish smashing the plugs on the surface in a shower of spray. We caught just one and thoroughly enjoyed the show that two dozen others put on.

Anyone who's fished with reasonable frequency over the years could reply with dozens of such stories. I've fished with Linda many times and think that I've gotten to know her far better than I would have as just her father. She and I first fished together when she was about six, and now, near forty years later, we still do, although very seldom. The first time, she caught just one small sea bass, and, by coincidence my very first saltwater fish was the same, when I was about twelve.

There's gotta be something mystic about it.

1978 Little Beach: Desolate Shore

Lou Zuegner

To the south of Long Beach Island the two adjacent inlets of Beach Haven and Little Egg are located, with the remnants of Tucker's Island in between. From the mainland a marshy peninsula sticks out like a bulging tongue almost plugging up these ocean entrances. On the south side of Little Egg inlet a long sandy stretch of desolate shoreline called Little Beach marks the beginning of the wildlife refuge. Because of the treacherous currents and shore breakers the beach is inaccessible from the inlet or the ocean. A couple of miles to the south the beach becomes marsh and is completely cut off by the Brigantine channel, the intercoastal waterway, and various other meandering thoroughfares and creeks, making any approach very difficult.

However, every piece of inaccessible land has its Achilles heel, and this is no exception. The northwest end of beach facing Little Egg Inlet can be approached in a shallow draft boat in a direct line from Rutgers University Marine Field Station on Sheepshead peninsula. A protective ring of sand-bars to the north, and shallow muddy flats spreading to the south, discourages sloppy navigation. A narrow creek spills out right at this northwestern tip and can be entered and ventured up to a couple of hundred yards even at low tide. This allows anchoring in calm water.

Scanning the horizon from Little Beach yields mostly roiling water, shell-covered beach and a flat marsh dotted with sandy clumps bristling with dune grass, just barely beyond the reach of the high tide's saline grasp. Off to the west is the rusting abandoned hulk of the old fish factory, slowly being reclaimed by the salt air and eroding waves; nature's justice for all the millions of moss bunker ground into fertilizer. Cross currents, tidal pools, and sandy shallows provide a handy playground a short distance from the safety of the ocean for small sharks and rays. Invariably sharks can be glimpsed at low tide rolling and finning among the shallow bars.

The sandy beach area is swept clean of most vegetation, perfectly leveled by the seasonal storms and moon tides. The lower lying areas, constantly submerged and exposed by the alternating tides, reveal the constant drama of survival.

The tracts of horseshoe crabs stranded by the receding currents display the daily life and death struggle. Dragging their heavy frames across the sandy floor and searching vainly for the elusive safety of deep water, some have consumed all their energies. Their trail spirals in confusion, culminating in their lifeless sun-baked shells. Others, much wiser, have spent their energies in burying themselves in the wet sands, patiently waiting for the first cooling wavelet of the returning tide.

Countless bird footprints catalog the frenetic tracking and checking of all possible food sources, their myriads of trails weaving randomly like so many drunken scavengers. Piles of shells indicate drop zones where gulls zero in with their cargo of unopened clams. By dropping them on the other shells, the concussion will hopefully crack open the difficult and uncooperative morsel. The whole beach is decorated daily, displaying the former

from *The Beachcomber* • September 14, 1978

Ray Fisk

"The rusting abandoned hulk of the old fish factory," circa 1980.

residences of razor clams, channeled whelks, large snails and scallops.

Certain dark, muddy areas, intensely heated by the searing sun and smoothed off by high tide currents, look like huge paved macadam parking lots. Intrigued by the look, one soon discovers with flailing arms and dancing legs that the crusty surface is supported by a lubricated, jelly-like mud base. Other parts of the muddy flats are decorated by millions of small snails, resembling a huge game of black and gray marbles.

In the center of this vista, pools of shallow water are filled with lettuce-like seaweed. Small schools of darting minnows scout around the edges, eager to take advantage of their neighbors who failed to change with the tide. The fragile empty shells of blue claw and calico crabs attest to the fastidious no-waste ordinance of nature. To the south, large dunes are carved by the constant winds. Their heads are covered with dune grass groomed in one direction by the constant winds. The etched faces on these small bluffs display multicolored layers of gray, white and black sand.

As I returned to my boat I glanced back on this tranquil scene to view my own two sets of tracks advancing and retreating, a rarity on this beach.

The fish factory ruins are still crumbling and rusting. It processed menhaden — known locally as mossbunker — into fertilizer in the first half of the 20th century. It ceased operations in the late '60s and, except for the metal framework, was destroyed by a fire in 1982. Tucker's Island has completely eroded into the sea.

1981 Making Waves: Surfing LBI

Cathie Cush

T he perfect wave took shape in Hawaii before recorded history. It swelled as it reached California,
gathering bronzed bodies and trendy sunshine in
its wake. And on its face rode men, at one with the natural force, until it
washed the eastern shore.

The first surfboards to hit the Island didn't make a very big splash.
In fact there was very little action until the early 1960s, when fiberglass
boards were introduced. Then, girls, hot cars and surfboards were uppermost in many minds for quite a few years down here — and not necessarily
in that order. Beach Boys, bleached blondes — for a while the whole West
Coast scene found an eastern home.

Local surfing legend Henry "Stretch" Pohl recalls the early days of his
career, when, as a lifeguard, he was introduced to the paddle-board used by
the National Red Cross, primarily for rescue. "In 1928 Tom Blake invented
the hollow surfboard. It was 14 feet long and shaped like a teardrop. In
1932 we got involved with surfing. After 1938-39 we started to go into the
balsa boards that were popular in California." He scoffs at the notion that
surfing was new in those days: "Captain Cook, in the 1800s, saw Polynesian
natives going down waves on a sliver of wood."

Beach Haven resident Tom Tatlow owned an early board made of marine
plywood. "Dale Baugh got the measurements and specs from Hawaii and
came back here and built it," he reminisces. "I bought it from Dale. It was
about 12 feet and weighed about 45 pounds. It was tough to maneuver."

Tatlow and Robin Nelson surfed 23rd Street in Spray Beach during the
summer of '54. At the time, Nelson was a lifeguard, and Tatlow about to
enter college. "We used to get hurt a lot, Tatlow says. "That board was so
big. And you spent a lot of time going after it." There was no way to attach
a leash to the unwieldy contraption, besides "if you did you were likely
to drown." The wooden boards had plugs to drain water out, lacked fins,

from *The SandPaper* • August 19, 1981

and the sides were squared rather than contoured, so straddling them was impossible, and catching waves was almost impossible. "The boards were much too heavy. You used to stand up maybe once out of every five times. The surf wasn't big enough to get up on those boards. The only time you could go really well with them was when you had a northeaster." Some things never change.

Over the next few years, the surf scene remained quiet until, in the early 1960s, the craze hit the Island like a tsunami. East met West and the West won. California dreamin' became a reality on Long Beach Island.

"Ron Jon's was the original on this Island — you've got to give him [Ron DiMenna] credit," says Bob Walters, whose Ship Bottom beach rental service began as one of the first surf shops on the Island. When Walters began to rent boards, "the only other shop was Ron Jon's — he was the first one on the Island, then me, then Ernie Koseff. We were the only three for a couple of years." Ron DiMenna learned to surf from the Reverend Earl Comfort of Manahawkin, a Baptist minister who was one of the first to bring a fiberglass board east from California, starting the fiberglass trend that brought about East Coast surfing as we know it. Before he opened his shop, DiMenna sold boards from a rented trailer.

Those early boards were a great improvement over the balsa and redwood boards, but were still a few steps below today's standards. "They were all long — ten-foot boards — the smallest thing was nine feet then," says Walters. "They were fiberglass. It was in its infancy then — a lot of fiberglass boards used to be pretty rough, but today they're pretty flawless. They know a lot more about resins and color."

One of the first of the surfing contests was held in Ship Bottom on August 8, 1964, and was sponsored by the Long Beach Island Board of Trade. Comfort and fellow officials Mike Howes, Cecil Lear, Charley Lang and Bucky Walters judged 77 surfers from all parts of the state. In a statement made to the press at the time, contest director Stretch Pohl said, "The Men's Open contest proved to be one of the most exciting events ever staged in this section of the country. The seas were whipped up by a strong southeast wind and presented an excellent opportunity for a surfer to demonstrate his prowess. Seven heats of ten surfers each were conducted. These were of twenty-five-minutes duration in which a surfer was to put together six of his best rides. The surfer who scored the highest points was then placed in a final heat to determine the winner. Ralph Hawn (Beach Haven) quickly won the plaudits of the viewers with his fine mastery of the waves."

Contests and competitions played a major part in the Island surfing scene for the next few years. But the real impact was made, not by the tournaments, but by the teams. There was an excitement in the air — surfers had a sense that they were on to something hot, something so new that any one among them might become the next superstar.

"The feeling was you were involved in something brand new," says veteran surfer "Holgate Bob" Muroff. "Everybody thought they could be the best." Although never a surfing team member himself, Muroff swam competitively for eight years. Surfing remained more personal. "For me, it's an individual thing, and I didn't care to join any clubs, any contests."

But for many others, the team was the thing. Most of the surf shops on the Island sponsored teams, which usually rode boards made by one manufacturer. "Koseff's team was the best on the East Coast," states Beach Haven surfer Jack McVey. "They won all the contests from Rhode Island down."

Beach Boys. Jan and Dean. Surfin' U.S.A. In those years between '63 and '67 when surfing was at its peak, McVey says "everybody was 'Beach Blanket Bingo' crazy." It was cool to be a hot surfer, to be revered — so cool, in fact, that many who never ever rode a board rented them to put on top of their car. ("I know that for a fact," Pohl comments.)

But heroes have heroes of their own, and one name recurs constantly in conversations about the heyday. Dean Ward. "He used to build boards for Greg Noll," explains Doug Smith, who rode Greg Noll boards for Koseff's back in those days. "He was the first California guy." "Dean moved here from Hermosa Beach," says McVey. "He influenced everybody on the surf team, who influenced everybody else. He was the hottest dude around for a long time."

Muroff, now forty-two, was a few years older than many who began surfing in the mid-sixties. He too saw Ward's impact. "He brought the California culture to Long Beach Island. He brought that lifestyle to a small, little town like Beach Haven. He was an interesting kid himself — he was doing things nobody else could. It was a little revolution."

By the late '60s the glory days were gone. New California obsessions had captured the public attention — skateboarding, roller skating — but surfing had taken hold, and was growing, although with less fanfare than previously.

Contests may have lost popularity for a number of reasons, among them the fact that so many surfers find the art too personal to be competitive. "Contests prove nothing — it's just an ego trip," snorts Pohl. "I like competition, but what does it prove? I ride a wave because I get a tremendous kick."

And as board lengths shortened, lengthened and otherwise metamorphosed, allowing a greater variety of self expression, contest judging — a matter of taste to begin with — became more so. "Judging surfing is a very subjective thing," explains Muroff. "How are you going to evaluate someone who is very loose and fluid versus someone who is ripping the wave apart, making radical cutbacks, cutting through the lip? How do you say who is better? But I don't think the sport had died out."

Signs indicate that Muroff is right. And competitive surfing may even be on the way back in. A group of young surfers from Beach Haven organized a contest earlier this summer. And this week, Y-Knot Surf Shop in Surf City is sponsoring a tournament, providing the waves reach a height of three feet.

"It's coming back," Pohl predicts. "It leveled off for a while, the only thing that bothers me is the cost of the board," which nowadays runs close to $300. "You have your hardcore surfer who doesn't give it up." Explains Pohl, who at age 70 still surfs occasionally. "And then you have some young guy who gets married and gives it up because he can't afford it."

Muroff says of those, like himself, who continued to surf, "we have stuck it out because we didn't have to leave it behind. A lot of these (other) guys didn't have the time. A lot of things come in the way." Muroff, who owns a trailer park in Holgate, still surfs to stay in shape, and because "I have never lost the enthusiasm for having a good ride. It's an exhilarating feeling to be part of that force. You have to know what that force is going to do next, and be a split second ahead of what that natural force is going to do. And no two are ever alike."

Like Pohl and Muroff, McVey has watched many surfers take up the sport. "Surfing just made me more attached to the ocean than I already was. I planned my life around being at the beach," he confides. "It's good for those guys to see somebody older, so they know you don't have to give up surfing when you get out of school. For a lot of them it's just a summer plaything," he observes. "There are definitely not a lot of people here my age who just hang out and surf."

The strains of the Beach Boys may be fading off into the distance, and the Island's surfing heyday long gone, but every day new waves break on the beach — and once that board gets in your blood you've got to go for it.

1987 Sittin' in the Box on the Bay

Gabriel DeCicco

The sneakbox is a Barnegat Bay tradition, and no sneakbox is more traditional than those produced by the Perrine Boat Works in Barnegat on the Mainland. Now a one-man operation owned by John Chadwick Jr., in its glory days the Perrine Boat Works shipped boxcar loads of the unique hunting and sailing vessel throughout the country. Sneakboxes even found their way abroad.

Chadwick works out of a small, corrugated tin building on School Street near downtown Barnegat. "When Mr. Perrine was in business, they used this and the old schoolhouse across the street," said Chadwick. "The town condemned the schoolhouse a few years back and tore it down." Despite the popularity of the Perrine sneakbox, large factory facilities were not required for production. "Mr. Perrine and later my father had a few

from *The SandPaper* • July 8, 1987

full- time employees and some part time ones," he explained. "A lot of the work was done on subcontract. That is, some carpenter would finish a boat in his back yard." This piecework production was efficient enough to allow boat builder Joseph Howard Perrine to advertise his wares nationwide in *Yachting* magazine.

Perrine was not the inventor of the sneakbox. In an 1879 book titled *Four Months in a Sneakbox*, author Nathaniel H. Bishop credits Hazelton Seaman of West Creek with its invention. A short time later, John Crammer Jr. improved the design, and Samuel Perrine, a sea captain and father of Joseph Perrine, made further modifications.

The boat is totally a product of the Barnegat Bay environment. It was conceived as a mobile duck blind for hunting waterfowl. The Barnegat Bay wetlands are a haven for migrating waterfowl, and not too many decades ago commercial duck hunters shipped barrels packed with the tasty fowl to markets in Philadelphia and New York. While summer tourists may find it difficult to believe, Barnegat Bay produced winter ice that was cut and stored until needed for shipment.

Hunters frequently built "sink boxes," pontoon blinds from which they could shoot the unsuspecting ducks and geese attracted by the wooden decoys unique to the bay area. But these boxes had to be towed. A portable, or mobile, blind that permitted a hunter to move about and sneak up on the feeding ducks under its own power was a natural evolution. Above all, it had to be a shallow-draft boat that could navigate around the marshes in only a few inches of water. It also had to have a unique method for anchoring the craft solidly on the muddy bottom of shallow water.

This environment not only attracted ducks and their human predators, the region also produced quantities of white cedar for boat building. Easily cut into planks, white cedar could swell up to one-quarter inch to provide watertight seams, according to Chadwick.

Allan Chadwick, John's uncle, printed a little booklet in which he said the sneakbox was fully developed by 1855. Originally, its design called for 12 feet in length and a four-foot beam. This is small enough to be propelled by sail or oars and roomy enough to store sails and oars out of sight. Naturally, it had to carry the hunter with all the gear he needed for the long vigil, plus a wide, relatively flat deck area for numerous decoys.

A sailing sneakbox off Surf City, 1983.

While Perrine never lost sight of the original purpose of the sneakbox and built them throughout his lifetime, he also designed larger vessels that would challenge yachtsmen. In 1922, the Barnegat Bay Yacht Racing Club recognized the Perrine 18-foot modification as a sporting craft, and since then the sneakbox has constituted a competitive class of racing sailboats.

Even before its official acceptance, however, sailors have met its challenges. *Four Months in a Sneakbox* is the story of Bishop's voyage down the Ohio River to the Mississippi River and on to the Gulf of Mexico. In 1926 the magazine *Yachting* published a three-part article written by F. Slade Dale telling of the adventures he shares with three comrades sailing a pair of twelve-foot "Barnegat boxes" from the Battery in New York City to Miami, Florida. The two sneakboxes, christened *Crab* and *Shelldrake*, used the Inland Waterway for their journey. But in 1926 their voyage was more than a Sunday outing. Even their crossing of New York Bay and their trip through New Jersey along the old Raritan Canal make interesting reading. Crossing Chesapeake Bay was a four-day adventure and was one of many the quartet of sportsmen experienced.

Although Dale chose to make his trip in 12-footers, Perrine had developed a one-design class of 15-foot gaff-rigged sneakbox by 1918 and, according to Alan Chadwick, sold over 3,000 of them. Perrine also made an 18-footer, and many of the original Perrine boats are still in use. The current proprietor of the boat works is frequently called upon to restore these now historic crafts, sometimes handed down through three or four generations. "I still have almost all the original forms and patterns," said John Chadwick. "Most of the calls I get are from around the Barnegat Bay area, but sometimes I'll receive requests from out of state."

For the past three years Chadwick has entered a sneakbox in the Ocean County Decoy and Gunning Show in Tuckerton. Judged by experts from a maritime museum, he has been awarded first place each time.

Are his prize-winners for sale? "Of course, but a lot of people don't like to pay $1,200 for a 12-foot boat," Chadwick added. "It costs $2,500 fully rigged." Nevertheless, current prices are only about two-and-a-half times what they sold for when J. H. Perrine and John Mason Chadwick Sr. were still alive.

The Barnegat Bay sneakbox has become a family heirloom, increasing in value with the passage of years. There are still some around that were built before World War I. More importantly, they maintain a Barnegat Bay tradition that began over 150 years ago. The sneakbox brought the name of Barnegat to areas of the world that had no idea where or what Barnegat is.

1989 A Sailor's Restless Urge

Don Launer

Spring has come, like a restless urge, like a rebirth. For sailors, it's intoxicating. In boatyards through-out the north the metamorphosis is taking place as, one by one, the boats, like living things, break free from their tarpaulin cocoons, anxious to spread their wings of sail.

It is the first spring day of the year, the end of our winter hibernation. The days are extending at both ends, with the sun climbing higher in the sky as summer drifts north. The buds are nearly ready to burst and children in school are spending more time looking out the window than at their books. Marine hardware stores are hiring extra salespeople and boatyards are no longer deserted. In the north the first day of spring is one thing, the first spring day another; the difference between them is some-times as much as a month or more.

As I head down to the boatyard, I pass little sandy beaches where, for the first time this year, kids have kicked off their shoes and are playing tag with the waves. Flocks of birds flying north hold a promise of summer to come, and the wetlands are active with new life — courting, nest building and territorial conflicts. The sun's heat sends shimmering waves on the road ahead and the chill wind of winter is replaced by a spring breeze.

How appropriate to begin our springtime rebirth by the water — the primeval boundary of our evolution. This meeting of land and sea not only attracts the boater in pursuit of his avocation, but there's also that elusive feeling deep within us all that hauntingly draws us to the water's edge.

Life jackets and cushions laid out in the sun brighten the boatyard. Some mallards swim in and out of the empty slips looking for handouts. As I walk to my cradled vessel, I see rolled-up shirtsleeves exposing sun-starved arms. Greetings are exchanged by paint-splattered faces and summer plans discussed.

"This summer we're going to take her on a long trip down the coast!" a

from *The Beachcomber* • June 9, 1989

Sailing, Little Egg Harbor Bay, off Long Beach Township.

Ray Fisk

friend eagerly promises, as he pauses and admires his newly painted boot stripe. "Yep, this year ..."

I know he won't get ten miles away and will probably never even take an overnighter, but his face glows with enthusiasm as he goes back to his painting; for it's the time of year when each of us has the opportunity to pursue our dreams.

The smell of fresh paint mixes with the warm salt air and suddenly the hat and jacket are no longer necessary. I loosen the tie-down lines at the stern of my boat and slide the ladder up under the boat cover. As I carry my new mainsail up the ladder, the Dacron crackles like wrapping paper. I can hardly wait to bend it on.

I sit down at the dinette table in the self-enclosed world of the cabin. It feels good to be on board again, like coming home. A lead sinker and fishhook are on the table.

"I meant to put those away last fall," I muse.

The cabin is a mixture of aromas: pervasive polyester, antifreeze and must. Last year's tide table marks my final log entry — decommissioning day in November.

I thumb through the pages of past cruises, remembering that day going through Barnegat Inlet when a wave broke over the boat, filling the cockpit and soaking me from head to foot. Then there was the day in the Florida Keys, when we helped a boat that had run aground in the shallows; and yet another entry — that delightful dinner of crab-stuffed flounder that the Barnegat Bay supplied us as we swung on anchor.

I pull down the charts. Although almost new they have the smell of books stored in the attic. Last year's courses, bearings, and times are penciled in. I remember one morning leading two other boats up the twisting channel of the Intracoastal Waterway in a heavy fog — laying out courses and watching with satisfaction as buoy after buoy emerged off our bow, right on schedule. I see a note on the Florida chart reminding me of that hot, humid day in the Gulf Stream off Miami when we dropped the sails and all dove in for a swim. And there are the times and speeds on the New Jersey coastal chart, the day we were trying to make the entrance into Cape May Inlet before dark.

How fragile my boat had felt at times. Yet the most fragile of shells has learned to live with the awesome power of the sea.

I think how spring is affecting those other shores I know — the southern islands where there is no fog, and the rocky coasts, so different in their nature — all linked by the unifying sea.

My prejudice against winter begins to fade. The temperature under the tarp is warm and comfortable. I curl up in the corner cushions of the settee, falling under the spell of being aboard again. All the hectic work schedules and job confrontations become less important now. The body and mind begin to relax and soar like seabirds.

So spring has come, bringing with it a nameless pathos. It's the blank pages of the log book yet to be filled, the new beginning, the fresh start that will, as it always has, wash away much that has gone before, as the waves wash away the sandpipers' tracks.

1990 **Bunking on *Buster***

Anna Leadem

Did you ever wish you could live on a boat? Some folks harbor that secret dream. Well, I did it, and believe me, life afloat can be a nightmare. It was like some personal circle of hell devised just for me. In late spring, my summer rental fell through; and with half my stuff in storage, the other half scattered hither and yon, and no immediate housing prospects, I realized I was homeless.

True, it was a self-imposed condition. Friends did offer me temporary lodging. But I'm a solitarian, one of those people who needs a lot of down time. I want to be alone. So while I scanned the classifieds for another rental, I went with the most appealing option: my father's 24-foot sailboat, *Buster II*, docked at a marina in Forked River.

"Perfect," I thought. "*Buster* is roomy and comfortable. There'll be peace and quiet. It'll be fun. An adventure."

But what had seemed like a brilliant idea lost some of its luster the first night on board. The marina was deserted. Clouds hid the moon, and the wind rustled the marsh grass. In the inky darkness that followed sundown, halyards hit masts with screeching fury, and hulls dragged dully against the bulkhead. Rigid with fear, I lay fully dressed in the V-berth, a blanket over my head. I kept thinking about the vagabonds who roam Rt. 9, and how effortlessly one of them could sneak through the gate and climb onboard, and how no one would hear my screams, and how I'd probably wind up as a *Beachcomber* story about boatyard murders. Every time the boat rocked a degree, I froze and prayed.

Snuggled up to a stuffed jib bag, I survived the first night, and in the morning I climbed out of the cabin with relief. And surprise. The sky was clear and blue, the birds were symphonic, and the perfectly still water reflected a glorious tangle of rigging. Mallards swam by, gulls soared overhead, and the sun beamed. It was lovely, and I had it all to myself. I

from *The Beachcomber* • June 9, 1990

thought, "Hey, this is all right!" And as long as I stayed up in the cockpit, it was. Below, in the cabin — well, that situation ran on another tack.

Even though I streamlined my daily routine drastically, boat living was utter chaos. Within a few days, I had clothes hanging from the hatch cover, books and papers strewn on the table, half-empty Chinese take-out cartons stacked in the tiny galley and wet towels draped over port and starboard berths. I couldn't find my toothbrush, my underwear, my keys. Things just vanished in the confusion.

I caught myself muttering madly and knew I had to take Thoreau's advice: Simplify, simplify, simplify. I jettisoned all but the essentials and pretended that made a difference. But even when it held only the most basic of gear, the cabin seemed to be shrinking day by day. I kept moving stuff, tripping over it, cursing it. I couldn't stand up straight; I had no place to sit. Whenever I tried to carve out a place to work or eat or sleep, I was sharply reminded that *Buster II* was not the *QE II*.

And it didn't get any better. One night, the boat's battery went dead, leaving me to read by flashlight. In the semi-darkness, I stepped on the hook from my brother's fishing pole which had fallen to the cabin floor, and used the last of the day's fresh water to clean up the blood. Giant mosquitoes ignored my citronella candle. Then the rain came through an open hatch and soaked my bedding — with me in it. A bottle of shampoo leaked in my duffle bag. A Big Gulp tipped over and drowned my books. And then disaster struck.

The head exploded. One minute it was fine; the next, it oozed vile turquoise slime all over everything. Hey, nobody ever told me what the red indicator is supposed to indicate. I mean, you have to be a rocket scientist to figure out how to use the Porta Potti 245 in the first place, and I was in no mood to have to deal with a sanitation emergency. The M&M Marine catalog claimed the head is simple to operate. I wanted to call M&M and let them deal with it. But of course I had no phone.

Ashore, I called Captain Dad and eventually got the indicator to read green again. At about this point, my search for an apartment, hitherto haphazard, gained new momentum. I wanted a home that did not float. Immediately. And I found one. But as soon as I did something unexpected happened.

I was out in the cockpit early in the morning, drinking coffee from a Wawa cup, feeding fortune cookies to the ducks and waving to the fishing boats on their way out to the bay. And guess what? I began to regret my imminent departure. I realized what a wonderful retreat I'd enjoyed, there on my father's pretty C&C sailboat. I'd had time to write and read and — best of all — think. Just to be. What luxury!

My last morning on the boat, a couple of noisy, nautical-type yuppies walked around the otherwise quiet marina. I surmised from their conversation that they were salesmen on their way to a meeting at the restaurant down the road. They stopped at my bow and asked me what I was doing there on a weekday. There I was, feet up in the cockpit, soaking up the sun in rolled-up pants and big glasses, editing a story for *The Beachcomber*. I said, "I'm working. I live here."

One of the guys turned to the other and said, "Hm. Isn't that the life?" In that moment, all the inconvenience became trivial. What nightmare? I just smiled and said, "Yeah, this is the life." And I wasn't lying, either

1992 One Whale of a Diver

Marion Figley

Every ocean swimmer old enough to remember seeing the original "Jaws" movie also probably remembers that moment of tingling, bone-melting terror in the gray-green Atlantic when they knew, just knew, that the odd movement they had caught from the corner of their eye — that funny rush of water pressing against their body — was something to dread.

Deb Whitcraft is no exception. "We were diving from George Clover's boat *Angler*, one of the first Island boats to book ocean dives, and Joe Zelotnick and I had just come up. "We were facing each other, and we were far astern of the boat. We didn't want to blow all our air looking for the anchor line from the wreck to the dive boat, so we had come up pretty far from the *Angler*.

"Over Joe's shoulder, I see this big fin come out of the water. I said, 'Oh, my God!' He thought I was kidding him and he wouldn't look back. The fin stayed straight up and it just kept coming at us. On the *Angler*, I could see all the divers with their spear guns pointing over the side, thinking we were going to get eaten up.

"There was nothing we could do; this thing's between us and the boat. There was nowhere to go. The surface is the worst place to be when there are sharks around. You don't want to be on the surface. Finally, Joe turns around and he says, 'Oh, my God!' Both of us are walking on the water, trying to get back to the boat.

"So by now, we're hanging on the stern of the boat, all these spear guns over us, and above us I can see George chewing on an onion and laughing. It turns out it's an ocean sunfish, but all of us had thought it was a shark. Joe never dove again."

But there was also the time that a leviathan did rise from the deep, about ten miles off Beach Haven, right under the flippered feet of Whitcraft and fellow diver Sue Scott. "We were the first two in the water, and there was 90 feet of water under us. We were just in the water, exchanging comments and adjusting things — when you go in the water, your equipment loosens up — and then something hard was underneath us.

"We just looked at each other, like this can't be happening. She went over one side of the thing, I went over the other. I mean — when you know that there's ninety feet of water beneath you, you just don't expect this. It didn't do anything to us; just aged us. I don't think we did anything else that day. We made it to the stern of the boat and of course, everybody on the boat thought it was hilarious."

It was hilarious because that unknown, rising gray mass turned out to be a surfacing whale. But Whitcraft and Scott were rattled enough not to dive that day.

Whitcraft doesn't dive much anymore, not because of mental "Jaws" images. She's very matter-of-fact about sharks which, she says, prowl New

Deb Whitcraft aboard the Black Whale.

Jersey's waters summer and winter, noting, "They never, ever, bothered us." But now she is too busy running casino trips, bay excursions and wreck fishing trips on her *Black Whale* fleet at Beach Haven Fishing Center, at the foot of Centre Street She has suited up countless times in the past, however, initially as a high-schooler who learned the sport of diving at the urging of a boyfriend.

That was back in 1971 and Whitcraft, petite and honey blonde, belied diving's "macho man" image while showing the strong personality that would popularize open ocean diving on the Island.

She coped with lousy-fitting equipment — everything was sized for men in small, medium and large — but she felt perfectly comfortable questioning her diving instructor on the way to Pennsylvania on a bus. "I remember telling him, 'We have all this water here. Why are we going on a four-hour ride to a quarry?' He told me that's where divers were certified, and if I could do it better, to go ahead and do it."

Whitcraft saw that as a challenge and accepted it. A year later, she opened up Innerspace Divers in Beach Haven Gardens, selling equipment and running dives during the few hours she had between working two full-time jobs at Foodtown and the Hand Store, jobs she needed to keep her fledgling business afloat.

People excited about ocean diving weren't exactly beating a path to her door because open water diving was so new. "Business was terrible because it was a business that really didn't exist here. No one promoted or encouraged diving here." It could also be that Whitcraft set tough standards for certification: five open ocean wreck dives. Jumping or wading into a still-water quarry is a far sight from facing a battleship-gray Atlantic Ocean on rocking waves, but Whitcraft thinks North Atlantic diving is the real stuff.

"Divers certified in a quarry carry the same certification card as divers certified in the ocean, but the North Atlantic diver deals with currents, more equipment, more weights, different waters. If you're quarry-trained, you're not used to that."

Or to strapping on a knife as requisite equipment to cut your way free from the miles of near-invisible monofilament fishing line, the leavings of frustrated wreck anglers that can snag a diver in a delicate but lethal embrace. "One of our local wrecks has a big, old Russian net on it. You get hung up on that and don't have a knife, you're going to die."

Whitcraft says that her business partner, Bob Yates, is the best diver she ever certified. Together, the two went on to introduce hundreds of people to the sport in a decade-plus of teaching, and Whitcraft maintains that women divers are equal to their male counterparts and that young teenagers make exceptional divers.

"You could take a female diver and put her up against a male any day;

with the exception of coping with the weight of the equipment out of the water, there's really no difference. The only difference, more times than not, is that a female diver will make better use of her air; they don't use as much." Whitcraft says that teenagers who understand the medical aspects and physics of diving generally are excellent divers because they have no bad habits to unlearn.

Whitcraft has always been a cerebral diver, stressing the classroom knowledge of diving as much as the practical experience, drilling her students on U.S. Navy diving tables and writing a long-running column for *The Beachcomber* that evolved through the years to what is today her biggest passion. Initially, she wrote about the practical experience of diving: what could be seen, how to catch fish and lobsters, how to handle emergencies, pending marine regulations, innovative equipment, collecting artifacts. Eventually, as she watched salvage divers destroy wrecks with explosives to get at marketable metals, she wrote more and more about the shipwrecks themselves.

New Jersey divers might not have tropical, emerald-green waters for diving, and they definitely have to struggle into wet or dry suits to cope with chilly benthic temperatures, but they also have a fairly shallow coast, dotted with a mother lode of shipwrecks, some 5,400 according to Whitcraft, who is determined to document the history of as many of them as possible. The wrecks might not be as glamorous as Mel Fisher's celebrated and controversial *Atocha*, but they could be a rich source of local history if only the waters to their dim, past fates were parted, says Whitcraft.

"For divers who are interested in historical shipwrecks, you'll never run out of them here. Per square mile, and I would bet anybody on this, New Jersey has more shipwrecks than any other coastal state in the U.S. During the 1700s we had Philadelphia, New York and Tuckerton, three major ports of entry, one north, one south, one in the middle of a 127-mile coastline," she points out. Early mariners were unaware of the configuration of the Jersey coast, that it bowed out and had large sand bars or barrier islands at a jutting angle.

Ever the questioner, Whitcraft remembers hating high school social studies and now finds herself asking her former teacher, another Beach Haven resident, why the local high school does not include the area's rich maritime heritage in a course. "No one cares about the historical significance of the shipwrecks as much as they do about their monetary value. The kids going to school here know nothing of their own local history, know nothing of these wrecks here. Kids around here don't know the important role New Jersey played in the Revolutionary War, Prohibition, the world wars," says Whitcraft. Most of the wrecks are within three miles of the coast, and many of those are in shallow water sites, 25 to 50 feet deep, and have historic artifacts, she says. "There are hundreds of them off Long Beach Island. They are heaped on top of one another. A lot of these ships went down not because of stranding or fire or navigational error, they went down because they'd strike the sunken, submerged hull of a previously sunk ship."

Along with the tides and currents that have broken up and scattered the wrecks, that convergence of wrecks complicates Whitcraft's research. "That's what we call a contaminated wreck site, one where you have one ship that went down in 1850 and another that went down years later. It's tough, if not impossible, to differentiate between artifacts and structural pieces of wrecks."

And then there are all those unnamed, unknown wrecks, the big "U" category. "On George Clover's boat I took my first open ocean dive and saw the *Gloria*, my first wreck. That's not its real name, just what it's called."

Of the 5,400 shipwrecks — submarines, gunboats, oil tankers, tugboats, freighters, schooners, fishing boats, barges — fewer than ten percent have been found. Of those 500-plus, maybe only half are identified by the vessels' true names, says Whitcraft. The other half, like the *Gloria*, were dubbed at a captain's whimsy, perhaps because he was fishing a wreck when his girlfriend was on board. The majority of the unidentified ninety percent have no name, period.

Putting a name on them is tough, but Whitcraft is trying. "I take these old accounts where they describe the location of the wreck; if it was before the 1870s in these parts, they might use the location of a house to place the wreck — and there might have been only a dozen people living on this sand bar at that time. Then I have to take a coastal chart from that period and overlap it on a recent coastal chart because the configuration (of the coast) changed greatly and try to plot the position of that wreck as the coast existed then, and then convert it to the way the coast is now," she says, describing the exhaustive process.

Her research has taken her to the National Archives in Washington, D.C., to Princeton Theological Seminary, to genealogical records and to cemeteries where stories of the shipwrecks were buried with its victims.

Among the successes of her detective work was the British barkentine *Ontario*, which veteran divers have explored for years with little curiosity for the vessel's past.

"Here is this 200-foot shipwreck, and they recovered some coins and old bottles, but no one ever took the time to find out what it was. It went down in 1876 off Beach Haven after it stranded and caught fire. It's in shallow water, only 25 feet. The crew was saved by men from Bonds Life Saving Station."

Her most intriguing research these days is a "contaminated" wreck that is at least two centuries old and has yielded fancy crystal and silver, ornate doorknobs, brass rails, zinc ingots and bone-handled tools. Fearful that the ship's history will be literally stripped away, she's keeping this shallow-water wreck a secret until her research is complete.

With twenty years of diving and studying wrecks, Whitcraft's research outgrew her home, so she put on an addition to accommodate it. Historical organizations and museums contact her regularly, asking for information or requesting specific artifacts for exhibits. With filing cabinets and boxes filled with bits and pieces of 5,400 wrecks, Whitcraft went electronic, hiring a couple of women to computerize and cross-reference the material into sixteen categories, including a vessel's name, captain, number of crew and passengers, type of cargo, ports of departure and entry, the date and type of the vessels' construction.

It's taken two years to store that material, largely because Frank Waston, a former Beach Haven resident and amateur maritime historian, bequeathed his fifty years of research to Whitcraft. The two had been pooling their research when Watson died. "We started at 'A' of the vessels' names, and the last time we worked together, we had gotten to 'S,' she says, sounding rueful that Watson left her with the largest category, "U" for unidentified wrecks. Like Whitcraft, Watson had concentrated on Jersey wrecks. "And he was a fanatic like me; it was just that he was at it longer."

What fascinates Whitcraft about the wrecks are the images they conjure up in her mind, images of people and a long-ago way of life. If Whitcraft had a past life, she's convinced it would have been as a Long Beach resident in the mid-1800s when she would have tried, with the other few shore residents, to save the shipwrecked from their often horrible fates. When she speaks of the *Kraljevica,* an Austrian bark that sank off Barnegat Light in a howling winter storm in 1886, her voice is solemn, "One of our finest lifesaving crew from Barnegat station was all but wiped out there, drowned while trying to make it to the wreck. Most of the crew of the ship had already rowed ashore and were safe in an old fishing shack."

Whitcraft cannot imagine living anywhere but next to the ocean, and specifically this ocean. When her boats head for Florida in the winter, she stays behind.

Although she brought others to love that gray Atlantic and loved teaching diving, her interests now remain historical. In fact, divers who took her course found themselves taking a three-hour shipwreck history class. "There's more to wrecks than diving on them," she says, hoping that she instilled a respect for the ships in at least some students.

She is proud of her divers' safety record and of the search and rescue courses she taught to local fire companies' emergency dive teams. Although divers must rely on equipment for their lives, she notes that in all the equipment she inspected for the state in diving-related accidents, few had malfunctioned. "Most deaths come from diver error, rarely from faulty equipment. Diver malfunction causes a diver to die."

But it's the days before modern rescue equipment that fascinates her now. "If I have to choose between diving and sitting in a cemetery researching shipwrecks, I'd rather be in the cemetery. It's more of a challenge. Viewing the actual shipwreck underwater is not what you have to do to identify the wreck. It's spending all those hours and days and weeks in cemeteries and archives and genealogy records tracing a watery history."

Deb Whitcraft's passion for the history and stories of shipwrecks eventually grew to become the Museum of New Jersey Maritime History on Dock Road in Beach Haven. It opened its doors to the public in July 2007. At that time over ninety-percent of the museum's contents were from her personal collection. Since then, donations of artifacts and research material have poured into the museum from up and down the coast.

1992 Gifts From the Sea

Margaret Buchholz

*O*ne never knows what chance treasures these easy unconscious rollers may toss up on the smooth white sand ... what perfectly rounded stone, what rare shell from the ocean floor. Perhaps a channeled whelk, a moon shell, or even an argonaut.

But it must not be sought for or — heaven forbid! — dug for. No, no dredging of the sea-bottom here. That would defeat one's purpose. The sea does not reward those who are too anxious, too greedy, or too impatient. To dig for treasures shows not only impatience and greed, but lack of faith. Patience, patience, patience is what the sea teaches. Patience and faith. One should lie empty, open, choiceless as a beach — waiting for a gift from the sea.

When Anne Morrow Lindbergh wrote these words in 1955 in what would become a perennial bestseller, *Gift from the Sea*, she was referring to the "easy unconscious rollers" of the mind soothed by an oceanside vacation, rollers that would toss up insights into life, when the word is spelled with a serious capital L.

The gifts from the sea that most shore dwellers and vacationers treasure, however, are the ones washed ashore by foaming rollers or uncovered by gouging waves.

The anchor from the Italian sailing ship *Fortuna*, wrecked off Ship Bottom in a storm in 1910, was one such gift, treasured by an Island resident from the time she first saw it peeking out of the sand. Carole Bradshaw campaigned hard to recover the anchor and have it showcased outside the borough's municipal building.

The Roman bronze coin, found on Beach Haven's sands by the late Chris Sprague and now housed in the Barnegat Light Museum, was another gift, as was a waffle iron from a coal barge that wrecked off Barnegat Light in 1926. Twenty-four years later, a storm pushed the iron, designed

from *The Beachcomber* • August 8, 1992

Long Beach Island beach glass finds, including a sand-worn section of an old ship's lamp (left), a 1930s milk bottle and a 100-year-old blue bottle.

for the top of a wood-burning stove, ashore.

These gifts from the sea can roll up to the feet of someone spending their very first day ever at the ocean, beneath the feet of someone treading clams for their umpteenth summer or beneath the trowel of someone gardening the same plot for 17 years. "Finding artifacts is a water-related thing," says Tom Williams, a volunteer at Ocean County Historical Museum in Toms River. "There is a relationship in the action between water and soil." That is why a woman who lived on Manasquan Inlet and who raked, hoed and tended a little garden there came up with a pistol that museum curators date from the War of 1812.

"It's not the beach, but it's within a mile of the beach," said Williams of the pistol's recovery site, pointing out that today's geographic coast is not the same one of a thousand or even a hundred years ago. "When you talk about a mastodon's tooth being found on the beach, you're talking about the land where our beach is located now. When the mastodon was living, the present-day beach was far out in today's ocean." According to naturalists at the New Jersey State Museum in Trenton, a forest of petrified trees lies off Cape May's coastline, relics of a time when dinosaurs basked along a warm water sea.

Those who search for gifts from the sea often do so methodically, with reference books at their sides. One source is Dorothy Mount's series recording archaeological sites. The other is Rutgers University's John Snyder's *Mapping of New Jersey*. Get out on the beach after storms, advised Williams, or get an old map. "They show old streams and whatnot. Find where there were brooks; those are the areas to go and then rake and rake and rake." These are the places where people generally find Native American artifacts — hammerheads, arrowheads and other hunting tools. "The Indians would be spearing fish and so forth or shooting at animals that come to the water," Williams said. Historic stream beds inland also yield petrified shark teeth or ancient brachiopods, clam-like shellfish.

For those who want to stick to the ocean and simply use their eyes for guides, it's still good to have a map, said Williams. "After any significant storm you go out on the beach," said Williams, "but first you figure out where something is — say, a wreck offshore — then see if anything washes up.

"The Revolutionary War and the War of 1812 meant that there were a lot of activities along the shore with gun runners and privateers who came in the inlets. Go to those inlet areas ... where, historically, there were pirating activities or known maritime activity."

One couple did exactly that, combining raking the bay with using a metal detector. "They made a business out of searching the bay," said Williams. "They donated to us a collection of all kinds of things from the British colonial period — a British officer's belt buckle, medallions, watches, rings, Spanish coins." But although people bring in their sea gifts for identification, most artifacts go into the finders' homes, probably for display on a mantle, said Williams. "It means a lot to the particular guy that found it."

And that is the true worth of a gift from the sea, that it holds value or calls up memories or evokes emotions for the finder. On a bitingly bitter February afternoon, an unchipped moon snail shell can bring flashes of brilliant blue skies, hot white sand and a cool surf. A single clam shell dangling from the rearview mirror of a car stuck in rush-hour traffic can carry the driver back to a summer job and her first love and moonlit walks on the beach.

A bit of hardened mud in Eleanor Smith's hand calls forth the startling sight of a truncated forest of cedar trees on a foggy shore. "It was one of those days when the mist is always ahead of you and you never quite catch up to it. All of a sudden I saw, coming out of the beach, tree stumps. Embedded in this mud, this sod, were these tree stumps, shoulder, waist high. This was in Harvey Cedars, and I suppose that there was once a meadow out there where cows had grazed." In the early 20th century, several Harvey Cedars residents recalled seeing tree stumps far offshore during blow-out tides. Smith, a Ship Bottom resident, is an inveterate beachcomber, never actually searching for gifts from the sea but accepting them eagerly when offered by ebbing tides or eroding sands.

On Barrel Island in Little Egg Harbor, Beach Haven residents Joan and Lincoln Dunkel found a jumble of large bones they thought probably came from a whale. The Newark Museum identified the whale, a pilot or "right" whale once hunted by Island whalers, and the bones came back to the Long Beach Island Museum. "We wanted the skeleton to hang like the ones that you see in museums in the city. Finally, I talked to a man at the Smithsonian who said, 'I could do it, but you wouldn't pay my price,' recalled Smith. Undeterred, she phoned Stockton College in Pomona where a graduate student articulated the bones. They went to Stockton in a jumble; a skeleton came back to the museum on a flatbed truck and is now hung on permanent display. The efforts of Smith and other museum volunteers who pitched in on that whale of a gift from the sea ended up providing a gift for all museum visitors to enjoy.

While Smith's advice to beachcombers is to scrutinize the sands after a northeast storm, gifts from the bay, like the pilot whale, are often a matter of chance. Gunners hunkering down on marsh islands find gifts, like the Viking figurehead carved about the time that Columbus set sail for spices and fame.

Other gifts have no maritime history, like the twig chair and table that floated out to a bare marsh island on some unknown storm tide. Treading, tonging and raking clammers find gifts studding the mud, bottles of every shape and size from days when glass was the only beverage container in a boat. While the shellfish are sold, the bottles are often retrieved and taken home, bay mud rinsed out, the glass slightly cloudy but generally free from encrusting organisms like slipper shells, barnacles or mussels. The bottles read like a book on the economy: small businesses giving way before the bustle of big, of modern: "Farmers Dairy, Manahawkin, N.J." and "Riley, M.I. & C.S. Co., Pitman, N.J.," both classic, quart milk bottles; "American Bottling Co., Dover, N.J.," heavy and thick with a swirled, dimpled glass pattern on its soda-bottled shape; "Holly Beverages, Mt. Holly, N.J.," the raised letters inside a wreath also of raised glass; "W. Worden, Forked River, N.J.," an even older soda bottle with a ball inside: the pressure from the gas would hold the round stopper at the washer lining the stubby neck.

On Cedar Bonnet Island, Jim and Georgeanne Snyder find gifts right behind their door and made a recent discovery that surprised both of them. After all, they had bumped into it a couple of times. Last week, the two hoisted a metal gear, about three feet in diameter, that Jim Snyder believes was used to turn the old rolling bridge when the railroad stretched across the bay. "My dad has lived here since 1929, and he told me what it is," he said, noting that the gear can be seen in a mural of the old railroad bridge in the McDonald's restaurant in Manahawkin.

According to Snyder, the first old bridge was not raised to allow boats to pass through it. Instead, the center portion of the bridge turned sideways. Finding the gear was pure serendipity. "I was coming in to moor my boat when I hit it with my propeller. At first I thought it was a brick or something down there. I had hit it before, but this time it broke my propeller." So Snyder decided to investigate and with his wife spent several days lifting the heavy piece from the bay. "We used a cable to pull it out of the water. We rigged it up and lifted it. It weighs about 250 pounds. It's probably one of the last pieces of the bridge left. When the railroad was dismantled, I imagine they dropped it in the bay and didn't bother to retrieve it," Snyder surmised. The bay's gift is destined to become a gift to Stafford Township Historical Society's restored Tuckerton train station. While the Snyders don't regard their "bay finds" as gifts from the sea, they have a collection of curious pieces in their dining room hutch.

An old spark plug has become a sort of *object d'art*, its utilitarian shape nearly obscured with generation upon generation of the shellfish and crustaceans that made it their home. One time when Snyder was putting pilings in the ground close to his house, he found a hand-blown bottle from Europe that dates back seventy or eighty years. The bottle was about five feet under the mud, but Snyder was nonchalant about it: handmade glass is a common find for the Snyders.

Unusual, however, was a World War I vintage hand grenade found at low tide one day. Snyder has also found coins in the water and mud. "I found one coin that wasn't worth anything because no one could identify where it came from. I'd say it was Greek, since I spent some time there in the service, but I couldn't say for sure."

While most people unreservedly accept sea gifts, others have high standards. Probably the most commonly sought treasure is beach glass, that wonderfully elusive reward for a beach walk. To be "ripe," say those with beach glass collections, a piece must have no sharp edges and feel minutely rough, like a quadruple-O sheet of sandpaper. The best fragments are sensually satisfying to touch and hold, like a worry bead from the Middle East, with well-rounded edges, the hint of a pattern and delicate coloring. If a piece is not "done," a real beach-glasser will toss it back into the water — even a blue piece.

Glassniks who are serious about their collecting say that cobalt blue is the most desirable color and the rarest. Kayaking out to Sandy Island one day, I saw a sparkle of blue sticking out of the sod bank. I squatted down to pick it up and it didn't budge — turned out it was a very old bottle encased in mud.

Most of the cobalt glass comes from Milk of Magnesia bottles and old letters appear in relief on the glass; paper labels eventually replaced the raised-glass trademarks. Shards of lavender are rare, too, with the deepest purple the most unusual. A worn piece of red glass is so rare that it is beyond desire, and if found, would send the beach glass fanatic into a rapturous nirvana. We know of one person who found a ruby fragment on a narrow Chesapeake Bay beach.

The majority of beach glass is opaque white and other lighter shades of pale. Clear glass that has been in the ocean for many years will develop a delicate shell-pink hue. Serious glassers — they're the ones who walk the beach with their head at a right angle to the body and straighten up and rub their necks at each jetty — won't even bend down for brown beer bottle glass; it's just not aesthetically pleasing. Green beer bottles, on the other hand, develop attractive shading patterns after they've been well tossed by the sand-polishing sea.

If it's possible that such a category exists, the granddaddy of all beach glass was picked up on a Loveladies beach four years ago, after a rousing northeast storm. The fragment is is a very thick third of a ship's lamp, seven inches wide, eight inches high, beautifully opaque.

So why do all the gifts from the sea fascinate? After all, many of them are nothing more that a shell among millions of its kind, a bit of broken glass that others might toss in the trash, a bone that is — well, just a bone. Perhaps it's because these bits of flotsam and jetsam open a small window on the past to connect us to history as no textbook ever can, instruct us on how little we know about inner space, and capture the marvelous seashore environment that continues to draw us to the water's edge again and again.

At the end of her book, Anne Morrow Lindbergh packs up to return to Connecticut and a hectic family and social life. As she feels the damp shells in her pockets she writes: "Island living has been a lens through which to examine my own life in the North. I must keep my lens when I go back. Little by little one's holiday vision tends to fade. I must remember to see with island eyes. The shells will remind me: They must be my island eyes."

1994 Message in a Bottle

Elinor DeWire

Who hasn't dreamed of finding a message in a bottle pitching in the waves or stranded on a lonely beach? Its contents could reveal the answer to some great mystery — the fate of a lost ship or the location of a castaway crew. It might generate a lasting friendship or an impassioned love affair, impart a verse of wisdom or bring its finder a fortune. Messages in bottles have accomplished all these things and more, but only at the whim of King Neptune's letter carriers. The sender takes a chance with a bottled letter: It requires no address or stamps, no mailbox or ZIP code, and is randomly delivered at an unpredictable pace. It may arrive express in a storm or on a swift current; or it may float about for centuries in some aqueous post office.

Because of their virtual indestructibility afloat, glass bottles make ideal couriers at sea. Barring an encounter with exposed rocks, coral, or other hard surfaces, a glass bottle's seaworthiness may span several centuries and thousands of miles. Roughly 50,000 bottled messages are released each year to satisfy a whim or to collect scientific data. Beachgoers and boaters enjoy sending them, and researchers still depend on these drogues for valuable data about currents, waves, ocean weather, and shore erosion. The chances of finding a bottle are better than you'd think, and sending your own is great fun.

The practice of sending messages in bottles is ages old. Some 2,000 years ago, the Greeks used ocean bottles to investigate currents in the Mediterranean Sea, and during the Age of Exploration, bottles served as proof of an intrepid voyager's travels. In 1492 Columbus launched a message in a cask containing a copy of his journal, hoping the news of his great discovery would somehow reach Europe if his ships failed to return.

Bottles proved to be stealthy receptacles for secret messages during the Elizabethan Age, when spies aboard enemy ships used them to communicate with the Admiralty. In Colonial times, Benjamin Franklin used bottles to study storm tracks and currents that affected the routes taken by transatlantic ships. His discoveries revealed that the mighty Gulf Stream could improve a day's sail by as much as seventy miles.

Similar to Franklin's bottles were the ones dropped in the sea from 1940 to 1960 by the U.S. Coast and Geodetic Survey. About ten percent of these bottles were recovered and returned, yielding important information about rivers, harbors, estuaries, and the open sea. The majority are yet to be found.

Other ocean bottles have been found that were sent with more discriminating aims in mind. A Swedish sailor once found a wife by advertising in a bottle thrown from the deck of the ship where he served and an Alaskan minister still uses ocean bottles to sermonize to an unknown salty congregation. Radio stations and department stores have launched advertising campaigns in bottles, and the keepers of remote rock lighthouses have used them to communicate with shore. Passengers aboard sinking ships have sent farewells to loved ones in bottles: A number were thrown from the *Titanic*, the *Lusitania* and the *Andrea Doria*.

A message that an American couple released from a cruise ship approaching Hawaii in 1979 was found off Songkhla beach, Thailand by a former South Vietnamese soldier and his family as they fled that country's communist regime by boat. A correspondence relationship began in 1983, and the couple worked with U.S. Immigration to help the Vietnamese family obtain refugee status in 1985 and move to the United States.

If you're considering finding or sending a message in a bottle, here are a few things to consider. New Jersey's low flat beaches make it ideal for launching or retrieving bottles. The best times to search are at low tide after storms and at times of the day and year when fewer people frequent the beaches. Early morning and late evening sun offer glint on bottles making them easier to see.

The National Oceanic and Atmospheric Administration reports that certain stretches of the New Jersey shore seem to capture more bottles. Sandy Hook snags many of those carried down the Hudson River or launched from New York City and Long Island. The barrier beaches between

Manasquan Inlet and Barnegat Inlet also seem to catch more bottles due to their near north-south alignment, and the peculiar way their offshore currents travel. Cape May grabs many of the bottles set adrift in the Delaware Bay.

If you're planning to mail a bottle choose a glass one that's round and smooth, such as a wine or ketchup bottle. Give your bottle some ballast by adding about a cup of sand to it, then insert the message, written in water-resistant ink. Stop tightly with a cork and seal the cork thoroughly with melted wax to waterproof the bottle's interior. Cork seals are best, rather than metal or plastic screw-on caps. Do not use plastic bottles, they are environmentally unsafe. The ocean actually recycles glass bottles; if they break, wave action and sand abrasion smooth the shards to create what beachcombers call mermaid's tears, or beach glass.

Mail your bottle as the tide is receding in an area where it can move out to sea unobstructed. Any of New Jersey's inlets work well. Fishing piers or breakwaters give bottles a definite sea advantage. Of course the best place to launch a bottle is from a boat. Next time you're on the water, consider tossing a bottle to King Neptune. Who knows where it may land?

1927: A Bottled Message

"In the not so distant past it was a common thing to find bottled messages on the beach, and though we have never personally had the good fortune to discover one of these free-for-all missives, we have seen and heard of choice ones. On June 25th, Dorothy Gordon Hay, of Beach Haven, found a penciled note in a bottle washed up on the beach: 'Greetings from the *S. S. Mohawk*, Clyde Line. All is well. H. Bolte, Ossining NY.' "

This brief item appeared in Charles Edgar Nash's 1927 newspaper, *The Sea Breeze*. Ironically, just eight years later all was not well. On a frigid January day, when the *Mohawk* passed off Mantoloking, it collided with another ship and quickly sunk. Hundreds of passengers and crew died.

2001 Puskas: Sunk, but Never Out

Mark Howat

He is, in a way, the godfather of the current generation of commercial fishermen in these parts. He showed them where the tilefish were; taught them how to fish for them when they could no longer fish for swordfish — which he'd taught them to do after they could no longer fish for cod, which were near extinction. It took him ten years of experimenting to find tilefish, learn how to fish them, and then create a market for them. "That," he says, "is when the fishermen here started making money." It's when Barnegat Light became known as the "Tilefish Capital of the World."

He led the battle to get foreign fishing fleets out of U.S. waters when there were up to 400 ships dragging bottom off the New Jersey coast. Now he is at the forefront of the wars to save long-line fishing. And, just for good measure and so you'll know he's not a sunshine fisherman, he's had three fishing ships sink from under him, two far out at sea.

Yes, Lou Puskas really is quite a guy.

We are sitting in the living room of his spectacular Barnegat Light home, built in 1884 — fifteen rooms, four fireplaces, three baths — and he has in front of him scores of newspaper clippings, letters and documents that record the history of this remarkable man. He is only the second owner of this house, which had been owned by the Archer Land Co. Puskas' hair and beard are gray now; his face weatherworn, lined and leathery, like a well broken-in baseball glove. He begins to talk and there's no stopping him. He has, in truth, given his life to fishing.

He started fishing as a kid. He caught a sunny, but it was really Puskas who got hooked ... for life. He was held back one year in school because he played hooky twenty-six days in row to go trout fishing. He built his first boat, the 32-foot *Gra-cee*. It's the only boat he owned that never sank. He got his captain's license and with the 48-foot *Gra-cee II* did 275 charters one year. In the winter, he'd go cod fishing. But the cod were practically

from *The Beachcomber* • July 20, 2001

Capt. Lou Puskus, with a catch of tilefish, at the Viking Village commercial docks, Barnegat Light, in the late 1970s.

wiped out by foreign fleets in the mid '60s. He began swordfishing, learning where and how to catch them, but after thirty-five people in Japan died from mercury poisoning, that practically put an end to-swordfishing.

He'd heard about tilefish but didn't know where they were or how to catch them. So for ten years he experimented fishing for tilefish, going out for days at a time alone, until he learned where they were and how to fish them. And when he caught them, he sent them to the Fulton Fish Market, where he sold them for thirty-five cents a pound. At first he did the fishing by hand in water 600-feet deep, hauling up tilefish weighing up to 60 pounds, and averaging 35 pounds.

Then on a frigid winter morning in March of 1972, with the wind chill at eleven degrees, Puskas and his 17-year-old mate, Kirk Larson — Barnegat Light's current mayor — headed for the Hudson Canyon for tilefish. They did well, with a catch of 3,500 pounds on board. Heading home, a storm kicked up. The seas were wild, the wind was howling and at four in the morning, a fire was discovered in the engine compartment. In minutes, the *Gra-cee II* was covered in flames. An inflatable rubber raft was cut loose from the top cabin and Puskas and Larson were quickly in it.

They lost the *Gra-cee II* and the catch. A passing tanker saw their last

133

flare, notified the Coast Guard and, after several hours in a life raft, they were taken aboard a cutter. Puskas suffered second-degree burns to the face.

In 1975, Puskas was aboard the 65-foot *Gra-Cee III* when it sank in Barnegat Inlet, and he and a mate jumped off into another boat. His boat was not lost, but in March of '83, the *Gra-cee III*, having just been overhauled, began taking on water 110 miles east of Barnegat. Again Puskas and his mates took to an inflatable life raft. Puskas' use of an emergency position-indicating radio beacon allowed the Coast Guard to locate and rescue the crew. At the time, visibility was only a half mile, cloud ceiling 100 feet. Waves were eight feet, and the wind was at twenty-five knots.

There are no more vessels named *Gra-cee*.

Puskas has spent several small fortunes fighting what he felt were intrusive government regulations. When the mercury scare occurred, he commissioned independent research and surveys that compelled the government to change its standard for swordfish from 0.5 parts of mercury per million to 1.0. He believes a safe standard could go as high as 2.5 per million if swordfish isn't eaten regularly.

He tangled offshore with the Japanese fishing fleet. "We could catch one tuna per day but there was no limit on what the Japanese could catch. I saw one ship catch 200 in one day and we were allowed only one. No one was regulating or monitoring the Japanese." So Puskas spent $30,000 of his own money and petitioned every member of the Senate, House of Representatives and other officials — 800 in all — and was able to get tough regulations passed. "Now the Japanese buy fish from us. What they once got for free they now buy from us. It helps our balance of trade, too."

Some of the trouble getting regulations passed was due to the Cold War, Puskas says. Our navy wanted to patrol off the coast of Russia, so they didn't want regulations on where foreign ships could fish off the U.S., he says. "We'd put out twenty miles of long-line, they'd put out eighty. They had huge ships capable of processing 300 tons of fish each. They would have cleaned us out. Now it's too expensive for them to come here and take a limited number of fish. So they buy from us."

Sportfishermen complain about long-line fishermen, he says, but last year they had the best year ever sportfishing. "They would not have

Capt. Lou Puskus in the wheelhouse, early 1980s.

experienced it if it weren't for guys like us. We really saved fishing — for ourselves and them," he says.

Today he no longer goes out fishing, although he owns the 78-foot *Olympic Javelin*, which sank once but was raised the next day. He plans to sell it when it is overhauled. He and John Larson, father of Kirk, own Viking Village and he is one-third owner of the Marina at Barnegat Light. Captain Lou Puskas is a fisherman's fisherman, one helluva guy who's led one helluva life.

2011 The Hunters of Winter

Joseph McCann

The alarm went off at four; not even dawn yet — actually, three alarms set a minute apart, as I did not want to be late for today's hunt. The fresh smell of coffee filled the house as the automatic coffee maker performed its wondrous job. It is my responsibility to provide coffee for the boat.

I laid out all my foul-weather gear the night before, as preparation means survival when duck hunting on Barnegat Bay. It is going to be one of the coldest days of winter, so today's hunt is no time for poor gear or miscalculations. One mistake, one slip, one fall into the icy water, and you may have only a few precious seconds to save yourself or a buddy.

I meet my hunting partners, Denis and Mike, at the Barnegat Light ramp. Together we we'll head outside the Barnegat Inlet for our first eider hunt ever. These large waterfowl don't usually come this far south, but the extreme cold this winter has pushed them to the mouth of the Inlet. Hunting eiders is like hunting a tank with wings, but we've been told they are very tasty.

Denis warms up the Carolina skiff while Mike and I load the gear: decoys, shotguns safely packed inside floating cases, ammo, and, of course, my huge Thermos of coffee and buttered rolls, the original Jersey breakfast. It is still pitch black outside and the winds are screaming out of the northeast at 15 to 20 knots. We share a few words about the foreboding weather forecast, but our excitement level is too high to deflate us and we shove off. We are a picture of unified determination — three friends heading out on the coldest day of winter to hunt ducks. Many would say we're crazy, but this is an annual tradition that we look forward to for a year in advance.

Denis and Mike are both retired New Jersey state troopers who worked in the Marine Division and were stationed at the Point Pleasant station. After working for several years on Barnegat Bay and surrounding waters they finished their careers as troopers. They knew the waters around Long

Beach Island and Barnegat Inlet like the back of their hand. Every cut, every island and every sand bar were ingrained in their memory should they need to get to an emergency on the bay. Both Mike and Denis were licensed captains and their boat handling ability was impeccable. They had worked so well together as troopers that they started a hunting guide service, the Barnegat Bay Waterfowlers. I was the lucky friend who was going to hunt eiders with two of the most experienced baymen I knew. Today, with the worsening weather, all of that knowledge would be tested by one of the most dangerous inlets on the East Coast.

As we turn northeast into the wind, the spray from the chop freezes instantly on the wheelhouse windows. I step out and use the squeegee to clear the icy buildup. To say that it is freezing is an understatement; I am wearing so much foul weather gear that the only exposed part of me is the area around my eyes, where the salt spray freezes on contact.

We steer out past Barnegat Lighthouse and watch the first sunlight cut through the night sky. I think how majestic the lighthouse must have been to a sea captain of yore on a night like this. Just then, the first roller approaches our nineteen-foot Carolina skiff, and we see the inlet is rougher than the weather forecast had predicted. We skirt the first roller and a second swell approaches. The engine roars and we cut across to the far side of the inlet for some protection from the wind.

We survey the situation and it does not look promising, but decide that if we did not at least try to get out of the inlet then we would possibly never have another chance to hunt eiders in the ocean. We continue driving towards the entrance of the inlet; the engine pushes us toward our destination as we breach the huge rollers. The skiff crests a wave and slides down the backside only to be met by another wave lifting us up and sliding back down again. Our skiff feels like a small dinghy. The rising sun slowly lights our way and we are stunned by what lies ahead of us. Waves are crashing across the breakers and the ocean is raging. The tops of the waves blow off into an icy cloud of spray by the powerful wind. We can see whitecaps hundreds of yards out past the foghorn. Some rollers are five feet high. Still, Denis suggests that we head out and see if there are any eiders outside the bay. I think to myself that it is crazy to venture any further. The wind is howling so loud that we have to huddle in the wheelhouse just to

Duck hunters break through a skim of ice on Little Egg Harbor Bay.

hear each other.

As we talk, I warn Captain Denis of a side wave heading our way. The engines roar again, and a roller picks us up and we are surfing back into the bay. I had been so excited about our eider hunt on the open sea, but it is clear that the winter wind is in the eiders' favor today. There is no way we are going to attempt to anchor the layout boat in the ocean in this heavy sea. We head back inside to safer hunting grounds.

We cruise to the leeward side of an island (I won't tell which one) and set out the decoys and layout boat. Mike and I take the first shift and settle into the boat. The layout is a nine-foot oval craft that creates a low profile in the water that the birds cannot easily see, so when you are inside, the water is near your chest level. It's a rather unnerving feeling to be so close to the water, especially when the bay is rough and the winds are blowing.

The Grand Architect of the Universe has provided us with a beautiful sunrise. Yes, it is freezing out and the ducks are flying in all directions, but watching the sunrise on Barnegat Bay in the middle of winter is simply good for the soul. We all agree that there is nowhere else we would rather be. We couldn't care less if we bring even a single duck onto the boat. Just watching nature and being outdoors is reward enough. However, the bay is loaded with the largest amount of ducks that any one of us has seen in a decade: Old squaws, buffleheads, broadbills, brant and mallards are flying everywhere. We take turns hunting from the layout boat, switching out every half hour to warm up in the wheelhouse. The decoy spread is bringing in the birds and we begin to fill our limit. After several hours of shooting we pack it up and head back to the ramp. Denis does an amazing job getting the skiff on the trailer, and Mike and I pitch in to secure the boat and gear for the ride home.

Our tradition is to stop and get breakfast after duck hunting, as we are cold and hungry. We decide on Scojo's in Surf City. Three guys, dressed in camo, sit down for a hot cup of Joe in a comfortable and friendly establishment. The waitress greets us with a big hello and asks us how we did today. We just smile and say it was a great day on the bay! We talked about the great shots of the day and the missed shots of the day. We discuss the positioning of the boat and what to try for our next trip. We laugh at ourselves, thinking we could set up in the ocean in such crazy weather. I say that several friends have asked me if I have any extra game meat for them. There is a new food trend called the Paleo diet that is gaining popularity. It suggests that we eat what the cavemen ate — wild-caught game such as duck, turkey, deer, and fish. Mike and Denis say that their friends have also been begging for some of the catch. Luckily, the ducks we have caught today will provide several meals for us and for our friends.

We pay our bill and happily leave the waitress a nice tip. Another great hunt is now a memory, and the tradition of gunning on Barnegat Bay lives on through three friends having a blast in the middle of winter.

Night **Beat**

Clarence Clemons at the Ketch, Beach Haven, 1982.

1981 The Last Picture Show

Lisa DiLeo

Summer nights may still be hot and steamy, but back seats at the drive-in won't have a chance to sizzle because the Manahawkin open-air movie theater closed this season. That long-standing lovers' retreat, the place to smooch under the guise of cinematic enlightenment, will become a shopping center, according to Alvin Frank of the Frank Family of Theaters, which owns all the movie theaters on Long Beach Island.

The reason for the changeover, Frank says, is the lack of profit drive-ins make compared to indoor theaters. "Drive-ins are not successful. The grounds are far more worth it as a shopping center." Movie theaters get $4 a head for films, which has drive-ins beat; they get about $5 a carload.

Frank, who owns theaters from Ocean City to Woodbridge and two drive-ins in Absecon and Atlantic City, says drive-ins other than his Manahawkin one have gone by the wayside. "The Toms River Drive-In has a

The Manahawkin Drive-in on Route 72 in 1967. It is now the site of Home Depot.

from *The SandPaper* • July 22, 1981

Ray Fisk/The SandPaper

The vacant Manahawkin Drive-in after it closed in 1981.

Kmart sitting on its site." The Laurelton Drive-in and Bay Drive-in, near Seaside Heights, also no longer exist.

Yet Frank isn't giving up hope for some kind of theater on Route 72. He is planning another indoor one in a new shopping center to be located near the entrance to Ocean Acres. He could give no date when the complex will open.

As for the old Manahawkin Drive-in, with its vacant billboard telling drivers there's no show, former patrons will find yet another small shopping center in its place. "I think there's going to be a lot of little strip centers on Route 72," Frank said.

But the heyday of the drive-in movie is gone. With the price of gasoline today, and cramped compact cars, the old reasons for watching three two-hour films consecutively can be thrown out the window with the old drive-in loudspeakers.

Now, Dolby sound and air conditioning have ushered in a more sterile, less passionate age of the silver screen.

1981 Pied Pipers of the Island

Sharon DiGiovanni

"So I broke into the church one night," Leroy Lewis reminisces, searching back thirty-eight years. Crawled through the cellar window ... But I didn't hurt a thing, you know. It's just that I saw that organ, and I had played piano before. But this! This thing was like — a Great Big Thing — big, like a whole orchestra. And I wanted to play it so badly.

"And so I got in and I played, you know, until they began catching on. And, oh, that church custodian, she was a mean one."

Now Lewis doesn't have to sneak. He is one of several "pied pipers" who have contributed to an Island tradition. His name is emblazoned on the Surf Villa billboard in Surf City — the very same which, short months ago, touted "Go-Go Lunch" — and a loyal crowd follows, their numbers swelled by organ-lovers from all corners of the vacationing country.

"They're never going to believe this back in Chicago," crows Keith Helbig. He catches his breath from the Indian dance in which he was star participant. (A toy headress is passed around the bar to the unrelenting rhythms of "Kawliga," until patrons brave or drunk enough take center stage and strut their stuff.)

Then there's the parade: a nightly event in Lewis' shows, a spectacle of which no organophile worth the name can easily be ignorant. "And I did not start that parade!" Lewis is quick to insist. "This was done as a joke on me one night. Some people from Pittsburgh marched through the door with a bass drum and a pair of cymbals. What could I do but start with the marching band music? And it caught on, and now people demand it."

Not only demand, it seems. Some of them work very hard at it.

On a recent Wednesday at the Villa, the opening strains of "It's a Grand Old Flag" sounded the call to arms at about quarter to eleven. A tall, thin majorette led the motley crew, her pale face compressed by a huge fake-fur hat that appeared insufferably hot. Behind her trooped the flag bearer, cym-

from *The SandPaper* • August 15, 1981

Leroy Lewis in 1959 at the Surf City Hotel, on the "Visual Grand Wurlizer Theater Pipe Organ."

bals player, someone on a whistle and a drummer in a most unlikely hat, strewn with an assortment of rabbits' tails. Above all rang the organ's clear, martial sound, slipping easily from song to song. By the time Lewis flowed into "Yankee Doodle Dandy," the hodge-podge quintet had become a dozen; each pair of arms, bunny-hop style, encircling the sweaty waist in front.

By the seventh lap through the middle of the room, the majorette had cast off her shyness and marched as though destiny called. The whistler came ever so close to exceeding the volume of the organ — no slight task when you consider that Lewis plays with some two-and-a-half walls of speakers. It was their shining hour. (With the possible exception of the cymbalist, who never did quite get the knack.)

Then the organ swirled into "God Bless America" as some snappily, some slowly, the entire roomful rose. It was hard to know exactly where to look — at the flag which had just been marched around the room, now proudly thrust into the breeze of the upright fan? Or at its replica on the bar's north wall, a hard-to-miss Old Glory constructed of hundreds of glittering red, white and blue spangles?

Exhausted, the marchers returned to their libations.

And without so much as a pause the organ played on and on ... and on. In the course of the next two hours, more listeners filed in. Hardly anyone left. Lewis launched into "Oh, 'Dem Golden Slippers." Five women across the bar, some in muu-muus, clapped time softly, nodded, smiled. "I'm Nobody's Sweetheart Now" gave way to a saucy jitterbug, and the dancers ventured out.

Then back to a slower tune. Snare drum brushes rasped, and shining from the whole length of the bar's south wall were the phosphorescent outlines of a trumpet, banjo and tambourine with two long strings of colored balls — orange, yellow, green — for the bells and chimes. And they don't just shine, they move. Sound is controlled at the console, and the instruments are animated on the elevated board, their own small speakers moving in and out, each like a breathing diaphragm.

"There are people who think all that stuff is new," Lewis remarks. "But, my God, that's old! 1924 at least. It's out of the Wurlitzer theater pipe organs. But we have it connected to the electronic organ instead. Ted Campbell (long-time friend and electronics ace) and I were among the first to do that."

The innovative pair had its start at Crane's Surf City Hotel, where Lewis played from 1957 to 1959 — his first paid organ-playing job on the Island (secured, he adds, after being turned down at Wida's as too young and inexperienced). At the Hotel, later heralded as "The Organ Capitol of the World," Lewis talked the management into installing a Wurlitzer pipe organ, available for a mere $2,500 after years of service at Hoboken's Fabian Theatre. "And that was a big thing at the time," Lewis recollects, "because nobody had ever put one of those behind a bar, you know. But now it's totally shot, really not playable. They're like big babies, those things, very temperamental."

The organ still resides at Crane's, where Jackie Vee and Paul Presto seem to use it sparingly, relying instead on an electronic model, augmented by melodica, sax, clarinet and a whole lot of sing-along.

In 1959, Lewis shifted to the Shore Bar (now Joe Pop's), playing opposite the Frank Burke Trio. "And we had this lovely lady there who was like 'the last of the red-hot mommas,'" he recalls. "Her name was Anne McKenna but she was nicknamed Apple Annie — 'cause she liked applejack." After the Trio and Annie decided to call it a day at the Shore Bar, Lewis followed suit "because, it would never be the same." A season at the newly-built Lighthouse Inn followed — to which he returned after four years in Panama to play for many years. After a spell in Pittsburgh he returned to the Island, played the Bayview for a few summers, then on to the Villa.

Many other area organists claim a similar patchwork history. Herb Feiler is one. He preceeded Lewis at the Surf City Hotel, and still plays at the Spray Beach Motor Inn. "Years ago, this whole Island was organ!" he recalls, listing performances at the Shore Bar, at Jimmie's, occasional sessions at the Beach Haven Yacht Club, at Nardi's. His friend Ed Matthews, leaning on the organ's top, notes that "Herb's the one who really got Nardi's started, as far as music." And Feiler, still playing, adds his memories of the thirteen long years when he both owned and played at the Riptide on Dock Road.

"At one time we had a 15-piece band there. The place held 300 people, and oh how the floor did shake! Used to be afraid the beer case would fall over. Said lots of Hail Marys back then," he smiles, his fingers never leaving the keyboards as he renders "Hello Dolly," eases into "East Side, West Side."

"And I guess the biggest thrill of all was when I played the largest pipe organ in the world. Just for a few minutes." Feiler explains that it was the showpiece of Atlantic City's Convention Hall and boasted 13,112 pipes. "Just to go through the catwalks behind it took three-and-a-half hours," Feiler adds, slipping into a medley of armed services songs.

And the Island, in its organ heydey, could boast of many other "greats" and near-greats. Lewis recalls that the Bonds Brothers, Ralph and Buddy, drew good crowds at the Surf Villa after opening there in 1960. They were known in particular for a midnight version of "Stormy Weather," complete with on-stage rain and lightning — an effect that Lewis and the Villa's owners hope eventually to restore.

"And then Dottie Ernst moved down from western Pennsylvania," he continues. "She's retired now, but played at Wida's for a long time, and she was very, very good ... and now Joni plays at Wida's, with Bob. She's a very good player ... And Buckalew's has used the organ quite a bit ..."

With so many Island organists rooted in the relatively distant past, do their audiences follow suit? "Not at all," contends Lewis. "We get everybody there at the Villa — old, young, middle-aged. And it's fun to be around something like that because it's very sad, you know, when the young don't want to get involved with older people."

And then there are surprises — like the day the rock band Impact came to hear Lewis play. "Well, I got fooled," he reminisces, laughing. "When they came in the door, I thought, "My God, they're going to hate this. But they loved it. They stayed. They even clapped! I almost fell off my bench."

And he acknowledges some changes introduced by the younger generation. "Like the word 'keyboard' that's used now instead of organ, and the kids started that. But! When they say 'keyboard player,' that doesn't make them a sensational organist or pianist, you know ... But I'll accept the terminology anyway." For Lewis, it's not age but attitudes — of audience and player both — that are most involved in enjoying organ music.

And Lewis has a few pet peeves. "Like you'll work on something for a whole week to make it — perfect. And the reponse is — zero. Though the musicians will respond. Then you play something like "Roll Out the Barrel," and it brings the house down. I do have to remember that they're on vacation. But once in a while, for my own sanity, I just have to play something pretty, like "Misty."

Of his many local colleagues, he feels, "The more in it, the better it is. There's enough for everyone on this Island." And, players aside, he feels the instrument's popularity is assured for a foreseeable future. "You can't consider that thing just an organ. It's a whole orchestra. It really is. It has something special all its own — and it doesn't have to take a back seat to anything."

Back at the Spray Beach Motel lounge, Herb Feiler seems to agree. "How long will I play this?" He laughs. "Until I die ... And the organ, that'll never die. No way."

1985 Tiptoeing with Tiny Tim

Curtis Rist

Tiny Tim arrived in Manahawkin twenty years after his hit song "Tiptoe Through the Tulips" catapulted him to a sort of neon and plastic fame in a drugged-out era. A successful freak among freaks, once a pet of Andy Warhol's, Tiny Tim arrived to perform with a circus. It was Monday.

He also arrived to shop.

But Tiny Tim's schedule in the Great American Circus is hectic. Although he performs only two ten-minute sets each night, he has been on the road to a different town every day since March, a schedule he will keep until the show closes out its season in November. While in Manahawkin, he stopped at a liquor store, the post office, Kmart, ShopRite, a prosthetic device shop and a diner for a fine lunch of two tomato and mustard sandwiches, a plate of hot roast beef, two birch beers, a coke, a flask of root beer schnapps, two pieces of goopy pie and two milkshakes. Everywhere he went, throngs of shoppers looked up from their carts to gawk and grab an autograph.

"This is the biggest thing to hit Manahawkin since the tornado two years ago wiped out the SuperFresh mall," said Arlene Stiziano, a starstruck Kmart worker.

If Tiny Tim was tired on Monday, it was because he hadn't had much sleep. He arrived in town at 2 a.m. after driving south from a performance in Point Pleasant in an Air Stream trailer towed by a baby blue pickup. The trip didn't end quickly, however. In Manahawkin, he noticed that one of the two gas tanks in the truck was half empty.

"I always have to have a full tank of gas," he said. "We had to drive about twenty-five miles to find a gas station that was open. Then we had to go to dinner, but the Roy Rogers was closed. We finally found a Big Boy's that was open, then we returned at four and got to sleep around five."

The drive wasn't simple, according to driver Fred Taubman, who is

from *The SandPaper* • July 10, 1985

responsible for transporting Tiny Tim and his latest wife, Miss Jan, wherever the circus beckons. Taubman, who doubles as a trumpet player in the band that accompanies the performer, has been Tiny Tim's driver for about a week, and replaced another driver who lasted for about the same amount of time.

"He's really paranoid," Taubman said. "He told me last night that if we had to drive all night, we would get that tank filled." But unfamiliar with the road, Taubman ended up driving off Hilliard Blvd. to the "Bridge to Nowhere," in the marshes of Stafford Township. "We were driving along, and all of a sudden the road turned to sand, and then it ended," Taubman said. "I'm not used to driving with a trailer, so it took me about an hour to back out. If I did not want to play with the band so much, I would have dumped him there on the spot."

It may have been a long road to the gas station on Sunday night, but it was an even longer road for Tiny Tim's career from a starlet of the *Tonight Show* and *Rowan and Martin's Laugh-In* in the late '60s to a circus sideshow in the eighties. Some critics, including *The Wall Street Journal*, have called Tiny Tim's new job the comedown of the century.

But the performer disagrees. "It's the greatest thing that ever happened to me," he said. "I've made a new generation of fans."

Not only is he making new fans, he is making new recordings, and hoping for another hit song. "All I need is one more hit and I'll be set for the next twenty years," said the Tim, who gives his age as closer to 55 than 51.

Tiny Tim continues to record despite failures over the last few years. During the gas crisis in 1979, he did a remake of the Tulip song entitled "Tiptoe Through the Gas Lines" (about which he said, "the gas got better; the song died"). Then he recorded the song "Highway to Hell" in 1983. His latest recording is "Rats in My Room," which is his first heavy metal number. "I'm excited about it," he said. "I think something can happen with it."

But until Tiny Tim can make it big with another hit, he will have to stick to the circus route and watch his budget. Although he makes $2,500 a week for his routine, according to his driver, his expenses are big. From his salary, $500 a week goes to his agent and $500 goes to his wife. Another $65 goes toward child support payments for his daughter Tulip, who is the product of his 1970 marriage to Miss Vicki, whom he married on Johnny Carson's

Ray Fisk/ The SandPaper

Tiny Tim testing a fan at the Manahawkin Kmart.

Tonight Show. And nearly $700 a month goes to the telephone company.

"I've got three phones. I love the telephone," he said rolling his eyes back so that just the whites showed as a point of emphasis. "When Alexander Graham Bell or Thomas Edison or whoever invented the telephone, they had a customer here." Tiny Tim loves the telephone so much, in fact, that the phone company is one of the few organizations privy to the performer's real name. As he pulled out a wad of money orders from his wallet that he uses as a stuff sack, he wrote the name Herbert Khaury on three of them, then sent them off to the phone company by Express Mail with a return receipt request at a cost of $11.45. "I've never yet — Praise the Lord — been late with the phone bill," he said. "I was a day late once. It was awful, but it was the mail's fault, not mine. This time I've paid the bills a week early."

Tiny Tim may be extravagant with his telephone bills, but other than that he has a tight budget. "He's a real nickel squeezer," Taubman said. "He said his wife told him she would leave if he had financial problems. So he pays her to keep her around. Then he'll go shopping and he'll have to put half the groceries in his cart back on the shelf because he doesn't have enough money to pay for them. That's what happened in Princeton last week."

But Monday was payday for Tiny Tim, and he was ready to shop. The first stop — before noon — was Roxie's Liquors. He bought four large cans of beer, a bottle of root beer schnapps, a bottle of schnapps that has gold dust floating in it, a can of peanuts coated in honey, and a bottle of Jim Beam mixed with cola. He tried to buy a lottery ticket, but there were none for sale.

"These peanuts are the best," he said, eyes rolling. "They're made by Budweiser and they serve them on airplanes. He opened the Jim Beam and cola in the car and swooned again. "Boy, they know what they're doing at Jim Beam. This is even better than the new Coke," he said, gazing at the can in his hand. "Jim Beam, we were friends before, and we're definitely friends now."

After stopping for some drinks and mailing money orders to the telephone company, Tiny Tim got down to the serious business of shopping. "We have to go to Kmart," he said. "Miss Jan's back is bothering her, so we have to find a pillow or something to make her feel better. Oh, I love her so. I'm so romantically in love."

On the way to Kmart, however, Tiny Tim was waylaid by some auto-graph seekers, and ended up in a drugstore where he bought a copy of the *National Enquirer* and three other tabloids. "I always read the *Star*," he said, "Look at this, 'Seven Ways to Turn on a Lazy Lover.' Believe me, I'm one of the laziest. The worst, the worst." The tabloids tell the truth, Tiny Tim said as he looked at a headline on *The New York Post* that read "Disco Bandits Die for $4."

The New York Times is great for an encyclopedia, but it's absolutely the worst paper in the world for horse racing," he said. Tiny Tim's faith in the tabloids goes beyond horse racing, however. The newspapers guide him in his intimate life as well.

"The *National Enquirer* actually saved my marriage," he yelled in headlines as he waltzed through ShopRite with three bunches of bananas that he said are "good for the bedroom." When he married Jan Alweiss of Valley Steam, N.Y., last year, there were no witnesses, so the marriage was void. "The *Enquirer* was the first to report that. The scandal sheets saved me." Miss Jan was married to Tiny Tim again in June between performances at the circus.

After a whirl through Kmart to buy an electric fan, a folding chair and to check the prices of Hefty trash bags. ("The ones with the pull strings are the best bags in the world," he said. "And look at this price. That's a good deal. I'm gonna be back for these.") Tiny Tim ended with a photo finish at the checkout counter in which most of the store workers and lots of the customers grabbed cameras to pose next to him.

At the ShopRite, Tiny Tim concentrated more on the subtleties of the products for sale than on his fans. In the toothpaste aisle, where he picked up both Crest and Aquafresh — "for my breath" — he was appalled to find that some of the Crest boxes were bent. "This is dangerous," he said, look-ing frantic. "You can't tell if it's just the box that's bent, or of the tubes are actually broken. Poison air can come through." He grabbed at the tubes, and knocked six or seven others onto the floor. He checked the bottoms of a row of mouthwash bottles to see if they were past the expiration date.

Tiny Tim became philosophical when asked why he is on a crusade for un-dented cans and un-expired food. "You don't know what goes on in this world," he said, dressed in a suit that was decorated with lyrics and notes

At the Bay Avenue Diner in Manahawkin Tiny Tim eats with a knife (because "forks have herpes").

from "Waltzing Matilda." "In this world, we have to correct what's wrong," he said earnestly. "If we've helped mankind even in the slightest way, then we've helped everyone else."

With a shopping cart filled with Wheaties, a jumbo assortment of individual boxes of cereal, lots of apples, three bunches of bananas, lots of little cans of orange juice and some lactose-reduced milk, Tiny Tim was ready for checkout. He spurned an offer to be let through ahead of all the other shoppers. "I don't want any special treatment, or anything," he said.

With the shopping behind, and only some coffee, peanuts and a Jim Beam and cola in his stomach, Tiny Tim, who weighs much more than 250 pounds but won't say exactly how much, was ready for lunch. At the Bay Avenue Diner, Tiny Tim ordered a Coke. ("The new Coke is the greatest travesty that has ever occurred."). Then he changed it to birch beer, so that he could pour half a bottle of the root beer schnapps in it. He finished the glass before the rest of the order was taken. "Boy, this thing hit me," he said, as he grabbed his side. "It doesn't usually do this. Where's the rest room?"

When he returned, he ordered a mustard and tomato sandwich with a special request of pickles that he took off and plopped onto the placemat without eating. Clots of mustard and bread caked to his teeth, and little beads of mustard formed in the wiry, reddish hair that hung in front of his face.

When his roast beef came, he asked for Heinz ketchup with it, which came in a plastic squeeze bottle. He opened it up and smelled it to make sure it was Heinz, then shook it up. Ketchup spouted all over the tables and over his tie. He didn't notice.

For dessert, Tiny Tim ate a piece of lemon meringue pie with a knife. "I will eat with a fork if I absolutely have to, but forks have herpes. As much as possible you have to try to keep away from herpes, AIDS and hepatitis. Most people don't eat with a knife, so you can trust that they're clean."

At home, he said, he keeps the same regimen. "Plastic," he said. "Everything is plastic and throwaway, or at least as much as possible. The dishes and forks I have I wash with Comet. I never go for the shine of soap detergent." Except when he showers. Tiny Tim takes many showers, "one big one and two little ones, at least, every day," he said. He uses Ivory Liquid bath soap or Jergen's moisturizing soap for the procedure. Today, he smells like Jergen's.

As the meal wound down, Tiny Tim ordered a Coke ("Is it the new Coke?") to help settle his stomach. "It mixes with the meat," he said as he slugged down the soda. "It helps me to burp up the meat."

The check came, and Tiny Tim stuffed the receipt into a pocket

crammed with other receipts and slips of paper, and got himself ready
to head back to the circus for the evening's performances. Bonnie Lee, a
waitress at the diner, walked over to the table and asked him if he would
sign her son's cast.

Most in Manahawkin caught a glimpse of a bizarre star, but Fred
Taubman has to live with it. "He's a slob," Taubman said of his employer.
He also said Tiny Tim is as washed up as anyone in the circus. "For the
overwhelming majority of workers, they're in the circus because they can't
get up anything better," Taubman said. "And in a way, that's the same for
Tiny Tim. This is really all he could get."

The circus life is hard for everyone, including Tiny Tim. "He's not the
most popular act in the show," Taubman said. "Mongo Bongo, the gorilla
who puts on sunglasses, is the biggest hit. When Mongo comes out, the
place goes wild. But sometimes people don't even clap for Tiny Tim."

Tiny Tim first visited Long Beach Island when he was a headliner at Joe
Pop's and the Surf Villa in the late '70s. He died in 1996 at 64.

1987 Wow! Not What We Expected

Bruce Novotny

Mick Taylor is billed these days as an "ex-Rolling
Stone guitarist." It's not exactly false advertising,
as he did spend five very productive years, from
1969 to 1973, with the world's greatest rock and roll band. He is used to
the label, even though it's been well over a decade since he left Mick Jagger
and the boys, and he claims not to mind the tag.

It is unfair, however, for Mick Taylor is no aging rock star living off
past accomplishments. He is not even primarily a rocker. When asked to
categorize himself he says, "I'm a guitarist. Blues, rock, jazz — mainly

blues." He did, after all, get his start in John Mayall's Bluesbreakers, which also spawned guitar god Eric Clapton, and was featured on Bob Dylan's 1984 European Tour.

Taylor now has his own band that he's happy with, a four-piece unit that has been tuning itself in clubs up and down the East Coast for the past few months. He brought that band to Rick's American Café in Barnegat Light last Monday, the band's last gig together for a month or so while keyboardist Max Middleton returns to England before going into the recording studio. It was probably not what most of the patrons expected — that is, tunes from Taylor's Stones era — but those who left disappointed are to be pitied.

Mick Taylor and his band gave, quite simply, a scorching night of blues and beyond. Relying heavily on instrumentals, as is Taylor's style, the band shifted easily from blues to jazz-fusion to guitar rock and, although Taylor seemed a little disconcerted about the crowd's inability to dance, his band never let up. Taylor and bassist Wayne Hammond worked especially well together, and Hammond obviously enjoyed the gig. He is a talented musician whose jazzier work recalls the bass lines of Miles Davis' 1984 album, *Decoy*, but who can handle driving rock and roll just as deftly.

Before the show, Taylor had said that the foursome was "just about at that point" where the members know each other musically and really begin to jell. That's an exciting state for a band to be in, for the audience as well as the musicians. The solid two-hour set wasn't spit-shined and polished; yet there was an unmistakable engagement with the house. The rough edges that really shouldn't be sanded down were still there, but the music was exceptional. Professional but not routine, technically adept and still emotionally charged, the Mick Taylor band didn't give the people the Stones classics they wanted — not one — but they had them yelling for more of what they did give them, at the end of the night.

It is not really surprising that his 1979 album didn't sell more: instru-

from *the Beachcomber* • July 9, 1987

mental music, particularly music as varied as Taylor's can be, seldom finds a ready audience. It is a little puzzling why Taylor doesn't sing more. He's got a fine blues voice as he demonstrated on "Something On My Mind," a much finer voice than another celebrated English bluesman, Joe Cocker. But to listen to Taylor's band make the music they do is to render the question unimportant. It is hot, tender, inventive, expressive, exuberant. It is blues and it's rock and it's jazz. It's the music and feeling of African-American rhythm and blues filtered through a London-born guitarist of exceptional ability and unleashed through a strong collection of musicians who have a great deal more music ahead of them.

And by now it is clear that Rick's American Café is committed to presenting great music — this Friday's Bo Diddley show is another prime example — and is no longer just the best blues bar on the Island, but very possible the best on the entire Jersey shore.

1987 Riding with Flamin' Harry

Bruce Novotny

Agood rock and roll show makes anything that can be written about it irrelevant. But in the proud and superflous tradition of music journalism, the story must be told.

This particular story is not new to Long Beach Island, but it is a little bit irrelevant to the music that was poured out on the stage of Rick's American Café by Flamin' Harry and his band last weekend. Flamin' Harry is a Barnegat Light favorite and has been appearing regularly at Rick's for a few years. He is one of the reasons the place has a reputation as the top blues club on the Island.

Flamin' Harry is billed as a bluesman but, to split hairs, he really is a bluesrocker, in the Thorogood style. It is a style that completes a natural, synthesis, the spirit of rhythm and with the youthful energy of rock and roll. Harry's band is a classic trio; bass, drums and Harry on guitar, and they play the music the way it was meant to be played. They play it strong, they play it hard, and they play it unadulterated. It's not pop and it's not computerized. It is straight ahead blues/rock, which has been the true folk music of this country over the last three and a half decades.

Flamin' Harry demonstrated clearly through his show that his music is not about songs as much as it is about the music itself. It is a disappointment when a band plays familiar tunes, whether their own or covering another's, the same way they've been played forever, down to the last note. That eliminates the spontaneity and much of the joy of live music. The "Flame" and his band have lost none of the joy, at least on stage. They're a tight trio and they handle their material with ease. Flamin' Harry in particular appears as comfortable with his guitar as Douglas Fairbanks with a saber. Yet rather than look bored with what must surely have become routine, they played to the crowd, especially a healthy number who danced through every song. Standards such as "Johnny B. Goode," "Bad to the Bone" and "Route 66" were extended beyond themselves until the music, the basic chords and riffs became the primary elements and the words were just along for the ride. Original material like "Rude Shoes," the title song from their new album, rocked just as forcefully and none of the folks on the dance floor sat down for it, either.

This is not extraordinary, nothing that a hundred other bands aren't capable of. Yet it is something that is always rewarding for the listener, good hopping music played with spirit and technical competence, and especially life. Perhaps too few bands understand what playing live really means, or perhaps it is just the nature of live music that it can satisfy so well. It is an activity that demands emotional and physical responses, not intellectual ones. That is why dancing is so appropriate and music journalism is so silly. The appetites to which rock and roll appeal do not get bored so easily (as those of the mind) and more quickly grow hungry again. All the Top 40 bands on the Jersey Shore can do nothing to ease that hunger. They're just background music, while true rock and roll like Flamin' Harrys becomes

from *The Beachcomber* • May 28, 1987

life itself, for a little while at least. Okay, that's an exaggeration, but it's good to know that the "Flame" will be around again, and that the music will be important, and words like these will always be just along for the ride.

1987 Beach Haven's Joe Piscopo

Joe Zeff

More people recognize Joe Piscopo from his work on "Saturday Night Live" and Miller Lite commercials than from his work on a garbage truck for the Borough of Beach Haven. Yet Piscopo, 36, insists he had some of his best times as a Beach Haven garbage man. Every summer his family migrated from Bloomfield to Long Beach Island, where Piscopo learned life's lessons on a bar stool at the Hudson House, in an occasional fistfight at Schooner's Wharf, and on the back of a garbage truck along Bay Ave.

He came home last Sunday to Joe Pop's Shore Bar for a last-minute practice run of his "Miller Lite Momentary Madness Tour," which takes off tomorrow in New York and closes twelve cities later in mid-August. Joe Pop's was packed for Piscopo, who kept the crowd loud with his routines about Frank Sinatra, Phil Donahue, David Letterman, Andy Rooney, Brace Springsteen, Jerry Lewis and David Lee Roth. Piscopo was backed by the Rapped Deployment Band, which will accompany him on the tour, as will Rich Hall, the man responsible for Sniglets on "Not Necessarily the News."

Piscopo remains America's foremost two-legged light beer spokesman. He has portrayed in Miller Lite commercials such fictional celebrities as East German Olympic swimmer Helga and brain-damaged wrestler Python. His latest characters are Rappin' Fats, a round rap musician who sings

from *The SandPaper* • July 15, 1987

about Lite beer, and Bruce Lee Piscopo, a karate kid who also espouses drinking Lite.

Also upcoming for Piscopo, who got his start four years ago on "Saturday Night Live," is a horror-comedy film co-starring Treat Williams called "Dead Heat." He is also slated for a live HBO special on Halloween night. I spoke to him at Joe Pop's.

The SandPaper: *So what brings you to Joe Pop's?*

Joe Piscopo: We're doing a warm-up for this "Miller Lite Momentary Madness Tour." It's a major tour going across America, and Rich Hall will be opening for us. It's going to be a good night of comedy. We're going from New York to New Orleans to Texas to California, Milwaukee, Chicago, all across America. I needed to warm up some dates so I wanted to come back down the shore, because this is where I was really brought up, more or less.

SP: *You spent every summer in Beach Haven?*

JP: Yeah, man. All my life. Literally, all my life, since I've been about five or six. It just has a sentimental value to it. Long Beach Island — it's where the real people hang out. It's not like the Hamptons, not real snotty like the Hamptons. It's not like Malibu, California. It's like real people going to the beach, hanging out at a pizza joint or just hanging out.

SP: *Is that the real Joe Piscopo?*

JP: Oh, man, that's it. Having a fight at the Wharf or going to get some ice cream at that place, man, we used to go down by Rommel's Liquor Store — which I also hit a number of times. I can't remember the name of it. It's like an ice cream place. The Frosted Mug, that's it.

SP: *Where else did you hang out when you stayed at Long Beach Island?*

JP: Pretty much at home, on our street. It was in Beach Haven, and it was the closest thing to a neighborhood that anybody could really have here. I grew up in the suburbs, in northern Jersey, so every summer I'd come down. I had my best buddy living next to me, who worked at Foster's produce stand. And then next to him was my other buddy, who also worked at Foster's. I worked for the town of Beach Haven. I was a garbage man. You ain't picked up garbage until you picked up lobster that's two days old. We had a great time on the truck. To this day when I smell garbage I get ecstatic.

160

Joe Piscopo plays at Joe Pop's Shore Bar in Ship Bottom.

As a matter of fact, when we pulled up here tonight and we pulled right in front of the garbage Dumpster, and I know they did that just for me. They put that bin out there right beside the limo just for me. Some of the best years of my life, clearly, were working on the garbage truck. It was a lot of fun. We used to hang out at night, like on our porch, or on the beach, or just on the street. It was just like what I would imagine the old neighborhoods of the thirties were like. We're all still best friends. We all still see each other, and it's just incredible. I try to do that with my boy. I bring my boy down so he gets that feeling, too.

SP: *Let's switch to show business.* Saturday Night Live *must have been your big break.*

JP: Well, I used to play down here. I used to go up in the attic at home with my Fender amp — and I still have it and use it on stage — and I would have my friend drum for me, and we'd like entertain people. We would play all the current songs, and I really liked to entertain. We would play everything but kids' birthday parties. Then you have to take it serious after a while. That's when I went to New York, at the Improv; that's where I started doing a little of everything. Doing a stand-up at the Improv gave you a way to showcase yourself, by yourself, so you didn't have to go to an audition with four-hundred other actors. I've literally gone to auditions with three-hundred other actors and stuff, and I came close to Broadway shows and things like that, and things started to happen for me. I went to "Saturday Night Live" after that.

SP: *Are you still tight with the people you worked with on* Saturday Night Live?

JP: Yeah. Eddie Murphy and I are very tight, and Timmy Kazurinski is someone I talk to a lot. When you see somebody from *Saturday Night*, it's amazing, the camaraderie. You went pretty much through a battlefield on that show. Trying to churn out comedy every week like that was almost impossible. We're all pretty tight still.

SP: *The Miller Lite commercials have really been a boost for you. The new one, featuring Rappin' Fats, is hilarious.*

JP: It was my idea. The other ideas, I've got to hand it to Larry Sokolove from Backer & Spielvogel, the advertising agency for Miller Lite. He came up with Python and Jumping Joe and Rhino and Helga, then I said I want to do a Rappin' Fats commercial. Like a rapping commercial. He wrote that song, and it's very funny. And then the next is a Bruce Lee commercial (I have to do a voice-over tomorrow afternoon for it), where I play a karate master, very funny. For the karate spot, we had a Bruce Lee film festival, and I watched all the Bruce Lee movies ever made, and it's really wild.

It's out of hand. I always liked doing characters, and Miller Lite came to me and asked if I wanted to do these characters. It's been great. Now I can turn down the silly television shows that get offered to me, or the film scripts I don't want to do. The idea is to keep yourself out there, and these commercials do that for me

SP: *You probably couldn't ask for a better arrangement.*

JP: I'm very grateful to Miller. Don't tell them that, though, because I'm renegotiating my next contract.

SP: *The partnership works well for both parties, especially with the upcoming tour.*

JP: Exactly. They knew I was on the road, and I go to colleges and everywhere, and they said, "Why don't we send you out on the road?" So now I'm going to meet all the distributors across the country. It's not just a tour; it's a handshaking kind of campaign for Miller Lite. It's an American product. I always say, I drive American cars … since Grandpa came over from Italy, man, we buy all American products. We're good American boys.

SP: *Naturally, whenever you walked into Village Pub you ordered a Miller Lite.*

JP: You know where we used to go? The Hudson House on 13th Street, not with the current owners. I was about 16, and I literally cracked a vertebra in my neck surfing. I went to the doctor in Toms River, and the guy just said I had to wear this brace, so I couldn't surf. My buddy — the Fat Man, Dave Strokoff — had an appendectomy, so he couldn't work. So the two of us, I mean we had our ass prints on stools at the Hudson House all summer long. We were sixteen, but we were bigger so we could get in. They didn't have Miller Lite so I drank Miller, how's that?

If we weren't at the Hudson House we would go to Buckalew's. We had a ball coming down here, and I want to shoot a film down here one day. I want to get financing and shoot a low-budget film. People don't know about the whole Jersey Shore scene. The off-season. We'd be driving down, and the way guys take their lawn furniture and sit on the front of Bay Ave. and watch the cars. Man, people don't know about that. It's hysterical. And they liked it; I couldn't believe it. These are like guys my age. It's not bizarre; it's just very interesting. People aren't aware of that, and I really want to capture that on film.

SP: *Do you mean that seriously?*

JP: Oh, yeah. As a matter of fact, I'm coming close to getting the financing for it. I want to do it low-budget where I have total control of it. That's the problem, getting total control. It's a good place, Long Beach Island. It's also a pleasure for me to be coming back here like this.

Island
Storms

Margaret Thomas Buchholz/The Beachcomber

78th Street and the bay, Harvey Cedars.

1930s Lighthouse in Death Throes

Excerpts from accounts in an old three-ring-binder of yellowed clippings left at The Beachcomber *office in the '70s. The stories date from 1919 to 1939.*

August 1933 hurricane: At Barnegat City there were fears that a return of heavy weather would undermine Barnegat Lighthouse, situated on the extreme northerly point of Long Beach Island. Last night the 75-year-old tower, which stands 168-feet high, stood only fifteen feet away from pounding seas. All Monday night great waves tore away thousands of tons of sand and earth on the western side, which is unprotected from the wind and sea. A small wooden jetty originally built to protect this side has been washed away and the Atlantic crept up steadily, cutting out a ledge 15-feet high. Local baymen said that just one more heavy northwester would eat away the remaining earth and allow the seas to undermine the foot of the lighthouse. [This late August hurricane swept over northern Virginia and passed inland of the Jersey Coast.]

Its original place in the lives of those who dare the sea — now replaced by a floating beacon off the dangerous inlet — the old lighthouse still remains primarily a cherished landmark, as a memento of the days when it flashed storm warnings or guided numerous craft into Barnegat Inlet, which gave ingress to the Barnegat bay region, then abounding with coastal shipping.

Year after year the furious gods of wind and tides have stretched their greedy maws toward the tower. Numerous times, reports of its destruction have arisen to end the story of man's efforts to save the beacon from the in-roads of the sea. But each time when gale subsides, the tower stood erect to belie the worst fears of the hundreds of persons who view the Lighthouse with veneration and pride.

Scores of visitors anxious to see the death throes of the red and white monument, and to see if it succumbed to the violence of the five-day storm

Erosion at the inlet threatens Barnegat Lighthouse, August 1933.

which has raged along the Jersey Shore, claiming its toll of nine lives, and dealing heavy damage to coastal resorts, went Tuesday and Wednesday to Barnegat City, certain that the high winds which developed in the last twenty-four hours would give the surging water sufficient reinforcement to eat away the 15-feet of sand, which is all that remains to fight back the currents from the very foundation upon which the tower rest.

Slowly but surely, the sand is crumbling into the furious inlet. To the east, man's efforts to ward off the ravaging waves have been more successful. Encouraged by stonework, a considerable stretch of beach has been created; where the beacon faces its enemy to the east, the battle has been won. But to the west the elements began a flank and rear attack, where the defense is most vulnerable. Danger today lurks on the north and west sides of the structure.

November 1935 northeaster: The northeaster of last Saturday and Sunday changed the status but little of Barnegat Inlet and Light, and little cutting away occurred at the base of the ancient marine beacon. The steel protecting wall built around that space has proven a decided advantage in its protection and acted as a strong barrier against the ravages of water and wind. Although the members of the Coast Guard crew stationed there reported they were not in danger, it was felt that some action would have to be taken by the government to repair the surrounding beach before the next storm.

Barnegat Inlet is at present unsafe for navigation, although it is used by many who are forced to do so by necessity, in order to earn a livelihood. It is hoped that the opening of the new inlet may prove a benefit to Barnegat Inlet. [The northeaster created a new inlet through Island Beach, to the north. Two-hundred-fifty-feet wide and seven to eight feet deep, it closed a few weeks later.]

November 1935 editorial: We who live in a sector that receives periodic batteries from a storm-swept sea, who can realize the potential danger that is forever dogging this part of our coast cannot understand why the federal government has not allocated funds for coastal erosion prevention work. The government has spent huge sums in boon-doggling projects, making work where none exists [a reference to the Works Progress Administration of President Roosevelt's New Deal], throwing money right and left for projects that will benefit but a few people; but when it comes to spending federal money on worthwhile projects that would protect our natural assets for all the people, there seems to be an endless ribbon of red tape to cut. Something must be done and done quickly or else we will see our valuable beaches and property slashed to ribbons with losses too great to estimate.

September 1936 Hurricane: At Barnegat City the famous Barnegat Light was being rapidly undermined by the battering ocean. Its base of sand was being washed away and the structure was leaning dangerously. It was feared that it might topple over.

From Reilly Sharp, Historian, Barnegat Light Historical Museum: The most the feds did to protect the Lighthouse was the steel wall (petticoat collar) around the base in early 1934. But that was just a Band-aid. The town built most of the rocks and groins that ran along the shore around the Lighthouse. The town constructed even the first jetty, which went out just thirty or forty yards into the inlet. The state government took responsibility for the north jetty on Island Beach in 1938, which ultimately received some matching federal funds and the contract was awarded to the Army Corps of Engineers. Any federal work on the lighthouse after the petticoat collar was few and far between, until the jetties were expanded in the '80s, as I understand it. From the 1910s to the 1940s it is a long sad, story of bureaucracy at its worst, as the town did everything it could with Washington and got stonewalled; then outright sabotaged by the Light-house Bureau head, who didn't care what happened to the historic beacon, because they were hot-to-trot over lightships.

1944 Trapped in Car in a Hurricane

*W**ritten a month after the 1944 hurricane, this letter is in the Long Beach Island Museum archives. We do not know the last name of the family. Bob had gone fishing that morning, September 14, 1944, and when the sky clouded over and he came in, a neighbor said a bad storm was coming. He and his wife Ellen, with their little boy Lee and baby Ruth, decided to drive home to Trenton. As they left Harvey Cedars, a little before four o'clock, the ocean was coming down the street.*

October 16, 1944

Dear Muriel, Charles and Donald,

We went about two miles down the road when we came to three cars stopped in water up to their hubcaps. I shifted into second and slowly went ahead. I passed the cars then a wave broke on our left side, splashing in my window and killing the engine, so I decided to pull ahead on my starter and

The day after the 1944 hurricane: All but about half a dozen of the oceanside homes between 78th and 74th Street in Harvey Cedars were destroyed.

battery. Then a garage floated toward us and stopped about twenty-five feet ahead of us — half on the road, half off. I was afraid to continue past it for fear a wave would push it over on top of us, or my battery might go dead. If it if that happened we could be turned over and trapped in the car.

I backed the car across the road and put the rear end toward the ocean. By that time the water was up to the seats. The breaking waves were terrifying; we opened all of the windows and just sat there. I held Lee and Ellen had Ruth. When a breaker came over us we would hold the children close to the ceiling. As the car completely filled we would hold our hands over the children's mouth and noses. When our faces went under we would shut off their breathing until we could breathe again ourselves.

The car filled rapidly but the water also ran out the windows rapidly after each breaker. We were by then sitting in water up to Ellen's elbows and we were scared to death, although neither of us mentioned it. The breakers came about 150 yards apart and were about 10 to 15 feet high. After a few minutes a huge wave floated the car about forty yards off the road towards the bay and turned it halfway around. We were then facing the ocean. We continued our same tactics with the breathing until a large breaker nearly turned the car over. My side went up in the air. I climbed

from the *Long Beach Island Museum* archives

out the window and held onto the top with my weight as far out from the car as possible and it finally settled on its wheels again.

Ellen held both children and I just hung onto the steering wheel through the window. I went under the waves and if the car tilted I would put my weight out and kept it down a couple of more times; finally we floated directly broadside to the ocean. I got all the way back in as I was sure we would not turn over.

We did. The next breaker turned the car over two or three times and Ellen's side landed on top. I quickly climbed out the top window and Ellen handed me the children. The depth of the water was just to the top of the car as it lay on its side. I pulled Ellen out and told her to hang onto the window jam with one hand and hold Lee with the other. He put both arms around her neck and just screamed. I held on with my right hand and put Ruth over my right shoulder and supported her back with my left hand. When the water went over us, I would try to pull my left shoulder and head around so the force of the wave would not hit Ruth's head.

As we hung there we went under the breakers, just like diving through them in the surf. They went about ten feet over our heads. After each one I would look at Ruth. If she wasn't crying I would hit her back and she would then vomit up all she had swallowed. We did that for quite a while, I really don't know how long.

Finally I saw a huge wave coming. It really looks like a small tidal wave. I told Ellen to hang on tight as a big one was coming. After it went over us I looked for Ellen and Lee and saw them floundering about fifteen or twenty yards behind me. They were in a clump of bayberry bushes that grow between the ocean and bay. The thought uppermost in my mind was, "We are done for anyway so we may as well all go together."

I let go of the car and staggered and swam with Ruth. Luckily the swift current landed me near them. I got Ellen to hold onto a limb of the bush and she did; Lee was still screaming so I knew he was okay. Ellen and I were so very tired and still the huge waves came. The water following a breaker was up to Ellen's neck and half the time we couldn't stand so we just hung on and prayed for the waves to stop. The ocean and the bay were all one and the current was so very swift. As we hung there holding on to the bush we saw a beautiful home on the ocean go by us one piece at a time

Six months after the hurricane, in the spring of 1945, Carolyn Wilcox stands at the oceanside of 78th Street, Harvey Cedars.

— the roof, windows, gable end, water boilers, tables, chairs and so on. We could see them riding the crest of the waves and only a few yards to our right. It was certainly a miracle that we were not struck by floating debris. I really believe that the height of the waves saved us. We went under the breakers and the articles floated over us. The next house, second from the ocean, turned part way around and shifted off its foundation. I really thought we were done for when I saw that whole house move toward us.

The wind was still coming off the ocean and I prayed for it to shift. We held onto that bush until dark. I kept Ellen in front of me and if the breakers came and knocked her off balance she would come up against me. It was more strain on me but I knew she would have to break my grip before she got away again and the four of us would be together. The bay was only about twenty yards behind us. I know if we got swept beyond the high growth we would be goners. Ellen can't swim a stroke, you know.

Finally, just before dark the wind changed and blew in from the bay. It helped ease the waves and finally the weather cleared. The stars came out and the wind blew strong and cold from the bay. The water still ran waist deep, but the breakers had stopped; it was like standing in the strong river current. We were so tired we could hardly stand up. I took the two children then Ellen hung onto my belt and we staggered to our car and rested against the back of it. The sand had piled up about two feet high so that we stood in water between our knees and hips and just leaned against the car, exhausted.

───────────────────

The family finally staggered to another car and rested there with another family until close to midnight, when they were rescued by police. They were taken to the Surf Villa, where they were warmed, the children fed, and Bob drank a beer glass full of whisky. The Red Cross drove them home to Trenton. They returned two weeks later and when they dug out the car to see what they could salvage they found Ellen's purse with all their money in it.

1953 Just a Good Northeaster

Donald Craig

New Islanders who talked about the hurricane on November 6 were firmly squelched by Old Island Hands. "Just a good northeaster" was the description generally considered acceptable.

Yet many who had been through the hurricane of 1944 weren't so sure and took off for the mainland before noon. Others who stuck it out maintained an attitude of watchful waiting. As Mr. Sheppard down at the inlet said, "Just so long as the wind holds northeast, I'm not concerned. But if it shifts to northwest or any other direction, I'm leaving at the same time."

The ocean breakers weren't more than average full moon size, but the bay was plenty rough. Harold Clopp of Brant Beach, crossing the Causeway around 4:30, ploughed through six inches to a foot of water all the way, while waves broke over his car. Yet he reported more cars coming on the Island than off it.

Salvatore Pinto

The 1953 storm left this house at 85th Street and the oceanfront in Harvey Cedars leaning and wrecked. It had an interesting history; it was a composite of two buildings that were part of the 1926 Philadelphia Sesquicentennial Exhibition. The rear two-story section was originally the Japanese Pavilion and the front was a reproduction of Paul Revere's workshop. After the exhibition, Philadelphia sculptor Alexander Portnoff, one of the founders of Harvey Cedars' art colony, bought and trucked the structures to the Island where they were reconstructed into a studio and summer residence.

Many spots on the Boulevard and side streets and around Beach Haven were under water during the afternoon and evening, but it was rain, not bay water, that normal drainage couldn't begin to carry it off. We got seven inches in sixteen hours.

All along the bay small boats dragged and snapped their moorings, capsized, sank full of rain and spray, or tore away from docks. One Peahala Park resident estimates close to fifty boats went ashore, downbay, or to the bottom in his small area of bayfront alone. A Corson sloop drifted down from Gaskill's to the Spray Beach Yacht Club, rammed Bill Best's sneakbox, breaking the mast in three pieces and splitting the boom. Several Spray Beach Yacht Club boats sank or overturned at the club dock.

At Brant Beach Art Hocking's speedboat, worth several thousand dollars, went to the bottom, and the rain washed away about ten feet of beach and street in front of the yacht club.

from *The Beachcomber* • Christmas, 1953

Lindy's Fishing Station at Beach Haven Inlet reported three of their boats smashed up and one drifted out to sea. A 26-foot cabin cruiser anchored off Bond's drifted ashore, but was rescued by the Coast Guard with no damage.

Fishing for sport and for business stopped for the day. Andy Bjornberg of Barnegat Light pulled his garvey and bay boats out onto the beach, and sent his *Queen of Hearts* up to Forked River ahead of the storm. The *Black Whale* and other Beach Haven fishing boats were taken for shelter to Tuckerton Creek.

Toward sunset the western sky took on a sudden weird brightness, and later the wind did change to northwest, but no hurricane developed. By late evening the stars were out.

1962 Desert of Sand after Storm

Excerpt from a somewhat exaggerated newspaper story headlined "First Trucks Reach Harvey Cedars; 67 Homes Left, but Most are Damaged."

What is left of Harvey Cedars is a desert of sand tortured by sea and wind into craters and plunging dunes. Until yesterday Harvey Cedars was accessible only by helicopter, but army engineers and private contractors have succeeded in bridging it. Last night a four-wheel drive National Guard truck sloughed through the sands of Harvey Cedars, one of the first vehicles into the beleaguered borough. Of the 500 homes that were here only 67 remain, but most of these are damaged beyond repair.

The houses have been wrenched from their foundations and washed to new locations — some are half buried by sand; others are no longer recognizable as houses. Utility poles thrust from the sand at crazy angles.

It was an eerie, unreal scene; the houses look more like toys left broken and scattered by a careless child than places were people once lived. There were no roads — all roads have been buried under at least five feet of sand. There are no landmarks. What houses are left are few and far between.

Mayor Reynold Thomas was happy to have a visitor. He said the worst aspect of the town's predicament was a total lack of contact with the outside world. "We were smashed to bits in the hurricane of 1944," he said. "But that was peanuts compared to this." His voice reflected the stunned disbelief of many of the islanders. "There was no warning and no let up. We kept expecting the wind to change to the west any minute, but it kept going and going, tearing the Island to pieces around us."

Like everyone else who lived through the storm Thomas had stories to tell. He told about Nancy Weiseisen, a 75-year-old widow who lives alone in a two-story home on 83rd Street. Tuesday night she was visiting friends near her home when the storm struck. Her friends begged her to stay with them but she insisted on going home.

• • •

The following letter written to her summer neighbors across the street, the Ingersolls from Philadelphia, turned up some forty years later:
March 21, 1962
Dear Mrs. Ingersoll,

I stayed in my house Tuesday, about 7:30 p.m. the ocean broke all the doors open. It came with such force that all the marble top tables and chests in the living room floated around like bubbles. The next thing that floated in from the kitchen was a rolling pin and a small bowl. The ocean was up to the windowsills in all the rooms. Every time the water receded it left sand. All this time I was sitting on the stairs in a wet coat and dress; by now I was wearing the last dry stockings and shoes. Each time the tide went out I would try to rescue something. Each time I was caught by the water. Also both pairs of overshoes were wet. When the house came off its foundation, it shifted the locks on the doors so I was unable to open the bedroom door where there were dry clothes and blankets. So, as the ocean

The view from the Harvey Cedars Bible Conference during the 1962 storm, looking across the cove toward the ocean.

came up the stairs, I went up another stair and now I was up as far as I could go, but by that time the ocean was receding a little, but I still could not get off the steps.

About ten o'clock Wednesday morning Michael Thomas and Michael Hill carried me out of the dining room window to a boat about three blocks away. We picked up Mrs. Silvermaster, her two huge dogs, Mr. Ullman and a young man and they took us to the firehouse where they had heat and electric made by the generator. By now everyone was emptying their deep freezer so we had plenty of food, and helicopters flew in drinking water. Some of the people were flown over to the high school. On Wednesday everyone had to leave the Island so they flew us all over in helicopters to the high school where people were sleeping in all the classrooms. Then by one o'clock people were offering to take people to different cities and a man living in Drexel Hill brought me to 69th Street where my brother and his wife met me....

They drove me back to Harvey Cedars on Saturday. Elsie Vosseller was delivering the permits, can't describe the destruction. Surf City did not seem to have been affected. McClellan's trucks were all out in front of their store. One lane of the Boulevard was cleaned up until we came to Harvey Cedars, where there was no road, only sand. Then the awful destruction of homes appeared; some of the streets have no houses, only foundations. On other

South end of Harvey Cedars after roadway was plowed.

streets the ocean made a clean sweep to the bay.

My house is really a wreck. I applied to the Red Cross for aid. All the east windows and doors were blown out; most of the living room furniture is torn apart. The dining room was not too bad. In the kitchen I could not see any of the furniture; all the marble tops were thrown to the floor. I'm hoping the sand kept them from breaking as they are my pride and joy. There is enough sand in all the rooms to make a good-sized dune.

The borough is pushing the sand up to the ocean, I'd say about 15 feet high. Cannot find my stove, water heater or furnace. Only about a quarter of the brick house is standing; the one on the ocean is on stilts but still intact. The Biddle house is gone.

Back to the Red Cross — they said I must be available so I will accept your kind offer of your house with many thanks. They think we will be able to come back in two weeks. I am sure it will take four to get my house in order. There is much damage to walls and doors and the door to the garage has disappeared.

Well, folks, I hope there will be more pleasant news next time; excuse spelling, I get upset when I write about the storm.

Affectionately, Nana

Mrs. Weiseisen's house was repaired and still stands at its original location on the northwest corner of 83rd Street and the Boulevard.

1962 First Night of the March Storm

Meriba Van Meter Walker

Meriba Van Meter Walker lived on Burlington Ave. in Harvey Cedars. She worked part time at Atlantic City Hospital and was a full-time school nurse at Southern Regional High School. This is excerpted from a long account she wrote about her 1962 storm experience twenty-five years later. On this day she was returning from the late shift at the hospital.

Traveling over the bridge at 1 a.m. it was only the sheer physical force in my arms that kept the steering wheel of my new Corvair in a semi-steady position. Fortunately, the wind was from the northeast and was hitting the car sideways rather than directly ahead. Several times with explosive gusts the car literally lifted off the bridge, bumping along for many yards. As I turned off the Causeway and headed north, the wind and rain hit me full force. Only my many years of traveling the same road accounted for my driving with so little visibility. There were no other cars and no activity at this hour.

When I arrived at Burlington Ave. I was met with the ocean rolling down the street. "Not to worry," I thought. This had happened many times in various northeasters. I drove to the end of the street and saw that the oceanfront house was severely damaged. Still not to worry. This had happened to the two oceanfront houses before.

I went to bed and in sheer exhaustion slept for two or three hours.

Page one of the Beach Haven Times *after the 1962 storm.*

Harvey Cedars Bible Conference (center) and Woods Island (front) after the '62 storm.

When I woke, the house was cold so I figured the pilot light on the heater had blown out again. I went to the window and saw that the house was completely surrounded by water. I figured it must be between four and five o'clock in the morning as this would be high tide. I took a flashlight to check outside and saw the gas tank had broken away from the house. The wind and rain was still very strong.

About seven o'clock, Grace, a teacher, called to ask if I were going to drive to school or take the school bus. I was horrified. I had never given school a thought. I told her I was not going to school at all because this was definitely a very severe storm.

We had a new school principal who threatened the faculty with insubordination whenever there were disagreements to his policies. Grace reminded me that I would be hit with insubordination if school was held and I refused to go. I laughed and said I would just have to be insubordinate. At this moment a red sofa floated past my window and I told her she should try to get to safety.

I then called the school and reached the vice-principal in charge of health services. Following is the conversation: "Ollie, is there really school today?"

From an unpublished private journal

"Yes, Meriba, there is school."

"Well I won't be there as a terrible storm is flooding the Island. Several houses on my street are destroyed completely and others are badly damaged. I think you should call off school as it is dangerous for the children in the buses."

His reply was that he would tell the superintendent and that he would see me when I arrived.

I arrived five days later.

This was the first night of the three-day northeaster. Meriba eventually took shelter at the Harvey Cedars Bible Conference, along with about fifty other residents. On the third day, from the building's tower she could overlook the town and saw where her house had been. She lost everything.

1992 Roaring Rapids in 'Cedars

Lisa Suhay

Gale-force winds, driving rain, massive waves beating away at the oceanfront, sleet, snow, flooding — the only thing missing from the portrait of biblical destruction was the locusts. For many, the brutal northeast storm that hit the Jersey Shore this weekend was an unholy terror. According to mayoral estimates, property damage for Long Beach Island ranged from $6 million in Beach Haven to $13 million in Harvey Cedars and nearly $20 million in Long Beach Township.

Dunes were completely devastated in Harvey Cedars and replenishment efforts will probably run close to $2 million, according to Mayor Harry Marti. Dune loss in Long Beach Township was estimated at $10 million and Beach Haven's dune loss was approximately $1 million. Estimates were not available from Ship Bottom, Surf City or Barnegat Light by press time.

But dollar figures can't convey the feeling of standing on an oceanside street, watching a fifteen-foot wave carry a sofa bed on its crest. Nor can they describe the frustration of some residents who, while stranded in their homes, watched their cars and other earthly possessions bob in waist-high water. After making an initial tour of Harvey Cedars, Marti said, "I'm just sick to my stomach looking at this. Right now I'm wishing someone else were mayor."

Residents of Harvey Cedars and North Beach took the brunt of the storm, watching helplessly as the ocean rushed in to meet the bay. Waves pounded away at the dune line, crashed through oceanfront homes and swept their contents to the bayside. About twenty-five percent of the 400 residents in the borough lost their electricity and water after high tides swept through electrical boxes; water mains were shut off by officials worried that roads would collapse under the weight of dump trucks and crush the lines.

The transition from mild flooding to roaring rapids took place in less than half an hour during high tide Friday. "We had just about everything float through our yard," said Harvey Cedars resident Howard Cook. "There were garden hoses, bicycles, furniture and washing machines." Cook and his wife, Mary Louise (known over the CB radio as Sand Dollar), rode out the storm in their oceanside home to keep the lines of communication between the mainland and Island open.

"Sand Dollar, Sand Dollar," came the staticky voice over the scanner, during the height of the storm. "What's happening at your end of things?"

"Well, it's looking pretty bad here. The water just keeps coming. We had gusts of wind up to 70 m.p.h. at 5 a.m." The high winds had ripped the roof off of an oceanfront home on East Burlington Ave., slamming it into the house behind it. The destruction didn't end there, as the roof dislodged and hit two more homes, finally ending up embedded in the roof of Roberta's Studio on Long Beach Boulevard.

"We had flagpoles snapping like twigs in that wind," said Borough Commissioner Jonathan Oldham.

from *The SandPaper* • December 16, 1992

When they weren't relaying news and weather updates to callers the Cooks occupied their time by looking through an album on the 1962 storm. "The De Cristofaro house looks just the same this time as it did back then," Mary Louise said. "That first floor got wiped out all over again." The home in question looked like a dollhouse with the back wall on the first floor completely destroyed and water flowing in the back and out the front door and windows. Furniture from the house was found on the lawns of bayfront homes. During a telephone interview from his home in Peapack, Michael De Cristofaro said he had not yet seen his shore home.

"The police just told me it was totaled," he said. "I find that hard to believe. I really thought the concrete blocks would keep it in one piece." Mary Louise added, "It's a shame to see how these houses get hit but they'll just build them right back up again. They never learn." She said that while the damage was severe, this storm was not as bad as the one in 1962. "The real difference is that in '62 there were less houses so the bulldozers could get through to replace the dunes," she said. "Now the houses are so close together there's no way to get the trucks in. They have to pile up the sand behind them until the tide goes down enough to get the trucks on the beach."

By Monday the borough was awash again, this time in news media and spectators. Television news helicopters strafed the shoreline alongside those of the Army Corps of Engineers. Private assessors in three-piece suits and camel hair coats milled past emergency workers in hip waders, looking for business.

"We're the good guys," said private assessor Dean Harcelrode of Andrew Knox and Co., Toms River. "We're here to help homeowners get all they're entitled to from their insurance companies. The important discovery we've made is that the land itself is not covered. That means landscaping and erosion."

Police were sidetracked from their regular duties to have reporters' and sightseers' cars towed out of the way of bulldozers. "It's been like Disney World all day with the photographers and TV cameras," said Barbara Aukstikalnis. "There have been people in our yard since 8 a.m." She and her husband, Tony, weathered the storm in their oceanfront home on East Cape May Ave., where they have been residents since Thanksgiving. Even after the worst had passed the couple was still pacing nervously along the edge of a sheer, 20-foot-high cliff, on which their $600,000 home now precariously sat.

"I'm a little shaky right now," Tony said. "It's beginning to look like a lot of these houses along here aren't going to make it after all. Every wave takes another stretch of sand out from under the house and high tide is a nightmare. We lost another three feet of sand just this morning."

Mayor Marti, who hadn't slept in more than three days, found himself faced with angry homeowners, devastated dunes and carloads of sightseers on Monday. "What we really need to do is get some funding to get the sand and trucks in here," he said. "It's not over yet. If we get another northeaster this week we're in big trouble. There's nothing left out there to protect us."

1992 Wild Walk Across the Bridge

Lisa Suhay

An eerie humming emanated from the Causeway bridge as high winds blew through the steel lighting fixtures Friday night. In the pouring rain and bitter cold winds, a few brave souls walked to the Island across the bridge, which was closed to vehicular traffic on and off for three days during the worst storm since 1962.

It took more than two hours, through rain and knee-high water, but Robert McKenzie of Surf City managed to walk with two fourteen-year-old boys from the mainland to the Island.

"The boys got out of school at Southern and wanted to get home to their parents," he said. "The bridge was closed off so you couldn't drive across, but police said we could walk. The kids really wanted to be at home and my family was waiting for me, and my house was under three feet of water, so I had to get there."

McKenzie said he understood police concerns over allowing cars onto the bridge ("they might get stuck and jam traffic or be a hazard") but was furious over the fact that "as we were walking over the bridge we got passed by no less than half a dozen empty National Guard troop transport trucks. They all refused to pick us up."

According to Ship Bottom police, there was no possible way for them to provide transportation to pedestrians since all but one of the department's cars had been "washed out." Police and emergency management teams as well as municipal workers on the Island found themselves on the go around the clock, catching catnaps and coffee wherever they could.

At 3 a.m. on Saturday, patrolmen and rescue workers gathered for coffee and a few minutes' rest during which they swapped stories. "There was one construction guy who went out to check on a house he was building in Harvey Cedars and fell into a sinkhole and the waves came up over him," said the clerk at 7-Eleven in Ship Bottom. "When they brought him in here to wait for a ride he just shook for close to an hour. Said it was the most terrifying thing that ever happened to him."

Patrolman Jerry Falkowski, who had just caught his first forty-five minutes of shuteye in thirty-six hours on a cot in the Harvey Cedars jail, said he had spent his day trying to get into oceanfront homes to shut off the gas and electric to prevent fires. "You can't get through to most houses because of the flooding, and once the water hits those wires we get electrical fires," he said. According to Long Beach Township Mayor James J. Mancini, "We had several houses catch fire on Friday and Saturday that we had to let burn to the ground because the fire trucks couldn't get to them."

Beach Haven resident John Coyle, who had flown up from Useppa Island to check on his Beach Haven home and Haven Beach business, was among the 3 a.m. crowd at 7-Eleven after wading his way across the bridge. Although he had to walk the whole way across, from midnight to three, he did manage to get a ride from the Beach Haven police once he reached the Ship Bottom convenience store. "That was quite a walk," he said. "I never dreamed I'd cross that bridge on foot, and especially not under those conditions, but it had to be done."

from *The SandPaper* • December 16, 1992

Many homeowners could not get onto the Island until Monday to examine the damage, and most found it nearly impossible to travel north of Surf City due to roadblocks set up to prevent looting and ease traffic problems. "We have a lot of heavy equipment operating and the last thing we need is more cars on these roads getting in the way," said Harvey Cedars Police Sgt. Thomas Laneve. "We have been requiring proof of residency so that we can be sure there are no looters."

Michael Stephano, owner of Cafe Mundo in Harvey Cedars, braved barricades and high water to get an employee to the mainland Friday. "One of my waitresses is seven months pregnant and she wasn't feeling well, so I decided to get her home to Stafford no matter what," Stephano said. The "no matter what" turned out to be a flooded Causeway and two flat tires. "As I was going over the big bridge I must have hit some debris," he said. "It was impossible to see through all the water what I'd hit, but it ripped open my tires and the tires of about seven other cars behind me." Stephano made his way across the bridge, borrowed two spares, changed the tires and got the woman home. He then got to a supermarket, stocked up on supplies and made it back to the High Point Volunteer Fire Co., where he stayed for the next thirty-six hours serving chili and coffee to volunteers and evacuees.

"This is the kind of town where everyone pulls together in a crisis," said Commissioner Jonathan Oldham. "I believe that if worse came to worst everyone in town would just hop on bulldozers and fill in the dunes themselves." Like most Islanders, many Harvey Cedars residents refused to be evacuated.

"People here are very independent," Oldham said. "People choose to ride out the storms. There's a sort of esprit de corps here. We get a few people who come in when the water gets too high, but they come and go with the tide."

2003 Deep-Six "Nor'easter"

Tom Halsted

Every year at least a half dozen big northeast storms churn up the Atlantic coast, delivering torrential rains or dumping upwards of a foot of snow, depending on the season. They tear vessels from their moorings, disrupt air and highway traffic, close offices, shops and schools, and make everyone miserable but the school children, who find themselves with an unexpected day of freedom.

Coastal dwellers can handle great storms. We've all seen worse, but that does not stop the hyperbole of the radio or television weatherman. Well in advance of every great storm, throughout its height, and in its aftermath, legions of these breathless commentators, alarmists, and amateur meteorologists give vent, as their calling demands, to dire predictions and fulsome on-the-scene commentary. And — particularly, with the winter storms — no word bursts from their myriad tongues with such frequency as the dramatic epithet "nor'easter." The eager, young TV meteorologist who intones, "Folks, we've got a big nor'easter on our hands," thinks he or she is describing something really awesome, truly profound.

Well, I've got news for those young whippersnappers. That gimcrack word "nor'easter" is a made-up, fake, pseudo-Yankee neologism that came from the same plastic cracker barrel as "Ye Olde Tea Shoppe." It should be shunned as silly and pretentious.

Fowler doesn't speak of it; nor do Mencken, Safire or any other lexicographer presuming to tell people how to talk American. Landlubbers all. But stand on a dock or a deck anywhere between Barnegat Light and Newfoundland and listen to a few working seamen; pretty soon you'll hear the difference. It's "nor'west" and "sou'west," "no'theast" and "s'utheast" — but NEVER EVER "nor'east" (Or, God forbid: "sou'east"). That counterfeit term should be reserved, if at all, for motels and drycleaners (as, indeed, one is so named in my town). You sound your "th" when the direction is easterly, and omit it when the wind blows from the west.

The distinctive pronunciation arose in the days of sail, when helmsmen needed to pass on commands in howling weather, and wanted to be sure to be clearly understood. "Nor'west" and "nor'east" might sound the same when shouted along the iced up deck of a scalloper or a longliner beating home against a winter gale with a trip of fish; but "nor'west" and "nawtheast" would sound distinctly different.

So reader, if you have a care for good English and a concern for preserving regional tradition, stick to your guns and hang onto your "th."

Well, brave words, I suppose. The sheer repetition of the vile word by legions of chattering weather people who don't know any better may in time drown out the few purists trying to hold back the sea. Indeed, I fear that it was a northeaster-driven tide that old King Canute was trying in vain to stop in its tracks.

2012 Sandy Slams Sea Shell

Scott Mazzella

The night of Sunday, October 28, the northeast wind pushed water south from Barnegat Bay, and by dawn on Monday, Little Egg Harbor was already overflowing. All that water was being trapped by more water surging in through the inlets and the sedge islands. The water then forced its way over bulkheads all over the Island, sending it into the yards and streets under the cloak of night.

On most streets, there was little evidence of urgency. Barbecue and outdoor furniture sat in backyards and on decks, kayaks leaned against houses. Few windows were boarded up, although some had the last-minute addition of a quick spread of a taped "X."

Down in Holgate, Charlie Potter woke up to water already filling some of the side streets and parts of his yard. To see the water this high this early was a surprise. The hurricane wasn't supposed to make landfall until that evening. He got dressed and took a walk around the neighborhood to check on friends and to see what else was happening. A few blocks away the ocean was already up to the beachfront pavilion at the end of Washington Ave. The sea looked like a cauldron of energy ready to boil over. The pavilion is built on top of a steep dune, and even though it's relatively high up, waves already washed up and around it. Potter ran into Don Kartan, who lives around the corner at Farreny's RV Park. Kartan said he was concerned about water making its way up from the bayside and from the end of West Street

Potter went back to the house. By 9 a.m. the water had risen so quickly that he knew it was going to get into the house — and soon. Potter raced to put the most important items as high up as he could get them — a scene playing out in homes all over the Island and in bayside towns on the Mainland. Potter cared deeply for an antique desk, a family heirloom, so he put that as high up on the couch as he could get it.

The water just kept coming. Soon it reached the steps, then the thresholds. Here we go, Potter thought, as water entered the house. As high tide arrived it brought two inches of water to every room. Realizing his son's toys were still scattered in the yard, Potter went outside to grab them. He stumbled a few times on objects under the surface. Even after the peak of high tide, the water did not ebb. It was staying and there was more coming.

By 11:30 a.m., Potter began wondering if he could ride out the storm. "The first high tide is never the worst," he thought. "The next high tide is going to be bad." He decided to leave. Many of his belongings and even his jugs of freshwater were already under saltwater. He grabbed his bag and left the house. "You just have to trust your gut and go with what you think. Where I'm heading is safer than where I'm coming from." He headed to the Sea Shell, which would have the food and cases of freshwater he needed.

So he began his trek to Beach Haven, two miles to the north. He knew friends and coworkers were riding out the storm at the Shell, so his plan was to head there — on foot. He sloshed through his flooded yard and trudged up Roosevelt Ave. to Long Beach Boulevard. Strangely, despite

Excerpted from the book Surviving Sandy

water being relatively deep in the yard, there were spots on the Boulevard that had no water at all, while other areas had more than six inches.

He walked north up the Boulevard and made it about four and a half blocks when he came to water rushing over the Boulevard between Jacqueline and Carolina avenues. It was ocean water. Sandy's initial high tide had completely eroded the dune between two oceanfront homes. There was nothing between the ocean and the Boulevard through that ten-foot-wide cut. He took a couple of photographs on his phone as the ocean water streamed onto the Boulevard and across the street toward Hurley's Motel and the homes behind it. The water coming through the breach rushed through as the waves broke, but brief breaks between waves allowed him to cross safely.

There were some more breaches along the way, but the dune line held its ground fairly well and Potter made his way to Liberty Ave., about a mile north of his house, where a National Guard truck loaded with more people from Holgate picked him up. The truck was heading back to Beach Haven and must have missed Potter on its way south as it traversed the side streets.

Potter made it to the Shell by noon, and the area was still in good shape. Bicentennial Park was untouched and the properties of both hotels looked relatively normal — aside from the firefighting apparatus parked in the Engleside parking lot. The only evidence a hurricane was on its way was at the beach, which was taking a pounding.

Walking into the main dining room and bar area, wooden boards blacked out the wall of glass windows behind the big oak bar that look out over a pool and the Shell's trademark Tiki bars. Aside from the wind, the blowing sand and the forecast, things felt secure. At least more secure than his flooded house in Holgate. But the feeling would be fleeting. Sitting at the darkened bar, the wind whistled as it blew against the boards covering the windows, Potter began to realize it was only a matter of time.

Tom Hughes, the owner of the Sea Shell since 1992, was not terribly worried about flooding. Historically, it had stayed dry in storms. When his father owned it, he didn't even have flood insurance. He figured if it ever did flood, he'd just open the front doors and let the water go through. Hughes left directions to have the electric turned off to avoid a fire. While

Superstorm Sandy deposits a car in flooded marshland by Little Egg Harbor Bay.

Ray Fisk

off the Island, he asked anyone still at the hotel on Monday to "abandon ship." Only one man was expected to stay and his job was to watch the roof, which had a precarious drainage system. Hughes wanted early warning if that were to go.

But his employees did not close the hotel. They called Hughes at home and told him residents were coming by looking for a room. The Engleside was full so they gravitated to the hotel across the street, even if it was not officially open. Hughes knew he could not turn them away. He told his employees to let them in, but to keep the electricity off. But the workers only shut off the electricity downstairs — or so they thought.

Potter and bartender Willy Logue tried to direct the electrical breakers in the building to only send power where it was needed, and where it was safe. They spent about an hour searching for breaker boxes so they could shut off nonessential circuits before the water found them.

Then a wave dislodged a door and sent water into the pool utility room, which shares a wall with one of the inside bars. The wall couldn't hold back the water and it began flowing in behind the beer cooler.

Realizing the water was now reaching electrical sockets in the building, Potter and Logue tried to shut off as many circuits to the bar as they could find. They thought they had them all, but they still heard fans to the beer coolers running. Making matters worse, the motors started smoking. Hoping to avoid a fire, they unplugged the coolers. They were heavy — about 350 pounds empty and they were still stocked for the fishing tournament with about a dozen cases of beer. Potter got behind the bar, pushed out the smaller of the two coolers and unplugged it. He couldn't budge the large one. He asked Logue for help.

As they gripped the cooler, a loud, thunderous crack stopped them cold. In a rapid chain reaction, a massive wave snapped the dividers between the boarded-up windows and wall of the bar. One-hundred-and-twenty feet of floor-to-ceiling windows crashed in on the ocean side of the wall. Water swept up debris, the remnants of the wall, the side of the bar, the beer cooler — and the two men. They careened into the other side of the bar. The bar broke in half and, along with the cooler, trapped both of the bartender's feet and pinned Potter's ankle. They couldn't move the cooler and they couldn't free their legs. Potter tried to shove the bar top away with his free leg, but couldn't.

They yelled for help. Another Shell employee heard them. He rushed into the room but could not budge the beer coolers. He ran across the street, through rushing water, to get help from firefighters stationed at the Engleside Inn. Within a few minutes, firefighters and some local residents showed up. Charlie asked that they get Logue out first. As they attempted to free his friend, the cooler trapping Potter pressed harder against his ankle. It hurt so much Potter at one point suggested cutting the foot off. That wasn't necessary. The men were able to get Potter's leg free. He was fine — bruised and numb, but able to walk away.

When they opened the front doors, water rushed out and took virtually everything with it. The entire inside was completely gone. All the bars were destroyed, the kitchens, the meeting rooms, floors, everything.

Potter hobbled upstairs and got his stuff. The Shell didn't seem too stable anymore. About a dozen people filed out of the hotel, crossed the river of ocean water to the safety of the Engleside.

2015 Beach Rain Falls Upon Us

Maggie O'Neill

I wake up full of Island energy, look out the window and see a dark navy sky. "Oh no," I think, "it's going to rain. No beach today." True to its color, the sky opens up and the rain falls. As the storm builds, I am mesmerized. I pay attention to the sound of the rain as it hits the roof and windows. It's nature's music, and I listen intently as the symphony unfolds. An unexpected peace engulfs me. I settle back into the old, overstuffed couch and feel myself start to relax. All the things on my "to do" list are suddenly canceled. I now have free time handed down from above.

The wild storm outside underscores the coziness of my shore home. Hardwood flooring creates a warm atmosphere. The knotty pine paneling is polished and shines against the fieldstone of the fireplace. An old, nautical lamp lends a glow to the room as only a lamp lit in gray daylight can do. It's comfy. I smile and turn my thoughts to rainy day musings, inexplicably feeling the urge to finally read the book on Long Beach Island history sitting on my coffee table. I start with the chapter on storms.

After a morning of dozing and reading, my lazy bones start to wake up, itching for a way to spend this gift of time. The rhythm of the storm beckons me. I throw on an old yellow slicker over my shorts and tee, grab my knee-high, red rubber boots and head out into the music of the rain. The weather gods forbid me to take my cell phone. Like a child, I delight in the deep running river of water in the gutters and laugh at the waves on the Boulevard. I skip in their wake, as warm rain mixes with the cold storm drain water from the bay, splashing over the top of my boots. What the heck, I think, I would be just as wet if I were swimming in the ocean. Throwing back my hood, I stick out my tongue to catch the raindrops. A car goes by, fast enough to produce another wave, and I smile as the driver gives me thumbs up.

I walk the Boulevard for longer than I do in sunshine, marveling at the grayness, the water, the sound of the wind and rain. The wet, salt air is thick with the smell of the ocean and it fills me with happiness. I stop in an open deli and shake off the water, like a retriever just out of a lake. The man behind the counter smiles and we share a laugh about the weather. I buy a cup of hazelnut coffee and sit by the window. The aroma is wonderful and the hot beverage soothes my spirit.

Soon it's time to bathe again in Mother Nature's outdoor shower. My hood is down, my hair is soaking wet, and I have not felt this good in years. My rubber boots make squishing sounds as I wade back to my little cottage. Stepping into the house, I realize that these walls have weathered a hundred storms, many much worse than this one. I am comforted at the thought and feel safe and protected.

By early evening the rain stops. I pour a glass of wine, dry off one of the chairs on my deck and sit. In the quiet of twilight I hear so many things that I often miss, usually too busy to notice the sounds of the day as it turns into evening. Birds chirp, one last roll of thunder echoes far off and drops of rain plop intermittently onto the ground, like a soft drum beat. The damp night air carries the muffled sound of neighbors laughing. I sigh with contentment and take a sip of wine. The lights in the homes around me flicker on, one by one, like fireflies in the dark night. Life is good.

Today was better than a day on the beach. Today the Island gave me a gift: time to experience the beauty of the rain. I survived the day without my cell phone, email, or text messages. I feel cleansed, refreshed, invigorated. Beach rain is different, I realize. Beach rain is special, and I am grateful for this late August storm.

The *Environment*

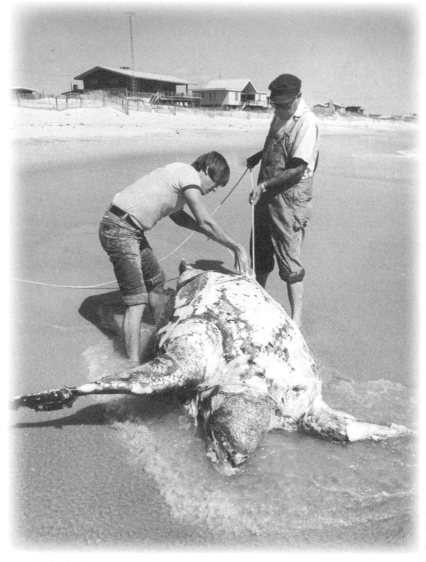

Ray Fisk

A leatherback turtle is retrieved by Bob Schoelkopf (left) of the Marine Mammal Stranding Center on the Loveladies beach.

1979 On Becoming a Birder

Brenda M. Holmes

When our house was built in Barnegat Light twenty-one years ago, and long before the backyard was transformed from a bare expanse of fill and sand to the forest of black pine, mimosa, olive trees and silver maples that is there now, we had a lot of birds. Did we have birds! You only had to break up a few pieces of bread and throw them out on the sand, and the ground would be black with flocks of redwings, grackles and starlings, and for all I knew at the time, Carolina parakeets, passenger pigeons, and auks (which lay square eggs, hence the name). It was like soot floating down from the chimney.

Before long we dug in some dead trees; with silvery branches, which were not only good-looking but provided a perch for the birds to fly to when alarmed. The limbs would be thick with sparrows, as if autumn-toned leaves had sprouted overnight. I started paying attention to the different varieties that patronized our soup kitchen, and got hooked on bird-watching. I had grown up in Australia, where there must be more strange and beautiful and exotic birds than anywhere else, and I never, never noticed them. There was just no way they could compete with the uniforms that filled my whole attention span then (World War II).

But now I was noticing birds and taking enough interest in them to buy a paperback field guide and a pair of binoculars. This last purchase might seem an affectation when you consider that the size of our lot is 50 x 125 feet, but I am a touch short-sighted. These aids to identification were left permanently on a kitchen counter under the window. It got to be so fascinating that after a while the birds were getting more food than we were, so that I could induce them to stay long enough to match them up with pictures in the guide. Was ever a chapter more fittingly titled than "Confusing Fall Warblers"? I must have changed my mind a dozen times over every little bird with a tiny beak and a touch of yellow somewhere on the throat or

from *The SandPaper* • October 4, 1979

Observing shorebirds on the beach in Barnegat Light.

wing or rump.

One Saturday afternoon I had the usual collection of blackbirds noshing on a cheesecake that was one of my less successful culinary efforts (too much salt). Apparently the birds didn't mind, because they were there by the hundreds. From my post at the window I noticed a pair somewhat different from the other; one was black with white on his wings, about the size of a sparrow, and the other, apparently his mate, was sparrow-colored but with something different around the eyes and beak. I flipped pages to the section on sparrows and there they were: lark buntings. But it couldn't be; the book also said they were prairie birds with a range from Minnesota to Nebraska, where there are more prairies than on Long Beach Island.

I called up Sidney Rothman, who knows everything, either personally or vicariously through his myriad contacts. Sidney says, "My dear, I couldn't tell a finch from a flamingo," or words to that effect. I mention the ospreys nesting on a telephone pole on his property as proof of his credentials as a naturalist. He says, "Is that what they are? I was having a cocktail party on my deck and this big bird swooped down and took all my anchovies." But he just happens to know someone in Loveladies who is a member of the Audubon Society and would like to hear about lark buntings. I call her and she listens with obvious disbelief, but asks if she can come up and see for herself. By the time she arrives with her binoculars a cocktail

196

party is in full swing in the house, and the only birds in sight are the Wild Turkey and Old Crow.

She is polite, refuses a drink, but looks at me with an expression that says she wouldn't be too surprised if I claimed to have seen a pterodactyl on the TV antenna. She takes up a position at the window with field glasses at the ready, however, and the birds obligingly come back, and there in the middle of them all is an honest-to-goodness out-of-habitat pair of lark buntings from the wheat fields of Kansas.

Early next morning there was a knock at the door and there stood what looked like a 100 percent body cast with feet and a pair of binoculars, asking if the buntings were still around. This accident victim, who had driven himself with great difficulty to the place of the sighting, was the husband of my visitor from the day before, and when I asked in astonishment if he couldn't take his wife's word for it, I got my first lesson in Life Lists: you have to see for yourself. By that time the lark buntings have checked out the dunes, bay and ocean, discovered a serious shortage of wheat, and were headed back to the prairies.

Another unexpected sighting occurred one Sunday morning, when I was having a cup of coffee at the window before going out for the papers. By this time we had a few real trees inching their slow pace heavenward, and on one of the branches I spotted a bird that looked like a purple finch but with a shade of red, more like a tomato than a strawberry. (What color-blind person ever named that bird?) Easy to find in the book: house finch. But the book also said that they did not belong in this area. That very day (these words have a hollow ring due to constant repetition of this story over what seems like centuries to my friends), *The New York Times* ran a story about pet shop owners who, facing penalties for caging house finches, had released several hundred pairs on Long Island, where they had domesticated themselves and started to spread north and south along the East Coast. Another triumphant entry in the book. Now of course, they are as common as purple finches on this island.

Over the years all the sightings were marked with the date alongside the picture of the bird. I did not have to say where I saw the birds; it was always Barnegat Light. One year I trustingly left the field guide in the house, which we rented, with the other books, and it was gone at the end of the rental season. One of the lost entries was of the horned grebe; that marked the occasion when my husband found one of these pretty little birds floundering in the surf one November weekend, covered with oil, and brought it up to the house. We cleaned it with detergent and kept it in a box overnight so that it would recover its buoyancy for swimming. At one point, when it was in the bathtub among pieces of bread that we hoped it would eat, and there were quite a few droppings as well (due, no doubt, to the harrowing situation the grebe found itself in), and whole place looked a mess, the real estate agent brought some prospects for next year's rental season. One peek into the bathroom convinced the prospective tenant that she would never, simply never, take a bath in that tub.

We took the grebe to the bay later, and it was worth losing a tenant to see the bird take its first few dancing steps on top of the water, as it beat its wings in happy surprise to be back home.

Besides these rarities we had a lot of live-in ordinary birds, including a robin (summer), mockingbird (winter), several cardinal families, purple finches by the score, and some blue jays with a passion for peanuts in the shell. The other day I laid a trail of peanuts across our deck, through an open sliding door and into the room where we watch the *Today Show* and drink coffee every morning. We could hardly believe our eyes when the male came inside without hesitation, picked up the nuts from the floor, and, made several return trips, first to the arm of the couch and then to the back where I had laid out nuts every few inches, and finally to the mesh bag lying around for a while until he got them all out. In the meantime the female hopped around outside the door, letting out little cries, but she finally plucked up enough courage to come inside, too. Now they wait on the deck furniture for the morning treats, and let out strident unmusical squawks if I am late with them.

The 1979 fall season of transients has begun. I was driven inside the house the other day by flies tormenting me when I was trying to do needlepoint in the back yard. The hose was spraying some draught-stricken shrubbery in the front, and flying through the mist was a bird I had never seen before, except that constant reference to Roger Tory Peterson's guide made the word "kingbird" pop into my head. While it ducked in and out of the spray I got tantalizing glimpses and decided first that it was too buff-breasted to be a kingbird, so must be a phoebe, except that it was not wagging its tail sufficiently for Mr. Peterson. Therefore, it must be a wood pewee, except that it did not have conspicuous wing bars. In any event it was a flycatcher, hopping around in a refreshing shower while all the flies were in the back yard, driving me demented.

An interest in birds has unexpected benefits for sloppy housekeepers. You don't have to wash your picture windows: if the birds can see through them, they'll try to fly through, with fatal results in a lot of cases. If you must wash the windows, close the drapes. Before I learned this lesson we picked up stunned little birds from the ground outside. Most were warblers, and it gave us a chance to study them much more closely than we otherwise could, until they recovered and flew away. Besides marveling at their beauty we were amazed that such tiny bodies had the endurance to fly from the Andes across the Gulf of Mexico to the northern reaches of the United States every spring and return every fall.

The point of all this is that although the birds are still around, after two decades, there are very few of them here except during migration. Where have they all gone? I don't know, but I know why they left. On our own street they used to nest in a vacant lot not far back from the dunes, in a profusion of cedar, holly, beach plum and other native growth. A big house is being built on that lot today. I can't blame the owners of the property for doing just what we ourselves did twenty-one years ago; no doubt it was good bird habitat until the bulldozers moved in. We do our best by planting shrubs and trees and feeding the birds in cold weather, but every house that goes up reduces the territory each bird must have to survive. It is all very sad, if not for reasons of ecology, then simply because there is so much pleasure to be had in birds and their beautiful presence.

1981 Global Warming Worries

Sharon DiGiovanni

If a team of federal scientists are on target, within the next century New Jersey's shorefront problems may become a thing of the past, as a warming trend could place the shoreline, ten percent of the state, under water. A seven-member team of atmospheric scientists, headed by Dr. James Hansen, recently published the results of research done under the auspices of the National Aeronautics and Space Administration's (NASA) Institute for Space Studies.

They've discovered a warming trend in the Earth's atmosphere over the past hundred years, and feel that, over the next hundred, the trend may continue at "almost unprecedented magnitude." If that happens, they contend, it might lead to the melting and moving of the West Antarctic ice cover, which in turn would cause a 15- to 20-foot rise in worldwide sea levels. This would, they add, "flood 25 percent of Louisiana and Florida, 10 percent of New Jersey, and many other lowlands throughout the world."

John Weingart, chief of the Department of Environmental Protection's (DEP) Bureau of Coastal Planning and Development, said of the report, "A number of studies have come to similar conclusions. A smaller number have come to opposing conclusions. Our reaction is one of concern."

Slow increases in sea level could actually worsen the state's shoreline problems. "Studies such as this have led the department to seek more ways to protect the oceanfront," Weingart commented. "Rising sea levels would contribute to our beach erosion problems, of course," said Jim Murray, director of the New Jersey Marine Advisory Service in Seaville. "But they're caused by a whole mix of factors, including man-made structures. But the trend they speak of is probably close to true. The problem in New Jersey," Murray continued, "is that on that type of scale, it's probably too late to do anything about it. New Jersey beaches are pretty much urbanized. If we'd played our cards ideally, we would've retreated as we had to. Now we've lost that alternative." Murray added, however, "I don't think we have to worry

from *The SandPaper* • September 5, 1981

Ray Fisk

Beach Haven's old post office is surrounded by a flood tide during a storm in 1983.

about it happening this weekend."

The NASA group attributes the warming trend to the "greenhouse effect" — carbon dioxide (CO_2) in the earth's atmosphere absorbing and holding earth's heat, which ideally, should simply dissipate into space. Over the past century, these scientists found, the amount of carbon dioxide in our atmosphere has increased from 280 to 300 parts per million to 335 to 340 ppm. During the next one hundred years, they expect that level to reach 600 ppm. And this heat-trapping carbon dioxide, according to a recent *New York Times* report on the team's findings, is largely the product of the worldwide burning of fossil fuels.

If, the study predicts, global use of such fuels is combined with other energy sources over the coming decades, an approximate temperature rise of five degrees Fahrenheit over the next century can be expected. However, the study continues, if developing countries use fossil fuels extensively to industrialize, the century-end temperature may rise a maximum of nine degrees F. Even the more conservative forecast, the scientists contend, means the earthly climate "would approach the warmth of the Mesozoic, the age of the dinosaurs."

However, claims Dr. Sherwood Idso, a climate specialist with the federal Department of Agriculture, "a doubling or tripling of atmospheric carbon dioxide would have little effect, except to increase global agricultural productivity by 20 to 50 percent."

Also it seems scientists have been charting global increases in carbon dioxide levels for years. But they don't agree temperatures have been rising correspondingly.

"I am sure the report will be looked at critically by people knowledgeable in the field," commented Dr. Raymond Dyba, a scientist with the DEP's Bureau of Air Quality Management. "Temperature trends are a controversial topic. In any case, such a change would surely be slow — no sudden waves of ten to twenty feet. I think the general thought is that we'd have ample time to adjust.

"But the long-term probability," Dyba concluded "indicates we can't go on blindly increasing our fuel consumption on a global basis."

This prescient article appeared decades before climate change became an urgent concern for the coast.

1983 The Island Is Too Low

William A. Geiger

The scene is a familiar one. A storm moves slowly up the Atlantic coast from the south, stalls just north of New Jersey, and for three days pounds the shoreline with heavy wind and rain. A northeaster.

One or two a winter is common, and even up to five a season is considered normal. But when that number doubles, as it did during the fall-winter-spring of 1982-83, an acute set of problems surface, not the least of which is often heavy flooding of Island streets. Heavy rainfall and higher than usual tides, which occur during most of the storms, pose serious problems for the people who run the road departments and other businesses on the Island.

"I've seen this happen for as long as I've had Tony's, and I just have to close up when the cars can't park out front," said Steve Ferringo, owner of Tony's Pizzeria in Beach Haven Crest. He pointed to the street outside the restaurant, where a good six inches of water extended from his doorstep to the right-hand lane of Long Beach Boulevard. "The rain this morning was terrible," he said one Saturday late in April, "and if the water doesn't go down soon, I'll have to close up for the whole day."

The rainfall during April has been unusually high, and when Ferringo was interviewed, the Island had just weathered another northeaster. A block north of Tony's, the A&W Restaurant, still closed for the winter, was completely surrounded by water. Even though the complex rises one full story above the road level, no car could possibly have parked in the lot had it been open. The water in most places would have been over the tires.

Ferringo is not alone in voicing his dismay over the flooding situation. Betty Creevy, a saleswoman for Crest Realty, situated between Tony's and the A&W, has seen, over the last few years, a drastic change for the worse with the flooding. "I have a Toyota, and I cannot drive a car that small

from *The SandPaper* • May 18, 1983

Tony's (now Joey's) Pizza in Beach Haven Crest, during a storm in 1983.

through the puddles and flooded sections," she said. "As a consequence, I have to waste a lot of time avoiding the sections underwater by going around blocks and backtracking." Creevy, an Islander for twenty-seven years, sees the problem as being one of poor planning. "I don't think the storm sewers were installed properly," she observed, "and with all the growth on the Island, the water has no place to run off. All the empty lots are being filled, and there are fewer places for the water to drain." Ferringo, too feels that new, larger storm sewers would help drainage, and thinks that this may be the only way to ease the flooding situation. He has tried to convince the local township authorities of his plight, but so far he has had no luck. "I took pictures, and I complained, but I have not seen anything done yet," he said.

One man to whom Ferringo has complained is William McGinnis, a Long Beach Township commissioner, and McGinnis readily admits that he has some concern about the flooding. "Sure it's a problem," he said. "Any time you have deep water, and a motorist is forced to avoid the area or have damaged brakes, you have a real problem."

McGinnis notes that some considerable flooding occurs in Long Beach Township, particularly from Culver Street to Rhode Island Ave. He feels that the main culprits are the storm drains installed along Long Beach

Boulevard. "When it rains heavily, they back up; it's that simple," he says. He has also tried to have the county install sluice gates, so that the water would only drain one way, from the Island downward to the bay. Sluice gates would prevent backup, he feels, since they would only open when water is draining, and not allow any to backfill into the pipes and come onto the Island. Another problem, he thinks, is the Island's geographic situation. "Parts of the Island are low, and you can't change the topography. The storm drains will work in the higher sections," he said, "but in the lower ones, outside of larger storm drains or sluice gates, nothing much else can be done."

Dick Crosta, superintendent of Public Works in Beach Haven, agrees with McGinnnis's assessment. "You can't do much about the flooding, outside of installing larger catch basins and storm drains." He says, though, that when a storm coincides with a high tide, even the best and largest of drains will not help alleviate the situation, since what happens essentially is that the bay reclaims part of the Island. "What the average person doesn't realize," he says, "is that much of the water that floods on the Island is bay water. That's bay water rising up onto the Island." So, when the elements act just so, nothing seems to help the havoc nature wreaks on the Island.

Both Crosta and McGinnis stressed that Long Beach Boulevard is a county road, and as such, county officials are responsible for the problem. Richard Lane, Ocean County engineer, said county officials are trying to keep up with the situation, but only so much could be done. "The Island is too low," Lane said, "and the storm sewer pipes cannot be dug deep enough under the roads in some sections of the Island; so they can't run to the bay and still stay above water." The higher areas of the Island experience little or no problem, and if it rains during a low tide, runoff is virtually ninety to one-hundred percent. But when the tide is high all the elements work against the system, and ponding, as Lane calls it, will occur.

Lane says larger sewer pipes would help drainage, but not in the lower areas of the Island. Lane sees a greater potential for flooding when larger pipes are used. "Sure, larger pipes would help, but remember, the bigger the pipe, the bigger the flow." He said, "If a larger pipe is put into the lower areas, we've found that when the tide is high, more bay water flows onto the Island."

Lane says sluice, or flap, gates only work up to a point. "We have experimented with flap gates; up in Point Pleasant we even tried to use pumps, but those darn machines were broken more times than they worked." Salt water is very corrosive.

During a hurricane, flooding would rise from inconvenient to dangerous. Heavy, torrential rains usually precede a hurricane, as does strong tidal action. If the Boulevard is the main evacuation route, some cars may not make it, especially smaller ones, like Betty Creevy's Toyota. All officials interviewed agreed that the hurricane question is a crucial one, but because of the Island's location and topography, nature may again hold all the cards. "We have tried many things," said Lane, "and we're still keeping our ears open to new suggestions."

Lane mentions that he has received many complaints from Island residents, but the most frequent complainers are the new residents. The older, long-time residents seem to recognize the flooding as the nature of the beast. "You have to take the bad with the good," he said, "and one thing going for us is the fact that the serious flooding only lasts a few hours. Then, when the tide goes down, everything goes back to normal."

The county is installing larger outflow pipes near the A&W Restaurant to help the situation in that part of Long Beach Township. McGinnis says he has purchased lighted barricades for the township so that night drivers would be at least warned of the situation and could avoid the area.

But while some things are being done, some businesses are still suffering. "April was a terrible month," said Ferringo. "I don't think I was open one full weekend all month. Something has to be done. I can't afford to lose all this business."

As engineer Lane asserts, they are searching for the right solution to help combat nature. And as he half-jokingly wished, "If we only could take a jack and raise the Island just a few feet."

Tony's Pizzeria on the Boulevard in Beach Haven Crest is now Joey's Pizza and Pasta and advertises "Occasional Waterfront Dining" on its sign.

1985 Island Could Be Submerged

Curtis Rist

While the rest of New Jersey suffers from a drought, the coastal communities could someday suffer from water problems of a different kind: inundation as a result of sea level rise. According to scientists and the federal government, sea levels could rise between three to fifteen feet within the next century, and could rise more than a foot within the next thirty years.

Since the barrier islands and coastlines retreat at a rate two hundred times the rate of sea level rise, that could put barrier islands such as Long Beach Island into something the scientists call "overwash mode." James Titus, manager of the Environmental Protection Agency's Sea Level Rise Project in Washington, D.C. describes what's in store for the Island paradise.

"Long Beach Island will erode and storms will push sand across the bayside to form land along what is now waterfront," he said. "The Island will move sort of like a tank tread, and will make its way closer to shore."

And Dr. Norbert Psuty, director of the Center for Coastal and Environmental Studies at Rutgers University, predicts sea level rise will "mobilize" all the barrier Islands along the coast, causing them to "penetrate" the mainland.

"You can build all the jetties and groins you want to prevent erosion, but it won't stop the movement of the sea," he said. "You'll end up with walking platforms wherever you build."

Predicting ecological disasters for the shore is nothing new among scientists. Every year warnings are doled out during hurricane season and a veil of pessimism among government planners threatens to dim the beach frolic.

And there is nothing new about predictions of sea level rises. For the past 3,000 years, scientists say, the sea levels have been increasing. If the

from *The SandPaper* • May 1, 1985

icecap in Antarctica and the glaciers in Greenland ever thaw, scientists warn, the coastline would surge to levels more than twenty feet what they are today and the coastlines would approach what they were thousands of years ago.

"Did you ever drive through the Pine Barrens and think to yourself that it looked like some sort of prehistoric beach," Titus asked. "That's because it once was a prehistoric beach."

The problem now is more immediate than the fantasies of global destruction. As a result of warming air temperatures resulting from increased carbon dioxide content in the atmosphere, known as the green-house effect (mainly because of emissions from fossil fuel combustion), there is a serious risk of the ocean rising by the end of the century.

According to some, more than half of that rise would result from the expansion of water already in the ocean. Just as air takes up a larger volume when heated, so does water.

"Since about 6,000 years ago, the sea level has come up about six feet, which is a relatively slow rate of increase," Psuty said. "Now we're talking about that same sort of a rise within one hundred years. That is a tremendous contrast of rates and the results would be devastating."

Some dispute the findings, however, and some meteorologists claim the Earth is actually beginning a cooling phase, in which the ocean levels would decrease.

"But we are focusing on the warming due to increasing particulates in the atmosphere which prevent heat from escaping," Psuty said. "The particulates are mostly dust resulting from large-scale agriculture, industrial pollution, and cutting down vegetation.

"As the atmosphere becomes more opaque, that will more than balance any cooling trend, and the result will be warmer climactic changes."

Although the changes would affect climates — and would alter the agricultural regions and weather patterns around the world — the effects might first be felt along the shore.

"The changing water levels would cause existing harbor facilities to be drowned, and would drown out existing estuaries. Salt water could infiltrate and contaminate the aquifers in the Pine Barrens. And Long Beach Island, according to this theory, would be completely submerged," he said.

A car abandoned on the Boulevard in Brant Beach during a storm in March 1984.

The problems of sea level rise are now being studied by the EPA, which has recently released a series of reports, including a chart titled "How to Estimate Future Sea Level Rise in Your Community."

According to Titus, the sea level rise is imminent.

"In the last interglacial period, 120,000 years ago, a one-degree centigrade change in temperature brought about a twenty-foot rise in tides. At the rate we're going, we will warm the temperature between 1.5 and 4.5 degrees centigrade by about 2040," he said.

The rise would be imperceptible at first, which Titus said is part of the problem: No one will take action until it is too late,

"Some predict the global warming will begin by the 1990s. At that rate, the sea level will rise by about a foot sometime between 2000 and 2010. But if we wait until then before we make any decisions on what to do about this, there won't be any time."

According to Titus, the rising seas will have to be combatted by large-scale erosion control projects, and may result in construction of an enormous sea wall around Long Beach Island to save the beaches and houses.

"At first, there would be dredging and pumping of sand on the beaches to offset the erosion. But as the seas rise more, the whole Island will have

209

to be raised, not just the dunes," Titus said. "That will be cost effective if the value of land is $1 million an acre, but it will only be cost effective up to a point,"

Donald Rippey, an agent for the Ocean County Cooperative Extension Service, included the EPA's findings and predctions in the agency's April newsletter.

Rippey said it was the first he had heard of the sea rise potential within the next few decades. "Why aren't we bringing air pollution under control that causes this problem? And this will affect Ocean County locally. We really have to be quite concerned about this," he said.

Titus said little can be done to bring air pollution that causes the greenhouse effect under control because the problem is global. "Even if the United States stopped emitting particulates and carbon dioxide, that would be only a small dent in the problem."

The approach of the sea level rise, Titus believes, is in management of the coastal resources. "We can't wait to make decisions that will be substantially effective. One of the approaches might be to restrict building in areas two feet above sea level and lower. Any rise there would obliterate those places. That's applying common sense," he said.

But, according to the Ocean County Planning Board Director Steven Pollack, it is unlikely any planning decisions will be made as a result of sea level rise until the damage has begun. "We have more pressing matters that we're concerned with now, such as garbage disposal," Pollack said. "I think the taxpayers would appreciate us spending our time on other things besides what the ocean will do in the year 2010."

Titus would agree with Pollock on some of that. "I have property in Brant Beach," he said. " I firmly believe the sea is going to rise, but I'm keeping my house until it washes under, he said. "I like the beach. People should be concerned about what is going to happen, but that doesn't mean they can't go to the beach."

Long Beach Township Mayor James J. Mancini, however, disputes what the EPA claims to have documented. "We talk about this all the time. What the EPA claims is conjecture," Mancini said. The coastline on the Island, he said, has remained constant for the past one hundred fifty years or so. "I've been taking care of the township beaches for twenty-four years and I look at the beaches with an affirmative attitude," he said. "Of course, many people take great pleasure looking at the beaches pessimistically."

But erosion and reduction of beaches locally and along the East Coast is an annual problem. Millions of dollars have been allotted to shore protection in this state, and millions more are required to finish the job. Even that is not enough, however, as management of the Forsythe National Wildlife Refuge has learned.

"We've already seen the effect that ocean erosion can have on the beaches, particularly in the Holgate section of the refuge," said David Beall, manager of the refuge. Fishermen have reported erosion of about two-hundred feet at the southern tip of the Island over the winter, according to Hal Laskowski, the division manager of the refuge for Barnegat. "The beach in some areas has eroded right back to the dunes," Laskowski said.

Although the winter erosion at Holgate is not attributable to a rise in sea level, it is another reminder of the forces of the sea and foreshadowing of what could become a rising problem.

But Mancini has hope for the beaches.

"There has always been a retreat syndrome when it comes to the beaches. Some people tell us to leave them alone and let them succumb to the ocean. That's the most absurdly ridiculous attitude a human being can have," he said. "Our beach will stay here, and we're going to take care of it. We will have great storms now and then, and some storm damage, but we will always put it back the way it was."

According to the American Littoral Society, since 1900 sea level along the New Jersey coast has risen at a rate of about one-and-one-half inches every ten years — nearly twice the global average.

1987 Protesting Ocean Dumping

Joe Saunders

D espite hasty preparations and less than perfect weather, the "silent show of concern" for the polluted ocean came off without a hitch on Sunday, and organizers say over 60,000 people took part in a hand-linked human chain extending almost the entire length of Long Beach Island, and many other parts of the Jersey shore.

"Long Beach Island was great," said Linda Hasbrouck of Save Our Shores, one of the sponsors of the event. "We had some really bad weather further north, but people still showed up. It was a public statement, and I think it got across loud and clear," she added, noting that all three major television news networks had carried the story both in Philadelphia and New York.

"It was phenomenal," said Karen Kiss, of the Concerned Taxpayers Association of Surf City, which coordinated the event on the Island. "People were standing shoulder to shoulder in all directions as far as you could see."

Kiss said organizers estimated that at least 60,000 people had taken part, after calculating the average amount of space occupied by one person and dividing it by the 18-mile length of the Island, a number she described as "amazing, considering the amount of time we had to prepare this."

The success of the event was due to a massive publicity blitz conducted by the taxpayers associations, which included flyers posted all over the Island as well as announcements which were made in churches on Sunday morning. "We asked the churches to read our letter," Kiss said, "that talked about what man and his industry are doing to God's gift, the ocean."

Richard and Jeannette Merion, residents of West Chester, Pa., who vacation every year in Harvey Cedars, heard about the event through both the publicity flyers and church announcements. Merion, a Republican committeeman at home, supported Connors' bill but felt that it, by its na-

from *The SandPaper* • September 9, 1987

Human chain "Hands Across the Island" rally against ocean pollution, 1987.

ture, wasn't going far enough. "We've got to do something about it (ocean dumping)," he said. "But New Jersey legislation only works for New Jersey. What about New York, Maryland and Pennsylvania? It has to be done on a federal level if it's going to be done at all."

However, both Kiss and Hasbrouck said they considered the event very successful in raising the public consciousness about the danger presented to the marine ecology by sewage dumping, whether illegal or legal. "It went up and down the state," Hasbrouck said. "We're very happy, very happy with the results."

"Awareness blossomed in this community that we have to do something about this situation," said Kiss. "People that were skeptical have really changed their feelings since they saw everyone there, from little babies to grandmothers. It's a finite planet, and we'd better learn to start changing the way we're treating it."

1987 To My Great-Grandson

Bill Hammarstrom

An opinion page commentary from a local bayman, fisherman, and naturalist written as a letter to the his great-grandson.

It grieves me not to be there by you, my great-grandson, but time dictates that I cannot. However, as you read this letter left for you in care of your mother's father, I believe you will feel my presence beside you.

Not being a very rich man in the financial world, I do, however, have some very important things I want you to have.

First off, I hope you live in a time of peace with good health and prosperity for all.

I leave you a still, frosty morning, broken only by the noise of your oars as you row down a creek in the Forsythe Refuge; your only companion, your retriever, shivering anxiously with excitement as if he knew what's ahead.

I leave you the thrill of catching your first winter flounder in the bay, as I did when I was your age.

I want you to have the surprise feeling when you bring up your first clam out from under your feet and experience the good taste as you eat it afterwards.

I want you to have the full feeling as you catch your first hard crab, with many more to follow.

I want you to have Barnegat Bay to fall back on to make a living to support your family, as I did when I was young when things got hard for me. I didn't make a lot of money, but it carried us over the hard times.

As you walk home in a storm, a pair of black ducks slung across your back, the rain pelting your face so hard it almost stings, I want you to have the wonderful feeling of being able to walk 100 miles in it.

I want you to have the full feeling as you bring home 10 bushels of hard

from *The SandPaper* • October 28, 1987

Man, dog, sneakbox, geese, Ship Bottom.

crabs in January, after spending half the morning breaking ice to the main channel.

I want you to have that feeling of pride when the judge awards you first place for whittling your black duck decoy, the same as I had when I was your age.

You now have the shotguns that I used. I told your father to give them to you when the time comes. Take good care of them and they will provide for your family, as they did for mine.

These are my most cherished possessions that I want you to have. I also realize that times change and nothing stays the same. As I am writing this letter, a power plant is slowly but surely destroying the ecology of the bay by destroying the spawn of clams, winter flounder, etc. Also, warming up the year-round temperature of the bay causes bay grass to grow in great abundance. There is talk of making the power plant put in a closed system, thereby eliminating the salt water intake from the bay. I will try and do everything in my power to implement this, but remember, I am only a fisherman.

There is also a proposed trash-burning plant scheduled to be built a short distance from the bay. I fear the tons and tons of pollutants from this plant will make the crabs, clams and fish unfit to eat and ruin the bay for years to come. We are begging the freeholders to either move the plant away from the bay or change the ways of trash disposal, but they seem oblivious to our cries. They only seem bent on doing things their way and to hell with the bay.

There is also talk of building a coal-fired power plant alongside the nuclear plant. I hear that some of the contractors in Forked River have bought up the right of ways to amass a fortune in selling the rights to the plant. I am also against this plant because of what it will do to the bay. They don't seem to realize there is only about an eight to ten inch fall and rise of tide here, and anything that goes into the bay will stay there because of the lack of tidal flowage.

I am telling you all this, my great-grandson, because I feel that you should know what I am doing to try to prevent all this from happening. Our lives here are not easy, fighting big business from ruining the bay. Enough of this talk. You're a young man, and although I can't be there to talk with you, I raise my glass to you across the years. If I fail in my attempt to keep Barnegat Bay clean, you will know it because everything will be polluted and unfit to eat, whether it be fish, clams or fowl, and you will have none of the wishes in my will. If I succeed, you will have all of the above mentioned in this letter — I salute you!

Your Loving Great-Grandfather

1987 Pollution Concerns Abound

Don Southwick

This letter to the editor was addressed to Governor Thomas Kean from an Island businessman, bayman, surfer and diver.

I'm sure that in the last few weeks you've received an abundance of letters and phone calls regarding the problem of ocean dumping. I hope that you haven't reached the point where they all seem the same and therefore start to lose some impact. First, let me say that I usually don't stop what I'm doing to write a letter to complain about just anything. It takes quite a large injustice for me to sit down at the typewriter and vent my anger. With the recent garbage, hospital waste and sewage sludge washing up on our beaches, I feel that I have watched an unbelievably gross injustice occur, and I would be guilty of an equal injustice just to sit back and let it pass. I have live here for thirty-three years, and my family goes back even further. Our family business is Southwick's Marina in Beach Haven Gardens and is very attuned to our ocean and bays. I grew up on the beach at the end of our street, started running boats at an early age in the bay, have been surfing on our Island for over nineteen years, have been scuba diving for fourteen years in the ocean and bay, and have basically shaped my life to work with the ocean. I mention these facts in order to impress upon you the importance the ocean holds for me. Up until this summer I have always wanted to live and work here on Long Beach Island. In the winter months, when it is too cold to be out on the water, I travel south to Florida, where I can again be in touch with the ocean. But now, with the events of the last few weeks, I considered for the first time the idea of moving to an area where people care about what happens to our ocean.

I'm not the type to throw up my hands and run away from a problem as soon as it develops. This is not the first time that we have had problems with wastes and sludge in our ocean. A big problem occurred in July 1976

from *The SandPaper* • *letter to the editor* • **September 16, 1987**

A bottlenose dolphin is removed from the beach in Harvey Cedars to be transported to the Marine Mammal Stranding Center for autopsy, August 1987.

Ray Fisk

when all the fish, lobsters, crabs, clams, starfish and all the underwater creatures that need oxygen to survive died due to an algae bloom of such massive proportions that it suffocated every living creature in our area. It made me literally sick to my stomach when I went diving on the wrecks off the Island that year. The water on the bottom tasted and smelled like a sewer as I swam over the seemingly endless underwater graveyard!

The algae bloom was caused by dumping sewage into the waters off North Jersey and New York. Not just at the 106-mile site, but just twelve miles off the coast of Sandy Hook we allow sewage sludge to be dumped into our waters! I am amazed that this practice was ever allowed to start, but I am even more amazed that it is allowed to continue after all the disastrous results we have seen and continue to see!

After that huge fish kill in 1976, governing bodies seemed to be upset and decided to do something about the problem. Somehow the ocean started to come back to life in the next few years. I seriously thought that we had learned our lesson that the ocean is not infinite and is vulnerable to abuse, so we should exercise great care in how we treat this planet's most valuable resource. However, it seems that once the headlines had faded from page one, we went right back to the same practice of dumping more and more sewage into the ocean. Once again, it was only a matter of a few years before our ocean could handle no more and decided to throw our waste back at us — right in our front yard!

I realize that dealing with waste, be it trash or sewage sludge, is a huge problem and cannot be solved overnight. Our concern should be with finding the best method of disposal, rather than the cheapest. In Long Beach Township, the cost for one year's sewage service is $265 this year. At a recent meeting of Chamber of Commerce officials and representatives from the DEP and EPA held on Long Beach Island, it was brought out the average cost for a North Jersey yearly sewage service is $35! The enormous number of people, generating an enormous amount of waste, are spending only a fraction of what the shore communities are spending, and their waste is being dumped upon our shores and in our waters!

Not only does this create a disgusting picture for all people at the shore, but it poses a serious question as to how safe the water is for people, fish, dolphins and all the sea creatures in our area. The fish that live in these waters cannot help but ingest more and more waste into their systems. How much is too much?

Already this summer we saw and continue to see bottlenose dolphins dying by the hundreds along our shore, and we don't know how many more are dying offshore! It wouldn't be possible for me to explain on paper how special the bottlenose dolphin is to me, but when intelligent creatures like the dolphins are being killed because the water they live in is so full of harmful bacteria, it really makes me, first of all, sick, then sad, and finally, angry. The dolphins can't escape their environment. They can't ride back to a home away from the shore and visit a doctor to help them get better. They are dying, and we come up with stories like "It's a naturally occurring algae bloom" or "We're having an ozone imbalance."

How stupid do you think we can be by sidestepping the real problem? Do we have to wait until people start dying at the shore? They are already getting sick, getting skin irritations and having difficulty breathing after swimming in the ocean for just short periods of time! Late in August I was surfing for less than three hours, and the very next morning I had a painfully sore throat that had to be treated with antibiotics. How long can we let this horrible abuse of our ocean continue?

Those opposing a ban on ocean dumping complain about a lack of alternatives. There are alternatives available — maybe not as cheap as dumping sludge directly in the ocean, but there are alternatives. In Ocean County, we have sewage treatment facilities. Plans are being realized for pelletizing sludge into useful fertilizers. These alternatives are all expensive dollarwise, but what we are doing to our ocean now is much more expensive, not only to the shore communities, but also to all the people who use the shore.

If only it were a matter of dollars and cents! No price can be put on a natural resource such as our ocean. Our entire life cycle depends heavily on the balance of our natural resources. Just as the forests are essential for oxygen production in the inland areas, the ocean plays a crucial role in giving us oxygen, as well as nutrients and essential elements. When we continue to pollute the ocean, we steadily reduce the beneficial aspects of the ocean and reduce it to an enormous cesspool.

When the ocean loses its drawing power as a recreational area, the shore is doomed to follow in the footsteps of the infamous ghost towns of the early West. No longer will families spend their vacations at the shore. With no people spending time or money at the shore, the property values will fall fast. Anyone living at the shore will be forced to move inland, not only for employment but also to maintain some standard of health. It will create overcrowding in an already overcrowded state, along with unemployment problems, and in short, it will become a disaster area because we are too pig-headed to start solving our waste problems now!

The ocean has always been a major producer of seafood in many, many different forms. When it can no longer produce edible or non-toxic seafood, a major chunk of what once was a healthy and vast supply of protein for human consumption will be erased forever. At the same time, the businesses and jobs related to the fishing and seafood industry will be eliminated. If something is not done soon to stop the dumping, people who love the ocean and all its creatures will be moving away from the Northeast states and relocating in areas where some concern is shown for our ocean.

I urge you, as a person in a position of power, to use that power to support the ban on ocean dumping and to enforce the legislation so that it will be economically unsound for anyone to dump sewage or trash in the ocean ever again! Yes, I understand that it will take much more money to enforce these laws, but what good is a law without enforcement? I do not and would not mind paying extra to clean up our ocean and to maintain the quality of the water. What I do mind is the people at the shore paying to handle our own waste and deal with it effectively, and then having North Jersey and New York take the cheap way out by dumping their sewage on us! This disgusting practice has to stop!

I have a terrible fear that after a month or so goes by and the tourist season is over, the gross injustices against the ocean and the shore will continue, and all the talk about stopping those injustices will fade away just as they have in the past. I hope that you will do whatever it takes to see that this practice of words without action ceases, and once again we can be proud and happy to live in New Jersey and not be ashamed of that fact, as I am now!

Don Southwick
Beach Haven

1987 Tracing Wastes' Origins

Kathryn M. King

I t became apparent last Thursday morning that the unthinkable, the unspeakable, had happened. High tides and an onshore wind had carried unacceptable contamination — not the "normal" tampon applicators — onto the soft sandy beaches of Long Beach Island right smack at the peak of the season in the middle of the hottest string of days at the Shore.

It was a vacationland nightmare come true, and it had its beginnings last Wednesday morning when lifeguards on several beaches called in ocean bathers as huge pilings and timbers, some with evidence of burning, skidded through the surf. By the next morning, Ocean County beaches were littered with wood debris, household garbage and hospital waste, including syringes and other intravenous equipment, drug prescription bottles, disposable hospital padding, tongue depressors and swabs. The Island's smallest community, Harvey Cedars, appeared to have the most trash on its beachfront. Surf City's public works department pulled in half-burned creosoted pilings 30 feet long and 18 inches in diameter.

On the Island, rubber-gloved lifeguards, volunteers and municipal employees began picking up the mess. "I'm collecting all the bills from the cleanup, and when I get them all I'll see how much it cost us," said Long Beach Township Public Works Commissioner DiAnne Gove. "Debris started washing up before Thursday, about a week before that. We can't understand all the piling-sized lumber we have picked up; most of it is new wood, not burned at all."

Gove, township lifeguards and municipal workers scoured twelve miles of the Island's beaches. But crews in all Island municipalities worked overtime, culling out potentially dangerous hospital waste from household trash and lumber. The unmistakable byproducts of a disposable society became a local problem.

Timothy Hilferty, director of the Long Beach Township Health Depart-

from *The Beachcomber* • August 20, 1987

Ray Fisk

Authorities examine medical and other waste on the beach, 1987.

ment that services four of the six Island municipalities, said Monday that criminal investigators from the state Attorney General's Office were here to segregate any refuse that could help pinpoint the source of the garbage.

John Eagerly, deputy press secretary for the Attorney General's Office, confirmed they are coordinating the investigation that should identify the culprit. The office will be collecting information from the federal Environmental Protection Agency, U.S. Coast Guard, state Department of Environmental Protection and State Police. "We have organized a special division of criminal justice, and we will be tracking down materials and their origins and then find out who is responsible for dumping them. We know tentatively that the hospital wastes come from two New York hospitals, but I am not in a position to indicate the specific origin of the trash," he said.

However, on the same day, Tuesday, a *New York Times* article said Albert Einstein College of Medicine in the Bronx and Horton Memorial Hospital in Middletown were implicated by debris found on the beaches. The article also said since January 1986 all hospitals in New York City are required to incinerate infectious or harmful waste. N.J. Congressman H. James Saxton said he has been a part of the investigation called for by Governor Thomas Kean after Kean made a helicopter tour, with state and federal officials, of offshore waters. "Garbage, if it was dumped in the ocean, was dumped there illegally. If we can find out who did it, they will be prosecuted," Saxton said.

Reimbursement for clean-up costs might be found from either the federal government or New York City, said Saxton. However, investigators would have to prove who is to blame. "These legal things have all sorts of problems. I talked to an attorney from the DEP who said you have to establish a continuity of possession of the evidence. They are trying to be very careful how they get this. For example, my aide has a place in Beach Haven, and he picked up a Federal Express letter on the beach, sent from California to a location in the Bronx. We can document that one. This has been a terrible experience for all of us ... It has certainly been a real trying week for everyone on Long Beach Island." Saxton added as an afterthought that New York City has been dumping oil for years, and it is time they stopped.

State Senator Leonard T. Connors Jr. this summer introduced legislation to halt ocean dumping of sewage sludge. Ironically enough, he noted on Tuesday, he recently received a letter from Hal Bozarth, executive director of the Chemical Industry Council of New Jersey, announcing the council's opposition to the bill which would impose a penalty tax on ocean dumping of sludge. Bozarth wrote that the ban would pose a financial burden on the state chemical industry.

Connors also said he can't see how New Jerseyans can complain about what other states are doing when six utilities authorities in North Jersey dump fifty-three percent of dry sludge, one million pounds a day, into the ocean twelve miles off the coast. He said we should start cleaning our own house and stop offshore sludge dumping. "The ocean is dying, that is a plain fact. Is there any wonder why dolphins are dying? Something has to be done; this is just the tip of the iceberg. Today is the day when we have to start to turn this around, to start going away from it. You heard it from me, the chemical industry is dumping. That's right." He said he is concerned that people who bathe in the ocean and eat its fish and shellfish may become sick if ocean dumping continues, "The plain fact is we got something going in the ocean that is just the tip of the iceberg. Over a year ago, more than forty doctors came to me and pointed this out to me ... I wish I had pleasanter thoughts on this shore issue, but this time I think it is just going to hurt. I don't know any other way to defend our Island but to call attention to the situation. I think something out there is wrong, and the something wrong is us."

Connors added that he finds it unbelievable that the source and responsible party for the garbage slick is not known: "It's a funny thing. If you decided to put in a couple pilings on the sly, or put in a bulkhead down around Beach Haven or anywhere on Long Beach Island or the coast, one of those helicopters flying over would pick you up in a minute. And could you imagine a barge or a tug carrying a load of crap can't be monitored by the same helicopter? I can't imagine all the money we spend on surveillance in the sky, nobody knew a barge was leaving. I can't imagine a slick that would go from Sandy Hook to Seaside Heights in an area a mile or two wide, and nobody saw it.

On Tuesday, another long garbage slick was sighted floating about three to five miles off the coast, from Beach Haven Inlet to Ocean City. The slick was spotted by Robert Schoelkopf, director of the Marine Mammal Stranding Center in Brigantine. Schoelkopf said yesterday that a large number of sharks surrounded the garbage which he believes indicated that the slick contained organic wastes.

1987 Dolphin Toll Reaches Sixty

Marion Figley

The deaths of more than 140 Atlantic bottlenose dolphins since mid-June, in an area ranging from Ocean County, New Jersey to Virginia, continues to puzzle scientists, including an expert on bottlenose dolphins who is part of a federal response team in Virginia.

Dr. Joseph Geraci, a wildlife pathologist of Ontario Veterinarian College in Guelph, Ontario, Canada, is heading a five-member response team at Little Creek Naval Amphibious Base, Norfolk. The team is performing necropsies on dolphins that are coming ashore in the mouth of Chesapeake Bay. On Tuesday, ten dolphins came ashore from ten miles north and south of Virginia Beach, bringing to 30 the number that has been reported to and by the team.

However, Brian Gorman, with the National Oceanic and Atmospheric Administration and a spokesman for the investigative team, said yesterday that tissue samples, collected by the team from six dolphins, have not yet yielded good test results. Those samples had been sent to the National Veterinary Service laboratory in Ames, Iowa to be tested for bacteria, viruses, toxins and pollutants.

"We did have some results on the tissue samples but they were only to say that the materials were not suitably fresh to produce any results. We haven't sent out any samples since Sunday night because we haven't had a fresh animal to autopsy."

According to Gorman, there are specific differences between the symptoms exhibited by New Jersey and Virginia dolphins. "It appears that the Virginia animals are in worse shape, that they have been dying over a longer period of time, over days or even weeks instead of hours. For the Jersey dolphins, it appears that whatever this disorder is, it has come on rather suddenly, whereas the animals here have appeared to have died more slowly.

from *the Beachcomber* • August 13, 1987

"The necropsies show in general skin lesions, large patches of skin that have sloughed off, large numbers of very small lesions inside the mouth, coious amounts of fluid in the chest and abdomen, lungs filled with fluid, enlarged spleens, emaciation and empty stomachs and coffee-colored fluid in the urinary bladder. All of those things suggest that whatever it is, it's taking a longer time (to kill them) than those in New Jersey." Gorman said that Dr. Geraci has performed fourteen hundred nicropsies on bottlenose dolphins but has never seen anything that remotely resembles these deaths.

In an attempt to examine a live dolphin and obtain fresh blood and tissue samples, the U.S. Navy will try to capture a dolphin off the Virginia coast, using equipment from Florida's Sea World.

In Brigantine, meanwhile, Robert Schoelkopf, director of the Marine Mammal Stranding Center, also has sent tissue samples from several dolphins to the Iowa lab and to the U.S. Fish and Wildlife Service laboratory in Madison, Wisconsin. "We're still waiting for preliminary results," said Schoelkopf, adding, "I still think that the animals have a natural disease which has erupted within and is spreading considerably throughout their species or, two, that they've been affected by some chemical or airborne pollutant, such as ozone which has been quite high this summer … And the still air which we have had here would have a tendency to hold the pollutant on top of the water where the animals are breathing it in."

Of the 57 dolphins that Schoelkopf has examined or collected since June, all but three have had signs of bronchial pneumonia as well as empty stomachs, discolored skin, ulcers in their mouths and skin lesions. Two dolphins had died of old age and one healthy-looking animal died with a stomach filled with fish. The latest dolphin reported on Long Beach Island swam slowly along the Loveladies surf on Sunday afternoon and came ashore in Harvey Cedars where it died on the beach. Lifeguards and people on the beach packed the animal in ice in order to preserve the flesh for sampling. Schoelkopf, wearing rubber gloves to handle the animal, loaded it into a metal casket, one of four supplied by the National Marine Fisheries Service to help the nonprofit center with its mounting costs from the large numbers of strandings.

Last week, a state wildlife pathologist had isolated a bacterium from the lung tissue of one dolphin. The bacterium is known to cause lung disease

Ray Fisk

A bottlenose dolphin, stranded on the beach in Harvey Cedars, is cooled with ice until volunteers from the Marine Mammal Stranding Center arrive, 1987.

in cattle and cholera in waterfowl. James Staples, a spokesman with the state Department of Environmental Protection, said Tuesday that other tests for viruses, conducted out of state, have not been finished. In addition, brain tissue from one dolphin was sent to the state medical examiner in Newark to check for hexane and xylene, chemicals that Staples said were rumored to have been dumped in the ocean in July. "The Coast Guard has been checking on this, but meanwhile, we decided to have the brain tissue examined." The two chemicals are known to concentrate in the brain. Lung tissue samples from two dolphins and blood serum from a third were also sent to Dr. Robert Webster, a virologist who has studied influenza epidemics throughout the world and who is associated with St. Jude's Children's Research Hospital in Memphis, Tenn.

Once a dolphin washes in, do not touch it, said Schoelkopf. "On Sunday, one lifeguard in Harvey Cedars had a finger down the dolphin's blowhole and was going to administer CPR. There were lesions all over this animal and ulcerations around the blowhole. The animals have skin lesions, and we don't know what is causing this or if it is contagious."

Lifeguards can help by roping off an area around an animal and by covering a live dolphin with a towel, said Schoelkopf. "Don't cover the blowhole and keep the towel wet with sea water," he advised. "If it's a dead animal or if it dies on the beach, it should be packed in ice to keep it as fresh as possible so we can get good tissue samples for testing." He again stressed that people should not touch the dolphins.

Fund-rasing T-shirt designed by Eric Bourgeois of Starving Artist in 1987.

1987 People Like You

Marion Figley

It may be a cliché but it is nonetheless true that bad times sometimes bring out the best in people.

People like Beverly Laird, her husband Ray and her brother Eric Bourgeois, co-owners of Starving Artist T-Shirts in Brant Beach. As more and more dead or dying dolphins wash up on New Jersey beaches, these three "were wondering what was happening and getting depressed," said Laird, when they decided to do something to help. That was a Friday.

Bourgeois designed a T-shirt with a dolphin on it and Laird's husband Ray printed them up. By Monday morning, they had 144 T-shirts to sell, to raise money for the Marine Mammal Stranding Center in Brigantine, which was picking up the dolphins and performing autopsies to try to determine the cause of death.

Their goal was to raise $500, but they sold out the first batch of T-shirts in three days and had to make more. In a week they had sold more than 500 T-shirts and sent a check for over $2,200 to the Stranding Center, which was sorely in need of funds. "It made me feel good to know all these efforts will go to cure a problem. It's been a wonderful experience," says Laird, "I can't get over how people want to feel they have participated. I just wish I could sign the name of every person who's bought a shirt on that check."

Another group sending money to the Marine Mammal Stranding consists of Long Beach Island Realtors who banded together earlier this year to create a "Welcome to Our Island" campaign to make summer visitors feel welcome here. The group sold buttons as part of the campaign, and they plan to contribute some of the profits from the sale of the buttons to the center.

Then there's Thomas Sweeney, who owns the White Cap Canvas Company in Ship Bottom. He and his friend and fellow Ship Bottom

from *The Beachcomber* • August 27, 1987

resident William Dorris have put together a petition that Sweeney has been distributing up and down Long Beach Island. The two friends met for a beer on Friday night and complained about the ocean pollution. Dorris suggested he have his secretary type up the letter and run off the petition forms, which he did. The following Tuesday, they again met at the Gateway and began soliciting signatures. Copies will be sent to the Department of Environmental Protection of the State of New Jersey and to various local, regional and state elected officials. The petition asks the recipient to "enact legislation (to) prevent the recurrence of infectious waste coming to our communities."

Sweeney says he did it because "I want people (in political office) to know that we care and that I am interested in what is being dumped in the ocean. I was upset and I tried to do something about it." He has placed the petition with other local businesses, and this Saturday, August 29, at 12:30 p.m. he will hand out petitions at the Ship Bottom public boat ramp to anyone who is willing to stand at the end of any street at the beach entrance soliciting signatures. He hopes to have 60,000 signatures by the end of next week. "I haven't had anyone yet say they weren't interested or didn't want to sign it," he says.

Mary Henry of Warren Grove concurs. Henry is the manager of the Ship Bottom branch of First Jersey National Bank/South, which is where some of Sweeney's petitions are located. Her customers have covered a stack of paper with their signatures so far. Henry, who describes herself as "militant" about the environment, wrote to President Reagan enclosing newspaper clippings from *The Beachcomber* and other publications about the current ocean pollution problems.

"The dolphins (dying) I'm extremely upset about, but I think probably it was the syringes on the beach that really got me mad," she says. "How dare they! It's just gone on too long. It's got to stop. Everybody tells me I'm a hopeless optimist," but she believes "something will be done this time" by elected officials to end the causes of ocean pollution. "I wish I had more power," she says. "I wish I had the power to do something (directly) about this, but I don't, so we're all doing what we can ... I figured it was worth the effort."

Another person willing to put out a little extra effort is Michael Lorenzi of Ship Bottom, who owns a shop in Bay Village in Beach Haven. He and Ray Fisk of Harvey Cedars, a photojournalist who has seen firsthand and documented the effects of ocean pollution, are putting out a post card with a message to Governor Kean, demanding the immediate end of ocean dumping. On the front is a black-and-white photograph of hospital debris that washed up on the Island, taken by Fisk, which first appeared in regional newspapers.

Lorenzi says that a week ago, he and Fisk were talking, lamenting the current environmental situation. "We were just outraged," says Lorenzi. "We talked about a letter-writing campaign, but we realized the impracticality (of that), so we thought, why not a post card?"

The first printing of 50,000 post cards is being distributed free to any local businesses that will take them to be given out to their customers. The cards are pre-addressed to the governor; all the sender has to do is stamp the card and sign his or her name and address.

Lorenzi had originally planned to pay for the printing himself, but when other shop owners in Bay Village heard about the project, they offered to chip in, too. And when Scott and Marilyn Kipple of Coastal Printing learned what the printing job was about, they called Lorenzi back and said they would do the work at cost.

When summer comes to a close, Lorenzi is a social studies teacher at Southern Regional High School in Manahawkin. He sees a civics lesson in his response and the response others to the situation. He says, "It's what living in a democracy is all about."

Lorenzi says that a letter and petition by the Van Dyk Agency in Beach Haven Terrace and the T-shirts designed by Starving Artist are what really got him moving. "They inspired me to jump into action and do something," he says. Thomas Taylor, president of the Van Dyk Group, wrote a letter to Governor Kean. It was a forceful letter demanding action, and the petition was started to add support to the letter. Within five days, the petition had 3,000 signatures on it, "and it's still snowballing." The letter and petition were Taylor's idea. "I thought, how long are we going to stand for this? Enough is enough. Something's got to be done. Our livelihood, our values, our beaches, our water are at stake," he recalls. "We took a stand. We just hope everybody else does," he says. "By the response, I would say that they are."

1992 Please, Keep Off the Dunes

Marion Figley

I f you are a newcomer to Long Beach Island — either resident or visitor — or even if you have lived here for years, go up to Barnegat Light. Anywhere from 20th Street and north — the borough starts at 30th — take a walk to the ocean and be in for a real surprise.

Unlike the Island's other five municipalities, Barnegat Light has sand dunes in the true sense of the word — rolling, graceful dunes, two, three and four gentle hills deep — before the actual beach begins. Turn around at the water, squint a bit to blur your vision, and the barely visible house-tops disappear. You could be on 18th-century Long Beach, as it was called then, when all the Island was protected by a similar double deep stretch of dunes.

Each of the borough's very long beach access paths is protected by stretches of dune fencing. Crowding against the fencing near the street ends are pine trees, beach plums now in bloom, bayberry, holly, autumn olive, other hardwood trees, shrubs. Cardinals, blue jays and other song-birds, startled by your passage, explode across the path, then scold rau-cously from inside a tree. In those shady areas, you might discover a box turtle lumbering slowly along, well camouflaged by the decomposing leaf litter. Stoop down, look near the fencing, and you'll see mice tracks, part of the dunes' food web that includes the marsh hawk often perched on top of the treated wood posts marking street numbers on the beach.

Barnegat Light protects its dunes, but so, too, do the other municipal-ities with varying degrees of effort and results. The borough had a head start, with undeveloped oceanfront land it promised years ago to set aside. The other municipalities cope with building lines that back up right into the dunes. It is a common practice for investors and individuals to buy a small home that nestled at the western base of a dune, raze the building and bring in pile drivers to whale humongous pilings into the dunes.

from *The Beachcomber* • May 30, 1992

Barnegat Light dunes.

The northernmost borough also has an edge on dune protection because the heaviest beach use is in the more populous towns from Surf City south. In addition, both Surf City and Ship Bottom have large numbers of daily visitors, more foot traffic over the dunes.

And "over" is the right word. As fast as public works departments put up dune fencing, it comes down just as quickly in some places, the perfect kindling for the fireplace or a beach bonfire in the chilly, early part of the season. The signs at the street ends in all municipalities have warnings for dune-crossing violations and the $500 fines they incur. No matter, says Long Beach Township Commissioner Frank Pescatore. The warnings serve largely as deterrents because the dunes, for the most part, are private property of oceanfront homeowners.

Pescatore supervises the township's public works department and has this wry observation: "The main reason for dune fencing is to keep not the kids off the dunes, but the adults. Really. I mean it. Kids, at that age we can teach them what a dune represents, but the adults seem to feel that the fastest way between two points is across the dune and into the house. The biggest offenders of the dune are the beachfront owners and the beachfront renters. If you don't live by the dune or on top of the dune, how do you get to the beach? You're going to take the nearest street entrance.

"The guy who lives on the beachfront walks up along the dune, cuts a path across it to get to his house. I didn't understand it at first; my men would tell me about it. But I've been looking, I've been watching, and — zoom-o — they walk across the dunes.

"Not only that, but I've seen where we start building the dunes up and the people come out and cut a hole right through it so they get up to their house easier. We have those who rent homes to other people and decide you can get a few extra hundred dollars a month or whatever by cutting the top of the dune off so their tenants can see the ocean. We have a few who have done that. ... We have people coming out with shovels — not toy shovels — digging a hole in the dune for their little darlings to play in."

Taking dune-loppers or dune diggers to court does no good, said Pescatore, recalling a municipal court case in which a homeowner had flattened a dune top for a volleyball court. "Here we're teaching kids one thing about dunes and the law allows another," he said.

Still, Pescatore, responsible for approximately twelve miles of dunes and access paths, will make sure fencing goes up in front of dunes owned by what he calls "notorious dune crossers." "If we put up that fence in the morning and they're there for the summer, by afternoon they'll cut a piece of the fence right out so they can walk through it."

Pescatore is building a model of a dune, complete with miniature houses, to take into local schools. "I'm going to say, 'Please take this message home to your parents.' I'm also going to take it to local clubs and organizations to tell adults about protecting the dunes."

Harvey Cedars recently hired a firm to reconstruct its dunes, severely undercut and eroded by the Halloween storm. While the borough's beaches remain narrow — Monday afternoon's high tide left a skinny strip of sand for beach walkers — the dunes have been reinforced and have a wide, flat top.

Apparently, that made them all the better to walk on and scramble down, with some knowledgeable residents politely informing those who are ignorant of the dunes' purpose, "Please keep off the hilled-up sand." Oddly enough, homeowners are to blame as well: Already, like umbilical cords stretching from them, newly built stairways and walkways extend from oceanfront homes, over the reconstructed dunes, to the beach, this in a town that historically gets socked the hardest by storms.

If these homeowners were wise, they would forgo the minute or two they think they gain from using their direct access stairway and walk just one house north or south to the regular beach access path. It makes no sense to gouge out the dunes, as several of these stairways did, when these homes need every sand grain of protection between them and the ocean.

These are not rolling dunes, after all. They are not Barnegat Light dunes, the kind where a swollen, wind-pushed ocean can rise and rise, roll over one dune and just slosh a little up the next. These dunes are perched at the edge of the sea. Tides like those from the fall and winter storms will take them out again.

The public works supervisor in another Island town says this happens because most people simply haven't been around long enough to experience the worst storms. "We just had a phone call yesterday from a homeowner who was quite exercised because we were building the dune up in front of his house. He couldn't see the ocean. Those of us who were here in the big '62 storm would rather have the dune than have the view."

So go up to Barnegat Light and see what real dune protection looks like. And please, keep off the dunes.

1992 Dumping Ban: About Time!

Karen Kiss

T here was a very important milestone that was reached this past 4th of July — another declaration of independence of sort, which was missed by the vast preponderance of shore goers in all the normal 4th of July hoopla.

It had everything to do with New York City and the harbor, and it was about ships sailing in the harbor — but not tall ships. It was about large, flat garbage ships ... and the news that they were not sailing the harbor on their way to the open sea.

For the downright awesome milestone which was reached this 4th of July was for the first time in 100 years, the Atlantic Ocean was not the repository for millions of pounds of sewage sludge ... the infamous toxic cocktail of human and industrial waste from the residents of northern New Jersey and New York City.

In retrospect, it is utterly confounding how a people who took such pride in the accomplishments of their collective intellect, such as birthing the concepts found in the U.S. Constitution (which advanced human rights and values by leaps and bounds over previous civilizations), could also allow the very lowest instincts of man — greed and indifference — to pollute the life-sustaining waters from which they derive food and into which they bathe.

Yet, when the people finally stood on their beaches five years ago this Labor Day in silent protest to this travesty against nature, against ourselves, and against common sense, we were told sludge dumping couldn't be stopped.

They said it in Trenton.

They said it in Washington

But, this July, we, the people, prevailed.

The people, millions of common people, nationwide, working together, exercising their rights as citizens, stopped the sludge dumping this July.

The SandPaper • letter to the editor • July 11, 1992

What a fantastic tribute this 4th of July to the positive aspects of our political system!

Oh, you can be sure that as we speak, there are those working in Washington attempting to manipulate Congress into allowing future dumping in the ocean of this toxic sludge. What else is new? The price of liberty will always be eternal vigilance and you can be sure we will be following the trail of those who wish to make a fast buck at the expense of the environment.

For now, however, we pause to rejoice in this tremendous victory!

Congress banned ocean dumping in 1988, after a summer in which medical waste washed up on beaches and thousands of dolphins died mysteriously along the Atlantic Coast. Sewage sludge had been dumped twelve miles out from New York Harbor since 1924.

1995 The More You Look...

Jan Van Gilder

"Going to the beach" is a phrase we hear often along this shoreline. In my mind's eye, it entails lugging beach chairs, towels, bags of sunscreen, magazines, things for thirsty people to drink, paddles and balls, bellyboards, etc. It can be quite a production. One evening early in June, my daughter Katie and I decided to go to the beach around six o'clock. We took no paraphernalia. It was beautiful.

Walking onto the beach at 20th Street in Barnegat Light, we found a curving path bordered by snow fence, wonderfully mature dunes on each side and several rotund little children wrapped in towels, heading home. The sun was low in the sky, casting long shadows across the sand. The beach was wide and almost empty. A lone osprey was fishing. One woman remained reading. A fishing boat headed into the inlet. Newly painted red and white trash cans, a lifeguard stand on its side and an upturned lifeguard boat were the only indications of the summer about to come. The "Keep Off The Dunes" sign reminded us to keep our distance.

We were drawn to the dunes by the many tracks left on the otherwise smooth surface. As in so many cases, the more we looked, the more we saw. The windblown tips of beach grass had traced circles around themselves. There were tiny holes with what looked like the pattern of a zipper leading away from them. There were big holes that had been excavated with such vigor that sand had been flung in a broad arch. Footprint highways complete with right angles and abrupt turns (occasioned by nothing we could see) led to these big holes. Tiny paths made by ghost crabs wound around the grasses and between shells.

Along the foot of the growing dunes, shoots of new beach grass poked through the sand. Raised lines which looked like the veins on the back of a hand attracted our attention. Something little was burrowing very close to the surface. As we watched, red ants came out of a small crescent-shaped opening. Each ant was carrying one grain of sand. I remembered the lines about the beach from Lewis Carroll's *The Walrus and the Carpenter:*

> If seven maids with seven mops swept it for half a year, do you
> suppose," the Walrus said, "that they could get it clear?"
> "I doubt it," said the Carpenter, and shed a bitter tear.

Those ants may feel the same way.

On we went, still staying close to the dunes. Red-winged blackbirds serenaded us from the greenery. Grackles cackled. (A friend of mine mistakenly thought those big, boat-tailed birds were called crackles.)

Our next encounter was with a kite string. I wound it in, thinking perhaps a kite would be on the other end, but I ended up with a small ball of string. A deflated Mylar balloon was half buried in the sand. Better there than in the stomach of a hapless dolphin or sea turtle.

At this point, the water's edge started looking more interesting and we wandered down toward it. A 1993 beach tag appeared in the sand by my foot. What other unsuspected things lie under the sand's surface?

from *The Beachcomber* • August 6, 1995

A whole train of questions began. What is this substance we are walking on? It certainly is a commodity in great demand for summer visitors to relax on, and as a barrier between us and the ocean. We know it can be pumped from the ocean floor and added on to our existing beaches and we also know that it won't necessarily stay where it is put.

In an interesting and informative book, *Discover Nature at the Seashore* by Elizabeth Lawlor, I found answers. According to Lawlor, ninety percent of the sand on New Jersey's beaches is made of quartz. The sand was created by the mechanical deterioration of quartz, the main mineral in the earth's crust. Just as your concrete birdbath deteriorates if you allow water to freeze in it over the winter, quartz rock deteriorates as water enters tiny crevices, freezes, expands and chips the rock. Tree roots and other natural forces add to the mechanical weathering of rocks. Sand is also formed by the abrasion of rocks. I was surprised to learn that, although this is a process that has been going on for millions of years, the sand on the beaches of New England and New Jersey originated in and has been carried out to sea by rivers such as the Merrimack in Massachusetts, the Connecticut, the Hudson, the Delaware and the Susquehanna.

Those of you who have traveled to Florida know that northern Florida has coarse sand. As a child, I remember feeling like a piece of breaded chicken after coming out of the ocean in Florida and sitting in the sand. It stuck and didn't easily brush off. On the Gulf Coast, however, the sand was like confectioner's sugar, white and powdery. In Panama, I experienced black volcanic sand. It's very sparkly and extremely hot on the feet. The white sands of the Bahamas and Florida are made of pulverized coral and shells, and the skeletons of minute sea creatures. They are not quartz, but calcium carbonate.

Beaches change constantly. The endless interaction of the ocean and the beach alters the contours of the shoreline all the time. Waves bring sand into the beach and take it away, only to deposit it in another place. We are very familiar with the silting of channels and the erosion caused by storms. Perhaps we don't think of it as such, but the beach is a place of conflict and

Waves scatter the beach with a wide variety of shells: blue mussels, arks, surf clams, slipper shells, knobbed and channeled whelks, scallops, mudsnails and tiny coquinas.

contrast, where the strong currents of the ocean compete daily with the land.

Needless to say, through all this ruminating Kate had moved on. She ran back with some treasures left at the water's edge. In her hand was part of a sand collar. This is a circular object which looks more or less like a car tire which has been sliced in half, through the tread. On the underside are the eggs of a moon snail. She had also found a sponge. Razor clams, jingles, scallops, clams and mussels were the shells of the day. Snap weed and sea cabbage edged the high tide line.

The sun descended slowly, and now even pebbles were casting shadows. Immature herring gulls continued their endless hunt for dinner as we started home for ours.

Way Back *When*

The Beachcomber

During the summer of 1943 U.S. Navy blimps patrolled the Island, searching for German U-boats.

1833 Birth of a Resort Island

The season of the year having arrived when it is customary, and in many cases necessary, to partake of a change of air and scene, and, having myself witnessed the salutary and invigorating effects of the air, I would recommend to my fellow citizens an excursion to Long Beach on the sea shore nearly opposite the little village of Manahawkin in New Jersey, which I esteem preferable to many other watering place on the seaboard, as there is an extensive, shallow and placid bay to cross from Manahawkin, which unites the advantage of pleasant and safe aquatic excursions for ladies and fine shooting and fishing for such gentlemen as may wish to enjoy it.

A good stage, with four horses, runs every Monday, Wednesday and Friday from Burlington, immediately upon the arrival of the six o'clock boat from this city [Philadelphia], and returns on intermediate days. The House

Hudson Buzby's Mansion of Health, built in 1821, offered some of the earliest accomocations on the Island at the edge of the Great Swamp in today's Surf City.

from *U.S. Gazette* • July 13, 1833

[boarding house] is kept by a very attentive and competent person, Mr. Hudson Buzby, in the best order. From it is afforded an extensive view of the ocean, on whose white bosom may be seen a vast number of vessels passing, to exchange the commodities of different climes. The scene of the ocean, particularly at rising or setting of the sun, is truly sublime and will compensate anyone for such a journey.

Hudson Buzby was a Burlington County Quaker who invested early in Island real estate. Buzby's inn was called The Mansion of Health, located at what would now be near 7th Street in Surf City. It was destroyed in a fire in 1874.

1897 Spirited Salvage Operation

Edward Brown

A two-masted ship, on fire and low in the water, beats desperately toward the southern shore of Long Beach Island. It is the spring of 1897, a dry year so far, and this small Island was about to undergo a memorable pair of days.

The crippled ship was the *Francis,* come around the Horn from California, loaded with foodstuffs, wines and spirits. On the decks and stored in the holds of the vessel were great hogsheads of port, casks of sherry, crated bottles of champagne, butts of madeira, and puncheons of brandy.

The laboring ship had been seen from shore and the plain folk of Long Beach Island, true to the tradition of the sea, made ready their surfboats to do what they could to save the crew of the stricken ship. Soon all 25 crewmen were safely on the beach and the Islanders gathered to watch the ship burn and go to pieces beyond the offshore shoal. Even after the ship sunk the islanders remained on the beach, for the second part of the sea-drama was about to begin, and one not to be missed.

Cargo from the broken ship began to drift ashore and it was all casks, kegs, and crates. Now these were abstemious, God-fearing people, and there were a good many sober Quakers among them. They were accustomed to the bounty of the sea, and believing the garnering of worldly treasure (the better to do good works with, of course) to rank somewhere between cleanliness and godliness, they set about the salvage with a will. Spurning the gifts of Providence was blasphemous, so there was an immediate, Island-wide scramble to reap the harvest.

Almost at once one large cask of Catawba wine was breached by an impatient salver. Cups and mugs appeared as if by magic, and the curious, many of who had yet to taste the exotic Catawba, dipped down into it. It was deceptively tasty and sweet — surely no harm could come from such ambrosia, but as one cupful followed another, the Long Beach Island two-day drunk was off and running like a turpentined cat.

Gathered around the hogshead under the warm fall sun, those with the largest dippers were the first to realize the salvage operation was about to take a merry turn. Conversation grew animated, if a bit slurred. People began looking at one another — their friends, neighbors, relatives — with a new sense of warmth and friendship. A 40-year-old spinster in one of the best spots next to the barrel was seized by joy. She tore at her outer garments, leaped atop a beached sherry cask and began a mad dance to the tune of something she heard in her head.

People gaped, but the spirit was with them by now, and soon everyone was cavorting on the sand. Bellowing men pursued squealing women into the high dunes back of the beach as inhibitions went the way of the afternoon winds and fully clad people dashed in and out of the surf, laughing and singing.

The good news spread like firewater. A gang of roustabouts, loading two railroad cars with iced fish for shipment to the Philadelphia market, deserted the station *en masse* and made for the water's edge. But the more people who showed up to sample and salvage, the more drink floated in at Beach Haven. It literally came in waves, casks and kegs wallowing in the surf like stunned, overturned turtles waiting for rescue.

from *The Beachcomber Book* • 1978

A drayman who had been among the first at the scene of the wreck was by this time an arm waving, knee-walking drunk, but he somehow managed to mount his wagon and drive the astonished team straight into the surf. The wagon overturned and 300 boxed chickens spilled out, to be saved by those on the scene still able to stand.

A milliner's assistant, sent up to the beach by his curious lady employer to find out what all the excitement was about, overstayed his errand. When he returned to the shop, flushed of face and full of himself, he took the proprietor in his arms and bent her backwards over the cutting counter, implanted long-suppressed and burning kisses on her lips. When he paused for breath, she recovered herself, thought for a minute, went to the door and put up the "closed" sign, then returned to her assistant.

One befuddled man, trying to get in the door to his shed, pitched his key into the sand, and in a fit of rage butted his head against the wood panel until the door gave way. Once inside, he forgot what he had come for and fell asleep in the feed bin.

Down at the beach by this time, the scene was pandemonium, a page out of bedlam. Amidst raucous laughter and yelling, elbows rose and fell with the regularity of metronomes. Once grave, gray-clad elders cavorted with an energy which belied their years, salvaged chickens squalled in discomfort, there was argument and a fistfight or two, and some people were taking naps just back of the waterline, oblivious to the noise and excitement.

The stationmaster at Beach Haven, known to be a sly man, managed to get a cask of sherry into a wheelbarrow and wheeled his load off to the depot, where he locked the cask in an empty boxcar to attend to later at his leisure. The stationmaster thought his cask safe, but when he went back to retrieve it some time later, he found it empty. Someone more devious than he had bored through the floor of the freight car and siphoned off all the fine sherry.

On and on it went, and practically all the Beach Haven villagers suspended business to go into the salvage trade. The workaday schedule of the south island ground to a stop, and later torches and lanterns were produced in order that the work not be needlessly held up by the darkness.

The party lasted two days, began to wane a bit near the end of the second day, and by the morning of the third, there was a great silence in

Beach Haven, broken only by the slow knelling of the church bell. The verger, driven nearly mad by rum-induced visions of demons, was tolling his bell to mark the end of the world which he was sure was at hand.

Others probably thought the end was near too, as they awoke to gray sunlight within their skulls. The hammers of remorse and retribution were striking everywhere. People felt their limbs, their heads, to see if, in fact, they were on the right bodies, for it seemed otherwise.

Children were wailing to be fed; the village idiot had somehow gotten into the general store's molasses barrel and was joyfully anointing with blackstrap every loose cat and dog he could find; overdue cows lowed for milking. The iced fish in the railway cars, abandoned two days back and no longer iced, were still at the station and setting up a half-mile stink that went from bay to ocean.

Later that same day the town fathers met and agreed (in low voices) to call out the Coast Guard and stand by to repel boarders in the event a sister ship of the *Francis* ever made Long Beach Island a future port-of-call.

1902 Barnegat Light Diary

Josephine Lehman Thomas

Barnegat Light built a one-room schoolhouse in 1903, now a museum, but before that, twelve children had classes in a building on 3rd Street. Both building and that part of the street were long ago claimed by the ocean, but the school journal the children started in 1902 was not. The long-forgotten diary turned up among papers in the attic of Isabel Soper, a former schoolteacher and wife of a lighthouse keeper.

Howard Steelman was the teacher who started that journal, choosing

from *The Beachcomber* • May 30, 1952

a different pupil each week as editor. The entries included news of local, national and international interest, what the classes were studying, who had whooping cough, grammatical errors noticed during the week, the weather and a quotation from a famous author.

In large, round, legible handwriting were noted such items as the elections of Teddy Roosevelt and William Taft, the anniversary of the sinking of the battleship *Maine*, the discovery of iron ore at Lake Superior, the opening of the New York Subway, Mount Vesuvius' eruption, Alice Roosevelt's engagement, the San Francisco earthquake, the start of the Panama Canal, the crowning of King Haakon of Norway, the first trans-Pacific cable, the beginning of a "railway" from New York to Paris, and the English Duke of Connaught's auto accident. (Auto accidents were news in 1904. So were automobiles.)

The children recorded Philadelphia Mayor Weaver's acceptance of the Reading Railroad's offer to build an elevated crossover at 9th Street, and that the people in Philadelphia were still trying to get pure drinking water.

In the winter of 1904-1905, two recurring entries concerned the Russo-Japanese war — Japan won it — and the condition of a Mr. Parker, who was ailing, had no home and a failing mind. His neighbors built a little two-room house for him and its progress was reported from week to week. When he could no longer live alone, they took him to an insane asylum in Trenton.

Not so neatly rounded off for the curious reader was the story of the whales: "Two whales, one 70 and the other 17-feet-long, washed ashore in an autumn storm." That is all they wrote. What we want to know is what happened to them? You can't just toss a beat-up whale into a garbage can.

Each spring, seasonal events went into the book. Mr. Sculthorpe left town to go up the Hudson River for the annual shad run. The Oceanic and Sunset hotels opened for the season. The summer train schedule, two runs a day, began. Vegetable gardens were planted. (No supermarket down the road. No road.) Mr. Applegate bought a cow. The cow had a calf. Fresh veal for sale.

School closed, so summer news was lacking. In September the Sunset and Oceanic closed, but the Social stayed open for gunners. Ducks were scarce, and then abundant. Seventeen barrels of bluefish were caught.

Vena Falkinburg, teacher (top row, second from right) and her eight students at the Barnegat City school in 1912.

Boats referred to as "naptha launches" brought hunters from New York. Salt hay was harvested. One train a day ran.

Autumn storms and the erosion at the Oceanic Hotel on 4th Street were noted yearly. In 1902 the sand hills behind the Oceanic washed away. The fire engine house on 12th Street blew over. Trains stopped running for two days after a northeaster. In 1903 the ocean broke through the dunes and spoiled all the drinking water in the town wells. The lifesaving station got twelve tons of hard coal. The ocean flooded the railroad tracks and froze; men spent days chopping ice from the rails. Mr. Sculthorpe built the first icehouse and filled it each winter from the frozen saltwater ponds.

A seven-masted schooner was seen passing by the inlet. A Spanish full-rigger with a cargo of bones grounded at Surf City. The lumber steamer *Charles Loring*, Savannah to New York, washed ashore after a collision. Lumber was strewn for two miles along the beach, and a special train brought workmen and horse teams to pick it up.

Al Brown, the railroad conductor, was married. So was Dr. Hilliard of Manahawkin, who went all the way to Washington, D.C., for his honeymoon. Lighthouse Inspector Thomas made his annual visit. The commercial fishermen got mad because the lifeboat crews were selling fish.

A new boardwalk was built at the lighthouse. The first street lamp was installed in 1902, the first bathroom in the Oceanic and the first phono-graph in 1904. The town seceded from Union Township and formed its own government.

Many names in the book are still remembered in Barnegat Light or on the Island: Applegate, Perrine, Devlin, Archer, Fenimore, Cranmer, Sprague, Parker, Peckworth, Sculthorpe. Over the years, five little Sculthorpe girls went to school there. One of the last entries in the book is that Mrs. Sculthorpe had a new baby — another girl.

As the pupils graduated, the ones who went on to high school usually boarded in Barnegat on the mainland. Their departure by train Monday morning and return Friday night was regularly recorded.

In 1908 Linden Cranmer, one of the first editors of the school journal, was back as teacher.

From a journal edited by Josephine Lehman Thomas, in the collection of the Barnegat Light Museum.

1917 Just Before Christmas

Edward Brown

It was the beginning of the cold winter of 1917, Europeans were killing one another in volume amid the mud of French battlefields, and the Yanks were coming. A world away, the seasonal northeasters rode Long Beach Island down, fierce winds making smoke rise off the bay and a stinging whiteout of the beaches. The Island was winter-withered and naked.

But for William Johnson, this dark 15th of December was a time of joy. Today he was bringing his wife and newborn daughter from the hospital in Lakewood back to their home on the north end of Long Beach Island, and just in time to get ready for Christmas. How lucky he felt!

"Martin's Box," a Manahawkin Bay stop on the railroad, survived until the late 1800s.

The small family was in high good spirits as they boarded the Jersey Central train in Lakewood. The baby was wrapped in a sheepskin over its swaddling clothes, and both the Johnsons were well clad in thick wool, and with good reason. Section hand Johnson, a trackman on the Barnegat Railroad, knew that the last part of this journey home was going to be in an open handcar. He didn't like the look of the weather making up either, but here near the stove in the passenger car they couldn't have been more cozy.

The Johnsons transferred to a Tuckerton-bound train at Barnegat, then got off at the Mud City stop in Manahawkin. The end of the line as far as rail service went on this off-season Saturday; from here to the Island the Johnson family was on its own.

William Johnson bulldogged a handcar onto the tracks, got his wife and child aboard, and began pumping the long distance across Manahawkin Bay. The threatening sky made good its promise and let loose sleet and then snow. A wind as merciless as any from a dark Viking saga sprang up and roared along the bay,

The doughty section hand kept the pump handle going and the car moving, trying to reassure his wife between strokes, a wife beginning to show signs of alarm. He looked out over the bay, baleful and grey it was, and something colder than the icy wind began to steal through him: fear.

from *The Beachcomber* • December 10, 1987

He fought it down and continued. Twenty minutes later, Johnson and his wife and child were coasting into the junction at Ship Bottom/Beach Arlington. They thought to shelter and warm themselves in the station house before making the turn north to start the run up to Barnegat City, but the station was empty and locked. There was not a soul to be seen anywhere on this winter-struck day.

They came out of the lee of the station to a deepening storm. Johnson's handcar was now heading almost directly into the howling northeast wind, and it was a punishing task to move the muscle-builder into it at any kind of speed. But the trackman was beginning to realize that speed was indeed of the essence. He had to get his wife and baby to shelter before this storm proved too much for them. His wife's face was pinched and blue in the cold. He saw his own fear in her eyes. He stole a look at their daughter. In her thick sheepskin she was sleeping peacefully, a tiny cloud of vapor coming from her face buried in the folds of the covering. She was all right.

As he frantically stroked the handcar over the rails grown slippery with ice, Johnson got the dreadful feeling that they were alone in the entire universe. The snow covered sand and frozen cedar swamps on this part of Long Beach Island spread out and away from the thin ribbon of track as if to the very ends of the earth. What few houses they passed were shuttered and aloof, grimly upright against the cruel wind. Alone, alone . . .

Even the hot work at the pump handle was failing to warm Johnson now, or perhaps it was the chill of fear which kept going through him, the fear that they would not make it through this maelstrom of snow and wind borne by a storm bent on destroying them.

A strong man has limits, though pushed beyond himself as never before. Johnson's weary arms slowed at the pump as the last of his energies gave out. He was fuzzy from cold and exhaustion, and it seemed he'd been pumping for hours, days even. It was eight miles up island to Barnegat City, but he knew now that they would not make it. His wife, clearly almost completely done in, huddled over the baby, ready to give up. They were going to die here on this empty track.

"Oh God, help me," Johnson prayed. A finger of light showed suddenly to the north. A sign? The trackman didn't know, but this was good enough for him. He worked his pump handles, trying to move the car forward by force of spirit as well as body.

He saw the light again, brighter this time. His heart leaped in his chest as Johnson realized what it was — the platform light at Harvey Cedars. The crew at the lifesaving station would help them. They were saved! Johnson pumped the last two hundred yards up to the platform, rousing his wife with the good news of their delivery. Warmth, safety, human kindness — all these were only a few yards away now.

There would be a Christmas after all for the Johnson family in this year of 1917 — and a life for them after that.

1926 Rumrunners and the U.S.C.G.

Thomas P. Farner

Back in the Roaring Twenties, when Prohibition kept the nation "dry" — more or less — rum-running was big business along the New Jersey coast. And the U.S. Coast Guard on Long Beach Island were cashing in by cooperating with the rumrunners.

On July 21, 1926, the *Asbury Park Press* ran a small story: "The charges are in the form of two affidavits implicating members of a crew near Beach Haven. The name of one witness has not been divulged. The other is Eugene Danley of Waretown, in whose home six gallons of liquor was found during a raid by Sheriff Grant last week. Danley said he bought the liquor from coast guardsmen." But this was only the tip of the iceberg; there had been ten arrests.

The story behind the uncovering of the plot had a strange beginning, with events not related to prohibition and rum-running. The *Press* the next day revealed, "The present investigation was developed from alleged

Smuggled alcohol captured at Bond's Coast Guard Station, Beach Haven, December 1931.

coast guard opposition to the activities of Game Warden Evernham of Ocean County, who also acts as a deputy sheriff. Evernham, last year, had information indicating that a certain club on Barnegat Bay was killing wild geese and duck out of season. He found that every time he went to the club to investigate, a flag would rise to the top of a mast a mile away. Suspecting that he was being watched, Evernham got Mrs. Mary Arnold of Point Pleasant to visit the club and order a duck banquet served for a number of friends. This ruse was successful and Evernham had club members arrested."

The duck hearing resulted in heavy fines, and among those penalized was Thomas Beer Jr., a son of Capt. Thomas Beer of the Loveladies' station. It didn't take long for the case to change from poaching to a federal crime. The *Press* story continues: "The sheriff's investigation then took him to Barnegat, where he procured from Thomas Driscoll an affidavit that in December a captain of a station with three others of his crew brought eight cases of Scotch whisky in a Coast Guard boat to Tuckerton pier."

Now Coast Guard officials took over. Soon they "called the captain of the station before them and got a denial of any complicity. A machinist's mate then was interrogated. He too made a denial, then broke down and is said to have made a full confession implicating the captain and others. The machinist's mate said that he had been assigned to water duty on the night the liquor was brought in, and that he had seen it piled on deck under a tarpaulin. He said the captain got in a truck and rode off for a half-hour. The captain, with the machinist mate's testimony before him, confessed and implicated the captain of a neighboring station." Like a house of cards, the conspiracy began to collapse.

This captain at first denied complicity, but broke down when the testimony of the first captain was shown him, and admitted he had received two dollars a case which he split four ways. He named captains of two other stations as sharing in the spoils. He said that "his wife had acted as go-between informing rumrunners when the coast was clear."

The day ended with a statement from M. W. Rasmussen, Superintendent of the Coast Guard's Fifth District: "The scope of the probe will be extended from Atlantic Highlands to Cape May. There will be a general house cleaning. Ten men are under arrest as a result of the disclosures, a dozen have been suspended and additional arrests are expected momentarily."

The illegal shooting of several ducks on Barnegat Bay had started a chain of events that put Long Beach Island on the front pages of newspapers across the country, with publicity not equaled since the shark attacks ten years before.

The Long Beach Island Coast Guard scandal of 1926 was quickly becoming a symbol of the failure of Prohibition, and the Volstead Act [January 1920] that enforced it. As the investigations grew, those opposed to the law argued that, instead of improving the nation's morality, it was corrupting its most trusted institutions and the government was trampling on the Constitution in order to enforce it.

The Philadelphia Inquirer of July 23, 1926 ran a special report: "Disclosures and confessions made during the last twenty-four hours will bring the entire Coast Guard patrolling Jersey waters under investigation. ... A number of towns along Beach Haven Inlet, including Beach Haven, Ship Bottom, Harvey Cedars, Barnegat City and Beach Arlington, are involved in the investigation. ... Among the four captains implicated is Captain Edward Falkenburg, of the Ship Bottom station, who has confessed that in December 1925, he transported eight cases of whisky across Barnegat Bay in a Coast Guard boat to Tuckerton ... Captain Falkenburg admitted receiving $100. The affidavit also implicated Machinist Mate Rider, of the same station, and two others.

Capt. Charles Rodgers of the Bonds station was also implicated. His wife is said to have acted as a go-between for her husband and the rumrunners, alleged to be an Atlantic City syndicate. She is said to have handled all telephone messages, and to have passed the money for distribution. … How the entire personnel of the Ship Bottom station unanimously voted to allow rum to be landed on the beach near the station was disclosed by Rider, acting captain of the station in the absence of Captain Falkenburg, who has been ill."

Coast Guard headquarters both locally and at Washington yesterday continued to veil the investigation with secrecy. Commander Yandell, executive officer in Washington, told the *Press* correspondent: "Coast Guard officers here had been cautioned by him not to disclose names of those arrested or questioned, or details of the scandal."

Concurrent with all this, an investigation of the death of Coast Guard Lemuel Gale, to determine whether he was killed because he knew too much about the rumrunners, was started by Ernest Burdge, Ocean County's Chief of Detectives. Gale had left his station at Beach Haven Terrace and two days later he was found unconscious in the beach grass, dying the next day. The initial speculation was that he was murdered because he knew too much about the rum-running operations. But a doctor diagnosed the case as apoplexy [stroke], and that was the cause of death given in the death certificate.

As the bootlegging scandal grew, the *Tuckerton Beacon* of July 29 carried an editorial urging calm: "We will admit, it looks now as if some of our own men, born and bred within a comparatively few miles, have fallen victim to this lure of a 'pot of gold.' We are loath to believe the stories in circulation and until it is proved, do not wish to publish the names of those under suspicion and so drag their names and reputations through this bootleg slime. It seems to be a part of human nature to spread this sort of thing and many newspapers revel in it, not giving a thought or caring about the probability of a mistake on the part of the investigators. It is much easier to besmirch a reputation than to clean and purify one."

Rumors continued, and one of the accused told a reporter, "We were darn fools to get in it, but what would you do if a $100 bill was smacked under your nose just to be blind for a little while? I'm only 22 and I still have my life before me, but I feel sorry for the old men whose lives will be ruined. This thing will nearly kill my wife. We didn't have many good clothes and no holidays and this looked like easy money to me. I won't cry; I'll take my medicine like a navy man and try to live it down."

Then on August 16, the *Press* broke a startling story: "Trial of eleven coast guardsmen accused of conniving with rumrunners has been in progress at the Ship Bottom station for ten days, it was learned this morning, despite efforts of officials to keep the hearings secret. The coast guardsmen are attached to stations between Barnegat City and Little Egg Harbor." The American people were about to find out what was happening behind those closed doors in Ship Bottom.

On August 18, *The Philadelphia Inquirer* was able to report news obtained inside the Coast Guard station: "From the lips of Captain Rasmussen came most of the amazing revelations of the alleged compact between rumrunners and coast guardsmen. Captain Rasmussen, a witness and at the same time a member of the investigating body, repeated a 'complete confession' he said the defendant, Falkenburg, had blurted out to him after a rather grueling examination, saying that rumrunners paid coast guards fifty cents for every case landed. It was also testified that when coast guards seized liquor from smugglers not in the compact, the liquor was promptly peddled to residents near the station."

The *Asbury Park Press* of September 15 reported: "The case was brought to a close today when General Lincoln C. Andres, Assistant Secretary of the Treasury in charge of prohibition enforcement, and the Coast Guard approved prison sentences for ten coast guards tried at the Ship Bottom station. The men are now on the way to the naval prison at Portsmouth, New Hampshire, where they will serve terms ranging from four months to one year. They were convicted of 'scandalous conduct tending to destroy good morals' by a Coast Guard court martial at Ship Bottom August 7."

Prohibition was supposed to improve the nation's morals. But as the 1920s drew to an end, some were beginning to question whether the "noble experiment" was working. Prohibition was repealed in December 1933, under President Roosevelt. Americans could now legally drink to forget the Depression — if they could afford it.

1949 Metal Wagons and Beach Tar

Carol Freas

It was ten o'clock on a quiet, dazzling, summer morning in 1949. Clothes washed in the small wringer machine on the back porch fluttered lazily on the clothesline in the soft breeze.

"Hey Mildred! We're heading for the beach!" My mother called out through the bayberry bushes and poison ivy to her friend who lived two lots down on the next street. Our little red wagon had already been loaded with our supplies for the day: metal shovels, small rusty tin buckets, a green canvas umbrella, some towels, a glass-lined metal Thermos of tea, and lunch — peanut butter and jelly sandwiches on fresh white bread, wrapped in waxed paper. Because preservatives weren't used, yesterday's bread was moldy, a victim of the heat, so my older brother bought a fresh loaf at Scottie's Market on our corner.

Off we went, up to the beach for the whole day. My 8-year-old brother pulled the heavy wagon, the 4-year-old pushed from the back, while Mom carried the toddler (another brother!) the two blocks to the beach. I twirled and danced, deftly catching whatever fell off the wagon.

Beach time hasn't changed much since then. Sixty years later, kids still dig for sand crabs, tattle on a brother, tumble in the surf, whine for candy, bury each other in the sand, squabble over the toys, and — Mom hopes — nap under a damp towel. But accessories and sun protection have changed. Back then, teenagers and adults aimed to get really tan with a mixture of baby oil and iodine, while the kids were lathered from the blue jar of Noxema plus zinc oxide for our lips and under our eyes.

By four, weary and scorched, with soggy sand inside the sagging cotton suits, our gang headed back down the street, wet towels dragging behind the topsy-turvy wagon. Black tar that had washed ashore from sunken World War II tankers still littered the beach; Mom scrubbed our bodies with kerosene from the bucket by the back door. Then, we hoped, there was

from *Echos of LBI* • Spring, 2010

Carol Freas on 11th Street beach in Surf City, 1949.

some warm water left in the 50-gallon tank on the porch to rinse off our sandy bottoms in the washtub.

In 1949, most summer cottages were simple, with few amenities. If the pan under the icebox hadn't been emptied earlier, the melting ice would drip down and water would run across the floor. If the screen door hadn't been latched, we'd be sent off with metal mesh fly swatters to attack greenheads and mosquitoes. Before using the backyard privy, Mom would scoot out any toads that hopped in.

Being tired from the hot sun, I can't recall what was fixed for dinner on the bottled gas stove in the corner. However, I do remember the sweet ocean smell of my nightgown brought in off the line. There were two double beds, a crib and four army cots in the big upstairs room, with colorful movie posters covering the unfinished walls. I could hear the surf tumble on the beach and the cars trundle over the flat wooden bridge.

Lying there by my brothers and drifting off to sleep, I heard my mother call, "Hey, Mildred, the kids are asleep. Come on over for a beer...."

Their cottage had been the old carriage house at the writer's grandfather's home in Burlington County. It was dismantled and trucked to the Island in 1927. In 1951, her father added an indoor bathroom, kitchen and gas heater for year-round living.

1953 New Homes on Old Wetlands

Donald Craig

A 1939 photograph shows the north end of Long Beach Island from about 78th Street in Harvey Cedars; at the top is Barnegat Inlet looking across to Island Beach. The piece of land which juts a square mile out into the bay between Harvey Cedars and Barnegat Light is today about two hundred acres of swamp grass and mud flats. Six months from now it will be taking shape as a swanky residential development, with a grillwork of lagoons for boats, private roads for Jaguars and Cadillacs and a growing number of $15,000 to $25,000 homes (350 are planned). It used to be called Sunken Sedge, and was sold at auction last year for $100,000, just $1,000 more than the bid from a group of Harvey Cedars and Loveladies residents. After a million cubic feet of fill are pumped in, the name will be Loveladies Harbor Estates, the latest in a series of real estate developments that have sprouted up and down the Island since Labor Day.

The Warren Webster tract in South Beach Haven rivals the Loveladies project, even to having similar lagoons and private, winding roads. Only 83 houses, however, are planned. Spier and Brogden are adding a big new section of houses to The Dunes, developed right after World War II, on the bay side of the Boulevard in Beach Haven Terrace, also with a lagoon or two.

In Haven Beach, some seventy new houses have gone up or are going up, together with a 150-foot pier with docking space for forty small cruisers. The Shapiros are adding to their vast production of dwellings both on the Island and on the west side of the Causeway, at Beach Haven West. Barnegat Light's first real development, the "Mellon Homes of Distinction," is taking shape along and near 25th Street, in the form of twenty or more trim, year-round Cape Cod cottages. Builders of individual homes, like Glenn, are raising and selling houses in every community from Barnegat Light to Beach Haven.

This means a big business boom for the Island. Several hundred dwell-

from *The Beachcomber* • April, 1953

Looking from 68th Street in Harvey Cedars north to Barnegat Inlet. The bay meadows (upper left) are where Loveladies Harbor would be developed.

ings have been built since Labor Day, or are in the planning and building stage. What the additions mean in terms of furniture, appliances, oil, boats, landscaping and general activity in such places as the movies, bars, restaurants, stores, gas stations and fishing docks can only be guessed. Worth particular note is that a large proportion of the new construction is going into year-round homes with heat and insulation.

The fascinating part of the whole business is that for most of these projects, land had to be "created." Because of this, Long Beach Island has this spring some hundreds more acres of habitable terra firma that it had on Labor Day. Most of the new acreage came from the bottom of Barnegat Bay.

To any seasoned-in-the-salt Islander, dredging is an old story. To the landlubber from West Philadelphia or Upper Montclair it is likely to be a somewhat mysterious business. For the benefit of the latter I shall sum up what I learned one bright morning last winter when Reynold Thomas of Harvey Cedars picked me up in his truck and gave me a conducted tour to show me what dredging is all about.

You may have seen one of his small red dredges anchored along the bay front, with a long snake of piping stretched on pontoons from the dredge to the shore. All dredges are fundamentally alike — a gigantic pump, usually powered by a diesel engine with the sucking end stuck down in the bottom of the bay, and the spouting mouthpiece at the far end of those pontoons.

Reynold's eight-inch dredge (that's the diameter of the pipe, not the size of the dredge) sucks 2,600 gallons of water per minute. With the water, it picks up ten to thirty percent solids — mud, sand, small gravel, clams, fish, eels, old shoes and anything else that happens to be in front of the hungry maw down below.

Our first stop that morning was in Brant Beach, where one of the Thomas dredges was anchored. Reynold had the job of deepening the channel at that point, and five different property owners had contracted with him to dump the bottom of the channel onto their land. That is, in essence, how most dredges pay their bills and make their money in a business involving heavy upkeep and risks. Every pound of muck and sand pumped from the bay bottom can be valuable soil for someone with a swampy marsh to cover. The sand settles, the water runs off, and gradually the "fill" builds up to whatever level the landowner specifies.

As we drove on past the Brant Beach Yacht Club, Reynold explained that the Club beach, the land behind it and in fact almost all of the solid earth on the bay side of the Boulevard had formerly been salt marsh or under water and had been built up by dredging.

We stopped again opposite the municipal building in Brant Beach, where a field of grimy looking sand had appeared since early fall. This will be the new township bathing beach and site for the Youth Club building. He explained how the grimy look would soon disappear as the mud in the sand, being lighter, washed away, leaving only clean, white sand.

We went on past Beach Haven Park, where Jerry Shapiro has used his own cutter dredge to fill in new land on which to extend his housing development. A cutter dredge has revolving knives in front of the mouth of the dredge that can chew up the bottom and enable the dredge to pick up harder clots than an ordinary "toothless" one. We passed Haven Beach, where fifty-thousand cubic yards have been added to the Island by the A. W. Kelly organization; and Beach Haven Terrace, where all the meadows opposite the Dunes development were being filled.

In Bay Vista [North Beach Haven], opposite Dotter's Jewelry Store, Reynold pointed to a high piled heap of sand and explained that is was a "spot pile" — a reserve of fill sucked up by his dredge and paid for by the contractors who need sand for places beyond the reach of the dredges. This pile, replenished many times, has resulted in deep water off the shoreline for Bay Vista boat owners.

Next stop was at the *Lucy Evelyn*. Reynold told me how *Lucy* had got where she was. A channel had been dug into the meadows, perpendicular to the shoreline, *Lucy* was floated through, then he pumped in sand under her, so powerfully that the *Lucy* was raised three feet. More dredging last fall covered over the old dump on the south side of the schooner, which will become the town bathing beach.

The biggest dredging project of all began last summer at Liberty Thorofare, the arm of the bay that reaches in past Little Egg Harbor Yacht Club, loops around Mordecai Island and returns to the bay again. Last summer the State of New Jersey hired the Hill Dredging Co. of Ventnor to deepen this channel for the benefit of small boat owners in Beach Haven, and that started something. The Hill dredges are gigantic affairs, worth half a million dollars and of great power. They require twenty to thirty men to a shift, operate twenty-four hours a day seven days a week and "make land" at the rate of 200 to 300 cubic yards an hour. It was the Hill Co. which built the Ocean City beach 300 feet out to the sea. Consequently, when a Hill dredge comes around, local property owners with big dreams jump at the chance to have some fill-in work done without having to pay the passage to and from Ventnor.

The first man to take advantage of the big dredge's presence was Warren Webster, who owns the big tract of land in South Beach Haven adjoining and south of Liberty Thorofare. He arranged to have the sand and dirt from the Thorofare pumped onto his marsh land, went on from there and has now in progress the luxurious development previously mentioned, stretching from Sherer's to the south end of Beach Haven. Before it left these waters, the Hill dredge did the fill-in jobs in Beach Haven, the Terrace and Haven Beach. None of this would have been done if the Liberty Thorofare project had not been worked out by the state.

The Hill dredge has gone home, but the story is not over. At Beach Haven Inlet the Coast Guard is thinking of building a basin and feeder channel to keep their boats, now berthed in Beach Haven. Surf City is planning development of two blocks of salt marsh in the vicinity of 5th Street. The state may yet again do some dredging near Barnegat Light to improve the situation there for small boats.

All and all, it is comforting to know that, however much the Atlantic may gnaw away at the Island beaches, dredging operations can be counted on to add as much as it takes away. And we have a wide bay to cross before we are pushed back to the mainland.

―――――――――――――――――――――

The Wetlands Act of 1970 and the federal Water Pollution Control Act of 1972, known as the Clean Water Act, put a stop to dredging sand from the bottom of the bay onto the salt marsh — the wetlands. Reynold Thomas, the founder of the Barnegat Bay Dredging Co., died in 1983. The company's work is now mainly keeping federal channels and inlets clear from New Jersey to Delaware.

1950s Sought-After Summer Jobs

Robert A. Freedman

Seems like this summer there are more jobs on the Island than kids to fill them. My brother swears he saw a sign outside of one local establishment, pleading: "Help Wanted — good or bad." It wasn't that way when I was young in the mid 1950s. Jobs then were prizes to be fought for. You started looking in April, and if you hadn't found something by June, your only option was to wait for someone to get fired.

My first job on the Island was delivering *The Philadelphia Inquirer.* I was ambitious — in the beginning — and developed a sizable route, maybe fifty papers a morning to deliver, papers that I first had to fold and fit into the front basket of my old balloon-tire bike.

That wasn't the hard part, though. Neither was the actual delivery process, which I kind of enjoyed — tossing those thick, rolled-up missiles (I still know how to make a perfect double fold — no rubber bands, thank you) wherever they might land. No, the hard part came on collection day.

People always seemed to be out. When I came to get my money, they were at the beach or on the boat. At night it was the miniature golf course or the movies. About the only time to catch them at home was early morning, and then they'd be grumpy and tell you to come back later — when, of course, they'd be gone. Some weeks I barely collected enough money to cover the cost of the papers.

The next summer I found a better job, delivering Western Union telegrams. Telegrams were a common form of communication back then, as not so many summer people had telephones in their cottages.

I was paid ten cents for each telegram I delivered and almost always could count on a tip of a quarter or more. With ten or so telegrams a day, I made out like a bandit. I stopped by the old post office in Brighton Beach two or three times a day to see if any needed to go out.

Sometimes the old lady who ran the post office would be taking down a message as I stood there, so I'd know what was in the telegram I was delivering. Usually, it was just ordinary stuff, like: "Will arrive on fourth-STOP-have beer ready-STOP-ha ha." But sometimes telegrams bore grimmer messages: "Father died on third-STOP-services will be Friday-STOP."

Those tough telegrams seemed to burn in my hand as I pedaled my bike to the destination. It was a curious mixture I felt — of fear, excitement, and of being a part of a grown-up process. Curiously, the receivers of bad news almost invariably tipped better than those who received messages of a more mundane sort.

As I reached an age where I could apply for the treasured working papers, eighteen, my job horizons broadened. I scoured the Island for a regular wage-paying job and eventually came up with a much-coveted position as a bag boy/shelf stocker at Marvel's Market. If my memory is correct, my beginning wage was 75 cents an hour. I was more than pleased with that amount.

At first, I was very nervous and made lots of mistakes. I packed bread and eggs at the bottom of grocery bags, put new stock in front of old, and once, while opening a carton of laundry detergent with a razor blade knife, sliced neatly through a row of twelve boxes. I quickly dumped the ruined and leaking boxes in the dumpster before Tommy Marvel (the boss) could discover what I'd done.

The job I most coveted at Marvel's was donut-maker. Marvel's made the best in the world, cinnamon and white-powdered and even chocolate-cake. Rich the Donut Man was in charge of the machines that mixed and cooked the sweet confections. On occasion, he would slip us stock boys a sack of fresh, hot donuts that had not turned out quite round or had broken in half while floating in the hot oil. We'd gobble them down in the back room with swallows of cold milk from a quart we'd pass around.

I used to dream about being the Donut Man. I'd wear a tall white hat and spear the sweet rounds out of my donut machine on a long stick. But it never happened. Instead, over the course of three more summers, I became a produce man — with the emphasis, I'll have you know, on man. That was almost as good as being a doughnut man and I was earning the outrageous sum of a buck and a quarter an hour. There in the produce aisle, I'd wait on customers, measuring out pounds of sweet cherries and bagging up ears of juicy Jersey corn. Some customers became regulars and each day they'd ask me what was fresh or if I'd pick out a ripe cantaloupe for them.

Sometimes older women would want to tell me about their daughters, who were always beautiful, and their sons, who all had just been accepted to Penn. One evening after work, when Tommy invited me behind the meat counter to have a beer with him and Tony the Butcher, I knew I'd arrived.

There were lots of other jobs over the years that took me through high school and college and even a year after college — when I resisted entering the real world. I drove a truck to the docks in Philadelphia to pick up produce and worked construction in Beach Haven West, pounding in long pine tree trunks as foundations for Shapiro Brothers' build 'em-quick little houses. I was a bus boy and a waiter and a Good Humor Ice Cream man of occasional bad humor.

I grew up through those jobs, each one revealing a new clue to the mystery of what it meant to be an adult. Long Beach Island summer jobs — no work could ever seem so right again.

1960 Memories of a Cottage

Jackie Ostberg

A devastating March storm showed no mercy when it swept across Long Beach Island in 1962. Houses, automobiles, and entire contents of homes were washed down streets and into the bay. Among those that stood fast and survived that storm was a small Sears Roebuck cottage on 28th Street in Ship Bottom. It was built in 1926 for members of the Summit-based Overlook Fish and Game Club, who wanted a place where they could salt water fish and go duck hunting. The 1962 northeaster had nudged one corner of the house off its foundation and filled the crawl space with seawater, but this relatively minor damage was fixed by adding a row of cement blocks to realign and raise the house.

My husband, Oz, became a member of the club in the 1950s, when our elderly neighbor who could no longer drive invited him to a meeting. After a few years, Oz became chairman of the Ship Bottom property. In the '60s, club members were encouraged to spend family vacation time at the shore whenever "fishing" members were not using the cottage. So, in 1960, we rented the cottage and set out for Long Beach Island, anticipating a great time on our very first Jersey Shore vacation. Our three sons, ages six, four, and one-and-a-half, could hardly wait to see the ocean. Every fifteen minutes, a voice from the back seat would call out, "Are we there yet?"

My heart sank when we finally arrived at our destination. What I saw was a tired little fisherman's cottage needing lots of loving care. For thirty-four years, it had stood steadfast through pelting rainstorms, raging winter blizzards, blustering windstorms and stiflingly hot and humid summer days. Why wouldn't it appear to be a bit disheveled?

Our kids saw the cottage through a different lens; they considered it to be a cool camping cabin. They dashed out of the car eager to explore the inside — what we found was one large all-purpose room, a sparsely equipped kitchen, and a tiny bathroom you could barely turn around in. The "great" room was a combination sleeping/dining/living space. An antique round oak table with serpent feet, plus six straight-backed chairs, indicated the dining area. At night, sliding curtains that were hung from metal tracks in the ceiling formed three sleeping enclosures. Clothes hooks had been randomly nailed to the walls. A janitor-sized sink occupied one corner of the kitchen. An enamel-topped rectangular table provided the only work space. A temperamental refrigerator stood in another corner. I wasn't thrilled with the amenities, but figured I could survive one week. I'll admit, though, it did have some redeeming qualities. The house was fifth from the beach and it was walking distance to DiFiglio's grocery store, the Ship Bottom Five and Ten and The Tagg-Along hobby shop. We found ourselves enjoying the carefree beach life more and more every day spent at the cottage.

In 1970, a majority of older club members voted to sell the cottage. Island Realtors gave three appraisals and bids from club members were to be considered first. Our bid, the one and only member bid, was accepted. Suddenly, we became the new owners of a fishing cottage that I once said I never wanted to see again.

Friends and relatives pitched in to help us renovate the cottage. Our sons were older now and were handy with a paintbrush. Not neat, but handy. A few pals from their Boy Scout troop helped paint the shingled exterior a warm sandy shade. Flower boxes under the porch windows were filled with red geraniums and white petunias. An American flag, placed in a holder by the door, waved cheerfully at passersby. New hinges were screwed into the sagging shower door.

Inside, Oz built captain's bunks with storage drawers below. I made colorful, striped draw curtains to replace faded ones. A neighbor who was re-modeling her kitchen gave us the cabinets she no longer needed. We added a four-burner stove and a newer used refrigerator. Final additions included a forty-gallon hot water heater (installed in the attic), a built-in closet where the janitor sink had been, a telephone and a TV. Paintings and photographs were hung on the walls. Our little house was looking mighty cozy. Every year, we managed to make more improvements. Eventually, a small pullout sofa was purchased for the porch to accommodate overnight guests.

We all fell in love with our fishing cottage. Even me! The boys named her "Blowfish Bungalow," after the funny puffed-up fish they caught in the

Tom, John and Paul Ostberg with a neighbor at "Blowfish Bungalow," Ship Bottom, in the 1970s.

bay. One year, we bought a red, 10-foot sailboat and took sailing lessons from the Clopp brothers in Brant Beach. All of our adventures were dutifully recorded in a log book: dolphin sightings, how many crabs were netted in the bay, who collected the most sea glass.

Visiting friends and relatives also wrote in the Log. Some even wrote poems and drew pictures. One couple wrote: "We left Indiana two days ago to spend our honeymoon on Long Beach Island. We're loving the beach. We've been steaming clams, boiling shrimp, and grilling fish, just like the natives!" A 14-year-old visitor wrote: "The weather was beautiful today. Mrs. Ostberg and I went sailing in the sunfish. We were going to jibe, but instead we capsized." A scary incident was noted after our 5-year-old niece wandered away on the beach. We searched frantically for an hour until, finally, we spotted a lifeguard leading a tearful, frightened little girl our way.

Traditions originated during the summer vacations spent at Blowfish Bungalow are now part of our family heritage. Nowadays, when grandchildren visit, we MUST fly kites on the beach; we MUST build sand castles; we MUST play miniature golf and lick drippy ice cream cones; we MUST gather on the porch in the evening to bet on the actual time the sun sinks below the western horizon; we MUST race back from the beach to be the first to use the outdoor shower while there's still hot water; and we MUST play Nana's favorite card game, Aces on the Corner. At times, the game caused shouting, yelling, and even some crying. Our boys accused my mother, Nana, of changing the rules. Her response was, "These are Chicago rules, boys." (Nana lived in Chicago). The boys argued, "But Nana, we want to play New Jersey rules!"

Many happy memories were recorded in that old Log Book. We hated to part with our Sears Roebuck bungalow, but it just wasn't big enough to comfortably enjoy our retirement years. More than a few tears were shed when we sold it in 1985. Today, we're spending our "golden" years just a few miles up the road in North Beach. But we will always fondly remember our Ship Bottom cottage.

1963 Splashback in Time

Margaret Buchholz

In 1963 the NJ Highway Department planned a four-lane freeway down the shore from Asbury Park, bridging Barnegat Light Inlet and possibly the one at Beach Haven (to where, we wonder). Fortunately this plan didn't take off any more than the one in the late 1920s (the Depression killed that idea.) In another project that year, the state wanted to replace the two-lane road with four lanes the entire length of the Island. They started with Ship Bottom, which had asked the state for an improved traffic circle to ease congestion, but the town could only have that if they would support changing the Boulevard to a one-way highway through town. Central Ave. would go the other direction. Officials, residents and businessmen alike fought the plan, and common sense won. Ship Bottom got the circle improvements anyway. But the Island was eventually bisected by four lanes.

• • •

Two years earlier, John Maschal had opened the Country Kettle Fudge shop in Beach Haven. *The Beachcomber* commented, "A little bit of a store, but a great big bit of business. People were glad to line up on the street to wait for their turn for the homemade fudge and ice cream." In 1963, the store moved to Schooner's Wharf, where a real schooner was beached at the wharf, the fabled *Lucy Evelyn*. (It burned to the ground in February 1972.) And whipping the fudge in the large copper kettle, set into an old barrel, was John himself manning the long wooden paddle. The business is now across the street in Bay Village, which the Maschal family developed. Third generation Maschals are still whipping.

• • •

The proposed Southern Ocean County Hospital had over $53,000 toward the goal of a hospital in the region. Volunteers started in 1954 to gather those dollars; the hospital was built in 1972. ... Long Beach Township increased its police force from 13 to 18 men in the summer. ... A movement took hold (yet again) to consolidate all the towns on the Island into one — and this issue would surface on and off for the next forty years.

• • •

Remember Tom Swifties? As in: "The poem on this ad doesn't rhyme, he said adversely." Or ... "When I wear my bikini, my navel shows, she said self-centeredly." They were so hot we published one every few weeks. ... Food prices in 1963: Leg of lamb and coffee fifty-nine cents a pound, five-pound bag of sugar sixty-nine cents, grapes thirty-nine cents a pound. ... A Boston Whaler cost $875. ... A new Island enterprise decided that the ubiquitous gravel that was covering most yards would look better painted green. Fortunately, that fad didn't last long.

from *The Beachcomber* • Memorial Day, 2013

● ● ●

Mike Thomas, my brother, broke the world speed record for his class of 280 cu. ft. hydroplane. The gala party was at Baker's Porthole Bar in Ship Bottom. Mike received a congratulatory letter from President John F. Kennedy, written three weeks before he was assassinated.

● ● ●

A stingray 5 feet long by 3 feet wide and weighing 65 pounds was caught off Flat Island. John Bauer harpooned it, and then the ray pulled loose, bending the iron harpoon and pulling John overboard. He and his buddy Ray Kabakjian went back to the dock, straightened the harpoon and returned to the chase. John harpooned the ray again and brought it near the surface. Ray shot it in the head with a spear gun. The boys then towed it back to the dock.

● ● ●

Although Stretch Pohl first surfed on the Island in 1932, the sport really took hold the summer of 1963. The traditional Hawaiian favorite made it big on the Island: "Surfers, who ride those long $100 boards, have insti- tuted a new way of life," we reported. A newly released platter with a jump beat, by Jan and Dean, bears the significant title, "Surf City." "If it hits the big time, our Island could become famous." It did, and we did.

● ● ●

Ship Bottom's 19th-century Coast Guard station on 26th Street was de- molished. ... Beach Haven's city fathers wanted to demolish an old garage on Engleside Ave. but some "men from the city" had a different idea — and it worked; the Surflight Theatre remodeled the building, which remained until 1987 as the theater workshop and warehouse. ... A warning against DDT: "When the sprayer comes down the street, do not let your children run into the poisonous fog; it is positively dangerous." The kids did anyway. DDT was banned in 1972.

···

A year after the Great March Storm of 1962, a letter to the editor read: "Residents of Brant Beach are up in arms about the new houses being built on the dunes that were destroyed in the storm and have been carefully built up over the past year. The authorities seem to be unable to resist the blandishments of profit-seeking developers. Mowing down sand dunes for building has seriously weakened our natural defenses and paves the way for future destruction. How can the authorities be so stupid? They should have prohibited the destruction of any dune." (Taxpayers have been paying for that stupidity for a long time.) A local builder commented with a shrug and raised eyebrows about a man building a new house fifty feet closer to the water than the one just washed away by the March storm. …

···

Alice Sutter, our longtime garden writer, told of the beneficial result of saltwater submerging Island gardens. A year later, they were more lush than ever, thanks to all those minerals and nutrients in the water. … Nine stone jetties were built in Beach Haven and Barnegat Light. The township contracted for 40 jetties at a cost of about $2.5 million. … The result of the Conservation Society's first Operation Greendike the previous October, when islanders planted beach grass on all the new dunes, was positive. The grass took hold and it was the beginning of the "lush green wall" that would trap sand and grow the protective dune line. …

···

In the December issue, we reported that some homeowners might collect insurance for the loss of their homes in the 1962 northeaster, following lawsuits in Delaware. Most did not.

Contributors' Notes

Marjorie Amon is a writer and photographer who lives in Barnegat Light and is the author of the book *Vintage at the Shore.*

Edward Brown, a longtime *Beachcomber* columnist, was the editor and publisher of a weekly newspaper in Medford and a favorite English teacher at Southern Regional High School. He died in October 2017.

Margaret Buchholz published *The Beachcomber* every summer from 1955 until 1987 when she sold it to *The SandPaper*; she continued on as managing editor through 2005 and then book and features editor until 2014. She is the author or editor of a number of books about Long Beach Island and Jersey Shore history, including *Great Storms of the Jersey Shore* (co-authored with Larry Savadove). Her other titles include: *New Jersey Shipwrecks*; the historical collection *Shore Chronicles; Island Album; Seasons in the Sun; The Long Beach Island Reader* (a companion to this book); and *Josephine* — based on her mother's journals as a World War I "government girl," as a globe-trotting journalist, and her life on the Island during the Great Depression. She lives in the home she grew up in on Barnegat Bay in Harvey Cedars, built by her father, Reynold Thomas, the longtime mayor of Harvey Cedars, and founder of the Barnegat Bay Dredging Co.

Dick Clements wrote the weekly "Fishing Around" column for *The Beachcomber* from 1951 until he retired to fish the waters of the Chesapeake in 1977. He died in 2005.

Donald Craig founded *The Beachcomber* in 1950.

Cathie Cush, a former *SandPaper* editor, got Beach Haven sand between her toes as a baby, in 1958. Her family's roots on the Island date to the early 20th century with a summer rental in Ship Bottom (then Beach Arlington) and extended family members who married and settled here. After summers working at The Frosted Mug and Schooners Wharf, and after college, Cush landed at *The SandPaper* as managing editor. Interviews with divers for an article about the Texas Tower wreck inspired her to learn to scuba dive in 1981 and she became a dive instructor and went on to write about shipwrecks and diving for many national publications. She is the author of several books, a fellow of the Explorers Club, and a charter member of the Women Divers Hall of Fame. She lives in Bucks County, Pennsylvania, but still considers Long Beach Island home. Cush got her first byline at age 14, when the *Beach Haven Times* published a poem she wrote about the stormy ocean.

Margaret Daley was a reporter for the *Asbury Park Press* for three years, a freelance writer for *The SandPaper*, and taught English at Southern Regional High School for most of her career.

Gabriel DeCicco wrote the "Offsides" column when he was a reporter for the *Beach Haven Times* and *Beacon* newspapers. He worked for *The SandPaper* and daily newspapers and was sports editor for four Gannett weeklies in Ocean County. He covered high schools, Pop Warner football and Babe Ruth baseball and published a book from his experiences, *Offsides*, in 2015.

Elinor DeWire is author of *Guardians of the Lights* and many other books with a focus on lighthouse history and preservation.

Lisa DiLeo, who wrote for *The SandPaper* and *Beachcomber*, has worked as a writer, psychologist, and school psychologist. She has conducted writing and teaching workshops in Kingston, Jamaica — and among her more gratifying experiences has been producing *Beauty and the Beast* with high school students in Jamaica. For the past decade she has been teaching the high school equivalency program to inmates at the Middlesex County Adult Correction Center. Most Friday nights she can be found singing at the Hopewell, New Jersey, "Bistro."

Sharon DiGiovanni was a freelance writer for *The SandPaper*.

Thomas P. Farner is the *SandPaper* history columnist, whose "200 Plus" column has appeared every week since the first year of the paper in 1976. His book, *New Jersey In History: Fighting To Be Heard*, a collection of his columns, includes some of the state's most remarkable episodes and colorful characters.

Marion Figley was a writer and editor for both *The Beachcomber* and *The Sand-Paper* from 1975 until she died in 1996. She also edited books for Down The Shore Publishing, including *Great Storms of the Jersey Shore*.

Carol Freas and her brothers were in the first classes at the new Long Beach Island Grade School in September 1951, and then Southern Regional when it opened in 1956. The first in the family to attend college, she earned an art teaching degree from Kutztown College in Pennsylvania and returned to the Island year round in 1986 with husband Ray and children Tara and Travis. She now teaches at the Long Beach Island Foundation of Arts and Sciences and Pine Shores Art Association and also exhibits and sells her award-winning watercolor paintings of the Island.

Robert A. Freedman is a former Long Beach Islander who moved to Oregon but never got the Island out of his blood.

William Geiger, long-time *SandPaper* writer, divides his time between Long Beach Island and Langhorne, Pennsylvania, where he teaches Greek and Latin at LaSalle College High School. His family has owned a home in Beach Haven West since the 1970s and he and his wife Mary Jane have a condo in Ship Bottom. When not writing movie reviews, he can be found cruising around the bay avoiding students.

Carole Garibaldi Rogers is an author of essays, articles, poems, and books; her book *Hidden Lives: My Three Grandmothers* was published in 2013. Reunions with her sons now take place by a New Hampshire lake, but she and her husband return to the Island for long fall weekends where they walk the beach and ride bikes to see all the old places once again.

Tom Halsted, a writer of maritime subjects from Gloucester, Massachusetts, served under two presidents working for the U.S. government on arms control and nuclear disarmament issues, including the SALT I and II negotiations. After service in the army, he began his career as an intelligence officer and photo interpreter at the State Department during the Cuban missile crisis, shuttling between the Kennedy White House, the CIA and Pentagon. A lifetime sailor, he wrote, "salt was in the air I breathed." He died at 84 in 2017.

Bill Hammarstrom, a bayman, fisherman and naturalist, lives in Waretown.

Mark Howat retired to Surf City after 43 years with *The Bergen Record*, of Hackensack, where he was senior editor. He wrote for *The Beachcomber* off and on for 25 years. Howat died in 2010.

Kathryn M. King wrote for both *The Beachcomber* and *The SandPaper* over the years and has had careers in marketing, art therapy, and addiction recovery. She is one of the fifth generation of Kings who have been a part of the history of Southern Ocean County. She grew up in Beach Haven.

Karen Kiss was a founding member and the first President of the Alliance for a Living Ocean (ALO), established in the fall of 1987.

William J. Kunze Sr. was *The SandPaper's* original fishing columnist who wrote "The Fishing Well" in the 1970s and 1980s. Grandfather of Deb Whitcraft, founder of the New Jersey Maritime Museum in Beach Haven, he died in 1995.

Anna Leadem wrote for *The Beachcomber* from 1987 to 1991 before sailing off to other adventures. A retired psychotherapist living in northwest Pennsylvania, she kayaks on freshwater lakes and daydreams about taking a broad reach across Barnegat Bay.

Donald Launer of Forked River was a longtime freelance writer for *The Beachcomber* who also published over 400 articles and six books on boating. He worked as a television engineer at the ABC television network from 1948 until his retirement in 1989 and won two Emmys for his work on Olympics coverage. He served as a sergeant in the army in Europe during World War II. He held a pilot's license for land and sea airplanes. Don designed and built his first boat, held a Coast Guard captain's license, and his lectures on navigation at the U.S. Naval Academy and hundreds of other organizations led to his 2010 induction into the Sailing Hall of Fame. He died in 2015 at 89.

Scott Mazzella is the author of *Surviving Sandy: Long Beach Island and the Greatest Storm of the Jersey Shore*. A 1999 graduate of Rutgers University, he worked as a staff writer at *The Beachcomber* and is now a history teacher at Jonas Salk Middle School in Old Bridge. He can't remember a time when he wasn't obsessed with weather. Some of his earliest storm memories include being mesmerized watching lightning from his darkened garage with his dad. "I was born a weather nut! My wife and kids claim that I go into 'storm mode' when severe thunderstorms are nearby. It's just a part of me."

Joseph McCann moved to Long Beach Island in 2001. An avid outdoorsman, he enjoys all four seasons, fishing, hunting or relaxing on the beach. He owns a financial planning and tax preparation service in Brant Beach.

Bruce Novotny was born in Atlantic City just before the legendary 1962 northeaster. His family ran a marina in Brant Beach which became a surfers' hangout and a source of inspiration for this surfer-writer. Bruce wrote a weekly culture and entertainment column for *The Beachcomber* during the 1980s. A graduate of Notre Dame, he studied in England, played soccer, and eventually moved to Southern California where he pursues a career in the film business, writing screenplays and editing videos. He is the author of the LBI-centered coming-of-age surfing novel, *Tales From An Endless Summer.*

Maggie O'Neill is a year-round resident of Ship Bottom and is a real estate agent at Mary Allen Realty.

Jackie Osberg lives in North Beach. She was a journalism major in college and was editor of *Modern Beauty Shop* magazine.

Curtis Rist had graduated from a college otherwise known for producing "people who go places," found himself listless on a Memorial Day weekend on Long Beach Island in 1984, and walked into *The SandPaper* offices, asking for a job. Mercifully employed, he wrote, edited, and "cut and pasted" to beat the band, back in the typewriter days when that meant actual scissors and glue sticks. Other jobs followed for the next three decades, at city newspapers, *People* magazine, and *This Old House.* Currently a dog breeder and singer-songwriter (to the endless amusement of old college classmates), he lives in Hudson, New York.

Christine Rooney, a special education and language arts educator, has vacationed on Long Beach Island all her life and moved here year-round in the 2000s. She is actively involved in Island activities such as the Lighthouse International Film Festival and the LBI Fly kite festival.

Joe Saunders wrote for *The SandPaper.*

Larry Savadove moved back to Long Beach Island, where he spent all the summers of his youth, after an adventurous career as a writer, ad man, and filmmaker. He spent another quarter century as a writer, editor, and columnist for *The SandPaper* and *Beachcomber*, living in an old oceanside Victorian in Beach Haven. He authored a novel, *The Oyster Singer*, set in Mud City, a remote backwater along our shores, and was co-author of *Great Storms of the Jersey Shore.* His first novel, *The Sound of One Hand,* published in 1960 won this praise from *The New York Times*: "It was the best novel about Japan I have ever read. He out-Micheners Michener a hundred fold." In his twenties, after editing the *Harvard Crimson* in college, he served in the army, working military intelligence as the conflict in Vietnam was beginning. After a decade in advertising in Japan and Latin America, he settled in Hollywood to make documentary films. His credits include "The Undersea World of Jacques Cousteau." His last "Savvy" column appeared in *The SandPaper* on Sept. 11, 2013. He had been working on a collection of stories, titled "Drunken Sailor," about his youthful adventures at ports of call on an oil tanker in the Gulf of Mexico when a long struggle with Parkinson's disease silenced his articulate, witty, thoughtful and humorous writing. He died in 2016.

Don Southwick is an Long Beach Island businessman, bayman, surfer and diver.

Lisa Suhay is an activist, children's book author, and has been a journalist for thirty years. She got her start at *The SandPaper*. Her career has spanned news, war coverage, social issues and commentary for national and international publications including *The New York Times, The Christian Science Monitor* and *The Virginian-Pilot*. She is the founder of the Norfolk Initiative for Chess Excellence in Norfolk, Virginia, a non-profit serving at-risk youth through mentoring and teaching the game of chess for critical thinking and life strategies.

Jan Van Gilder was a *Beachcomber* freelance writer in the 1990s, specializing in nature. "Growing up on the Jersey shore with parents who loved the outdoors, it is little wonder that I started observing nature early on," she wrote. "Although I settled in Washington, D.C., loving nature was always an important part of me. Now, my daughter and granddaughter are enthusiastic company on hikes. We are sure to put on our 'woods eyes' as we start off on a walk and they never fail to reveal something well worth seeing."

Meriba Van Meter Walker was a full-time school nurse at Southern Regional High School and worked part time at Atlantic City Hospital. She lived on Burlington Ave. in Harvey Cedars.

Roy S. Wolper taught English literature at Temple University. Among his awards are a National Endowment of the Humanities Fellowship in Creative Writing, and a Best Stories award from the British Broadcasting Corporation. He lives in Wyncote, Pennsylvania, and summered on Pearl Street in Beach Haven from 1961 until 2011.

Joe Zeff started coming to the Island when he was a high school student in Pittsburgh and jumped at the chance to spend his first summer out of college as a *SandPaper* reporter. That began a career in journalism that included jobs at *The New York Times* and *Time* magazine. He now runs a design firm helping companies tell more effective stories using apps, websites and videos. Every summer he returns to Long Beach Island from Montclair — for a week-long rental, a thirty-six-mile bicycle ride, or a hit-and-run for an Okie's sandwich.

Lou Zuegner, Beach Haven, wrote for *The Beachcomber* in the 1980s under the byline "Dirty Louie."

Acknowledgments

I thank all the authors for their enthusiasm, cooperation, and clarification as we dug their stories from the archives.

And for help with research: Perry Benson, Reilly Sharp, Richard Tramontana, Gordon Hesse, Neal Roberts, Amanda Devecka-Rinear, Capt. Jerry Mason USN (ret.), Elaine McClellan, Carolyn Conway and Victoria Clements. Also Gary Henderson, publisher of *Bay Magazine* and Cheryl Van Meter Kirby, publisher of *Echoes of LBI,* who also contributed her aunt's letter describing her experience in the 1962 northeaster.

I also thank SandPeople Pattie McIntyre, who tirelessly and endlessly (it seemed to her) input the paper copies into the computer; Jeff Kuhlman, willing help with computer problems; Sara Swan, who did some heavy lifting and looking, and Ryan Morrill, who pointed the way to old photos.

Tim Moersh / The SandPaper

If you enjoyed this book you may also be interested in these titles,
also edited or authored by Margaret Thomas Buchholz:

The Long Beach Island Reader
ISBN 978-1-59322-095-2

Island Album:
Photographs and Memories of Long Beach Island
ISBN 1-59322-087-7

Fisherman's Wife
ISBN 978-1-59322-040-2

Shore Chronicles:
Diaries and Travelers Tales from the Jersey Shore 1764-1955
ISBN 0-945582-77-3

Josephine:
From Washington Working Girl to Fisherman's Wife
ISBN 978-1-59322-062-4

New Jersey Shipwrecks:
350 Years in the Graveyard of the Atlantic
ISBN 978-1-59322-050-1

Four Seasons at the Shore:
Photographs of the Jersey Shore
with seasonal essays by Margaret Thomas Buchholz, Sandy Gingras,
Larry Savadove, Rich Youmans. ISBN 0-945582-91-9

*Down The Shore Publishing specializes in books, calendars, cards and videos about
Long Beach Island and the Shore. Visit our website:*

down-the-shore.com
Or for a catalog of all our titles just send us a request:
info@down-the-shore.com
Down The Shore Publishing, Box 100, West Creek, NJ 08092